2023

The Big Keto Diet Cookbook

for Beginners

1000 Tasty, Healthy, & Easy-to-Learn Ketogenic Diet Recipes for Your Whole Family and Busy People on a Budget

Alexanne Hyatt

Table of Contents

Chapter 3 Fish and Seafood

Chapter 4 Poultry

Chapter 5 Beef, Pork, and Lamb 56

Chapter 6 Salads 72

Chapter 7 Snacks and Appetizers

Chapter 8 Stews and Soups

Chapter 9 Vegetarian Mains   99

Chapter 10 Desserts   105

Appendix 1 Measurement Conversion Chart   114

Appendix 2 The Dirty Dozen and Clean Fifteen   115

Appendix 3 Recipes Index   116

INTRODUCTION

I struggled to find the best way to balance my diet with my busy schedule. Each week, my weight check-in never wavered, and despite my best efforts, I knew that if I didn't find a suitable diet management plan soon, things would not look good for my future health and wellbeing. What's more, I would have little or no chance of fitting into the expensive outfit I was saving for my twentieth wedding anniversary dinner! But, I had no idea just how severe my health outlook was until the results of my recent annual check-up left me reeling in shock!

"So, where to from here," I asked myself? First, I am too busy to waste time on diets that require foods to be weighed and measured. And anyway, I have tried more diets than I care to remember, and nothing much has changed for me.

Feeling despondent, I visited a friend I had not seen in a while. I was blown away by the dramatic change in my friend's appearance. Not only had they lost substantial weight, but their outlook on life had become more positive and cheerful.

I discovered my friend, who, like me, had tried several diets, had been introduced to the ketogenic eating plan. Since starting the ketogenic diet, they are happy to witness a positive turn in their health, weight loss, and lifestyle. And it certainly shows!

Delighted with my discovery of the keto diet, I dived straight into finding more about it. First, I wanted to find out how I could use the keto diet and if it would fit into my already hectic lifestyle.

As a busy mom of four children, who have several extra-curricular activities, I find myself running out of time for meal preparation. More than that, juggling my small home-run business with my family's needs keeps me on my toes.

The keto diet has been an eye-opener. Not only have I managed to keep the kids happy with the new meal plan, but they have become more supportive during meal preparations. Also, we all feel healthier since we started keto. In addition, I have noticed a marked positive drop in my weight, and I am sleeping better and waking more refreshed!

Suppose the benefits of the keto diet for my family and me have been so profound; I believe sharing our eating plan journey will benefit more busy people struggling to find a solution to maintaining their health and wellbeing.

So, without further ado, let's get into the essentials of the keto diet and how it can work for us all.

Chapter 1 A Complete Guide to the Keto Diet

Surprisingly, the keto diet has been around since the 1920s, designed to help people suffering from diabetes and epilepsy. However, the diet has gained enormous attention recently as a healthy and successful eating plan for people struggling to lose weight.

Our daily diets include 50% or more carbs for many of us. We probably eat more pasta, pizza, potatoes, and bread than any other food type. Our bodies break the carbs down into sugars, known as glucose, which gives us the energy to cope with our daily tasks.

So, what exactly is the keto diet, and how can it improve our health while helping us lose those extra pounds?

What Is the Keto Diet?

The keto diet recommends eating fewer carbs while increasing our meal's protein and fat content. The keto diet's radical changes to our eating plan may seem strange. Under normal metabolic circumstances, our bodies use glucose for energy. However, when we have too few carbs to support our bodies' energy needs, we have to make another plan. So, our bodies turn to the next best fuel provider, the fat stored in our tissues and cells.

So, instead of our bodies using carbs to power our essential life-sustaining processes, fat deposits are targeted. As our bodies burn the fat, they produce ketones manufactured in our liver. When the fat-burning process starts, our metabolism enters a state of ketosis, during which energy is produced.

When we starve ourselves, we consciously deprive our bodies of food and inadvertently use the premise of the ketogenic diet. Our insulin levels increase, stimulating the release of fatty acids from our body fat. The fatty acids are oxidized in our livers, where they become ketones used as an alternative energy source.

Types of Keto Diets

The ketogenic diet is perhaps one of the most flexible of its kind. The simplicity and clarity of the eating plan appealed to me from the get-go. So, when I started investigating weight loss programs, I was surprised to find several variations of the keto diet. Each of these benefits us, so we should consider our options before deciding which diet type best suits us.

Standard Ketogenic Diet

The standard keto diet (SKD) has an extremely low carb content of around 5-10%. It usually contains about 70% fat, 20% protein, and 10% carbs.

When we translate the standard ketogenic dietary requirements into grams per day, we should eat 40-60 gm of protein and 20-45 gm of carbohydrates. There is no limit on the amount of fat we can add to the SKD.

As we can see from these figures, most of our calories are supplied by our fat consumption. Thus, we can manipulate the SKD to suit our unique health and dietary needs. In addition, the SKD includes plenty of fresh vegetables, especially leafy greens and non-starchy varieties like carrots, eggplant, and mushrooms, to name but a few.

The standard ketogenic diet is recommended for those wanting to boost their glucose levels, lose significant weight, and significantly improve their heart health.

Cyclical Ketogenic Diet

The cyclical ketogenic diet (CKD) is successful because of its rotational system of carb backloading every two days following five ketogenic days, not to be confused

with carb cycling. Our bodies switch out of ketosis during the increased carb days to benefit from our brief high carb intake. Those of us who are more athletically inclined will potentially benefit from rotating a typical low-carb, high-fat meal plan with intermittent higher carb intake. The point of CKD is that we use an increase of carbs to help replenish the muscle glycogen lost during our workouts.

Targeted Ketogenic Diet

Another variation of the ketogenic diet is the targeted ketogenic diet (TKD), which encourages us to eat more carbohydrates before or after we exercise. The intent of TKD assumes that the increased energy our muscles require and what they need during activity and exercise is readily available from our increased carbohydrate intake.

High Protein Ketogenic Diet

The high protein ketogenic diet (HPKD) includes substantially more protein than the SKD by pushing the protein content to at least 35%. However, like me, some will benefit from substantial weight loss and may find the high protein ketogenic diet the more effective dietary option.

Potential Health Benefits of the Keto Diet

There are several potential benefits to the ketogenic diet. However, the eating plan may not suit all of us. Therefore, because each of our bodies is unique, before we start dieting, we should seek the advice of our medical practitioner.

At first, the high protein content of the keto diet helped reduce epileptic seizures in children. However, the low carbs combined with high protein and maximized 'healthy' fats in the keto diet elicit a dramatic change in our metabolic process. Consequently, if we seriously follow the ketogenic diet, we will feel less hungry and likely begin to lose noticeable weight within four days of starting the eating program.

During ketosis, less glucose is generated, thus helping us manage our insulin levels better. In addition to lower sugar levels, our cells will learn to function with increased ketones and less glucose. Hence, the keto diet is most likely beneficial for those of us with diabetes two.

As our bodies become increasingly efficient fuel-burning machines, the ketogenic process may help to reduce our low-density lipoproteins (LDL cholesterol) that block our arteries and raise our risk of heart disease.

Many of us suffer from a cluster of health conditions called metabolic syndrome. One is our excess of fatty tissue around our waists, a silent symptom of a serious health condition known as metabolic syndrome. Fortunately, the keto diet targets weight loss, thus decreasing our risk of heart attack and stroke.

When combined with regular exercise, an added benefit to ketosis is that our low-carb diet may support improved muscle health and strength.

Keto for Weight Loss

I would describe the keto eating plan as an extraordinarily low-carb diet that allows us to eat no more than twenty grams of carbs daily. Initially challenging though the keto diet was, I quickly realized planning is key to my successful weight loss. So, following the diet diligently for two months, I laid out a pretty strict framework within which I could operate. My carb intake was carefully divided to ensure I stuck as closely as possible to the required twenty grams. Keeping the carbs low meant my calorie count dropped accordingly. I recommend a similar routine for starters that got me into the keto groove.

Maintaining simple and repetitive meals made planning, shopping, and food preparation much more effortless. And, to my great glee, by the end of the first five weeks of the keto diet, I discovered I had begun to lose noticeable weight and the accompanying inches around my waist. What an incentive! By the end of the two-month trial, my weight had dropped by almost 18 pounds. I felt and looked so much better; lighter, brighter, and happier!

Keto for Prediabetics and Diabetics

It's important to note the positive effects of keto on people with a tendency to diabetes and those with full-blown type two diabetes. The high-fat, low-carb, and moderate-proteins meal plan prescribed by keto seems to reduce our blood sugar. What's more, the keto diet may help lower our dependence on prescription insulin.

Other Health Benefits of Keto

The keto diet has potential benefits for several conditions besides weight loss and blood sugar management.

Creative Menu Planning

When I was on the keto diet, I developed a flair for turning out some delicious and exciting meals. On the other hand, perhaps the fact that I had to seriously consider what I was going to cook in the first place made me more mindful of ways I could improve food flavor and serving. Either way, keto taught me that it's okay to be more creative in the kitchen.

Increased Energy

The healthy, balanced keto eating plan will support our increased energy and vitality. We may find keto helps us side-step the midday energy slumps we have come to accept as a part of our daily life. Because our bodies burn more fat, we are likely to discover a new lease on life.

Bust the Sugar Addiction

Perhaps one of the most significant benefits of the keto diet is that our sugar cravings will gradually disappear, leaving us in better health than we may have imagined.

Keto Food Pyramid

A food pyramid gives us a clear visual "food map" of what we should eat. At first glance, the keto diet appeared restrictive and challenging. I found it difficult to imagine how I could stick to a diet that offered so few options. How wrong I was. When I saw the keto food pyramid, I realized my food options are as many as they are varied.

Healthy fats form the basis of the keto food pyramid. The reason being is to burn fat, we need to eat low-saturated fats. As we move up the food pyramid, we find proteins, non-starchy and low-carb vegetables. Above these, we find full-fat dairy, and finally, nuts, seeds, and fruit at the pyramid's summit.

Understanding the food pyramid is fundamental to our keto diet success. We read the importance of each food group from the base of the pyramid to the summit. We should eat more food varieties listed at the bottom of the pyramid than those at the summit. However, the keto diet designates a balance of food varieties at every meal is critical for the diet's success.

Thus, we should have more servings from the food options at the base of the keto food pyramid and fewer of those foods closer to the summit.

Healthy Fats

The healthy fats at the base of the food pyramid will provide us with most of our essential daily calories. We can use ghee, butter, or oils like avocado, olive, and coconut for cooking and salad dressings.

Proteins

The level above the base shows us essential protein sources like fish, cheese, eggs, and lean meat. Protein is vital for muscle strength, building healthy neurotransmitters in our brains, and balancing hormones. And, because protein is satiating, we tend not to need to eat as often. Thus, we are likely to enjoy productive weight loss.

Low-carb Plants

The next level of food choice is the keto-friendly and low-carb vegetables that supply our essential micronutrients. Amongst others included are avocados, bok choy, broccoli, and asparagus.

Remember, because they have excessive carbs, starchy vegetables like carrots and potatoes are forbidden on the keto diet.

Dairy, Nuts, and Seeds—1-2 Servings per day

We find the calorific-dense, healthy variety of nuts at level four like macadamia nuts, almonds, hazelnuts, and nut butter—sunflower and pumpkin seeds are also included. So, again, we can enjoy these foods in moderation.

Foods to Avoid

There are many foods that we are discouraged from eating while on keto. I found the challenge of ignoring the prohibited foods from my keto diet daunting. However, I realized we could introduce small servings of off-limit foods now and again. The foods we should avoid are the following.

Grains

We should avoid eating all grain-based foods when we are on keto. Included here are crackers, pasta, cereal, and rice. What's more, all bread, including gluten-free varieties, has a high carbohydrate content.

Starchy Vegetables

I discovered that starchy vegetables low in fiber and high in carbohydrates should be avoided when we are on keto. Included here are beets, corn, and all types of potatoes. In addition, chips, crisps, and French fries are prohibited on keto.

High-Sugar, Fruits

We should avoid fruits like bananas, dates, and mangoes as they spike our blood sugar due to their increased carbohydrate content.

Sweetened Yogurt

We should avoid artificially sweetened foods as the added sugars boost our carbs. Instead, we can choose plain Greek yogurt which is rich in proteins and low in carbs.

Most fruit juices have a high sugar content and are thus not recommended for keto.

We should avoid all high-carb, sugar-based foods, syrup, and honey, no matter how delicious.

Five Best Keto Tricks for Beginners

Starting a new diet can be both exciting and a little daunting. My best advice is to have a precise diet plan and a food list. Here are five valuable tips I suggest so we can get a head start on our keto diet.

1.Start Simple

For me, a simple food plan is my go-to solution. We can kick start our keto diet by following three steps.

Step 1: we should choose a protein such as fish, chicken, beef, or eggs.

Step 2: we need a low-carb vegetable such as cauliflower, zucchini, broccoli, or bell peppers.

Step 3: we can add unsaturated fat such as cheese, nuts, or mayonnaise.

To begin, each meal should consist of these three steps. Then, as soon as we feel more confident about our keto diet meal planning, we can step up our game.

2.About Carbs, Proteins, and Fats

♦ Limit Carbs—Five to Ten Percent Total Calories Daily

I found it challenging to turn my back on carbs. After all, carbs formed the foundation of about 95% of my meals before keto. When we do keto, carbs are limited. So, we need to be strong and turn our back on temptation. I can agree that I am not sorry I did it! Limiting carbs helps kick-start ketosis, the keto diet's fundamental premise. We have two other macronutrients (macros) in place of carbs that help support our health.

♦ Protein is Target—Ten to Twenty Percent Total Calories Daily

The first macro we should consider is protein. Our protein consumption is paramount for keto diet maintenance. Too little may damage our health, while too much can upset the ketosis balance and nullify our dieting efforts.

♦ Fat is the Initiator—Seventy-Eighty Percent Total Calories Daily

Second, fat is another helpful macro. Once I have planned my carbs and proteins for each meal, I add the fat content. Fats help to keep us satiated and provide most of our energy needs. We can manipulate the fat content of each meal to suit ourselves. If we increase the fat content, we are unlikely to feel hungry too soon. Correspondingly, if we decrease the meal's fat content, we will likely lose weight. Because fat is an essential energy source, we must ensure it is included in every meal.

To figure out the ideal macro balance of each meal, we can use a keto macro calculator available online.

3.Portions do Matter

Despite portions and calories not being the main focus of keto, we still need to consider our meal size. The more considerable the amount, the less likely we will lose weight. When we keep our food portions smaller, we gradually train our stomach and brain to expect less food for the same gain. Fat is the key to ensuring our amounts have optimal value for weight loss and keto diet success.

4.Avoid the Keto Flu

As our bodies move into the keto rhythm by shifting from glucose and carb-based energy to fat-induced energy release, we may experience flu-like symptoms for a day or two. Though unpleasant, the symptoms soon fade, leaving our bodies ready for keto success.

5.Stay Hydrated

Drinking water is essential to our health. However, we should increase our fluid intake during keto to keep ourselves hydrated. Carbs encourage our cells to retain water, but the keto diet stimulates water release to flush out toxins. Hence, we should drink up to 64 ounces of water daily to stay hydrated.

Supplements for a Keto Diet

Supplements are recommended for most diets to cover our health bases. However, because the keto diet excludes several food options, here are several essential health supplements we may need to boost our health.

Magnesium—200-400 mg, Daily

For blood sugar regulation and energy support, magnesium is essential to help us meet our mineral requirements. What's more, magnesium is beneficial for improving our sleep, reducing irritability, and minimizing muscle cramps. Natural sources of magnesium are found in spinach, mackerel, and pumpkin seeds.

MCT Oil

Coconut oil is a source of medium-chain triglycerides (MCT). Therefore, it is a suitable supplement for those of us doing keto. I use MCT oil to increase my fat uptake quickly, increase ketosis, and support weight loss.

Omega-3 Fatty Acids

When we are on keto, omega-3 supplements support our overall health by reducing insulin markers and protecting us against inflammatory diseases. Sardines, salmon, and anchovies are rich in omega-3.

Exogenous Ketones

Our bodies produce ketones when we go into ketosis. However, we may want to consider using ketone supplements to increase our blood ketone levels and push us into ketosis faster. Exogenous ketones have the added advantage of boosting athletic execution and upping our speed.

Greens Powder

Vegetables, especially leafy greens, are rich in essential minerals, vitamins, and active plant compounds that help our bodies fight inflammation and infection. In addition, vegetables help lower disease risk. Green powder is an easy go-to way to boost our vegetable intake and support our overall health.

Tips for Eating out, When Following the Keto Diet

When I started keto, I dreaded eating out. What would I eat? And, how would I manage at social functions and gatherings? After some research, I discovered I could successfully manage these social events. The key is working out sensible, realistic ways to enjoy social situations while still maintaining my healthy keto diet in different locations. I have also discovered that many restaurants are keto-friendly if you know your allocated food groups. In addition, there are usually several choices of suitable protein dishes, including fish and meat. Here are some super-easy ideas to encourage you to eat out during your keto diet.

- ◆ I learned that I could easily replace the high-carb portions like French fries with extra vegetables.
- ◆ Egg-based meals are an easy, tasty alternative protein.
- ◆ Bunless burgers are perfect for a low-carb meal. Swap out the fries for extra salad, cheese, bacon, or even avocado.
- ◆ I love Mexican food, so I always add extra guacamole, sour cream, and cheese to ensure I have a balanced keto meal.
- ◆ And, for dessert, we can opt for a selection of cheese or perhaps a small serving of nuts and berries with cream.

Whatever your choice, enjoy eating out while you are on keto.

Chapter 2 Breakfasts

Vegetable and Cheese Bake

Prep time: 7 minutes | Cook time: 9 minutes | Serves 3

3 eggs, beaten
¼ cup coconut cream
¼ teaspoon salt
3 ounces (85 g) Brussel sprouts, chopped
2 ounces (57 g) tomato,
chopped
3 ounces (85 g) provolone cheese, shredded
1 teaspoon butter
1 teaspoon smoked paprika

1. Grease the instant pot pan with the butter. 2. Put eggs in the bowl, add salt, and smoked paprika. Whisk the eggs well. 3. After this, add chopped Brussel sprouts and tomato. 4. Pour the mixture into the instant pot pan and sprinkle over with the shredded cheese. 5. Pour 1 cup of the water in the instant pot. Then place the pan with the egg mixture and close the lid. 6. Cook the meal on Manual (High Pressure) for 4 minutes. Then make naturally release for 5 minutes.

Per Serving:
Calories: 237 | fat: 18g | protein: 14g | carbs: 6g | net carbs: 4g | fiber: 2g

Cauliflower Avocado Toast

Prep time: 15 minutes | Cook time: 8 minutes | Serves 2

1 (12-ounce / 340-g) steamer bag cauliflower
1 large egg
½ cup shredded Mozzarella cheese
1 ripe medium avocado
½ teaspoon garlic powder
¼ teaspoon ground black pepper

1. Cook cauliflower according to package instructions. Remove from bag and place into cheesecloth or clean towel to remove excess moisture. 2. Place cauliflower into a large bowl and mix in egg and Mozzarella. Cut a piece of parchment to fit your air fryer basket. Separate the cauliflower mixture into two, and place it on the parchment in two mounds. Press out the cauliflower mounds into a ¼-inch-thick rectangle. Place the parchment into the air fryer basket. 3. Adjust the temperature to 400ºF (204ºC) and set the timer for 8 minutes. 4. Flip the cauliflower halfway through the cooking time. 5. When the timer beeps, remove the parchment and allow the cauliflower to cool 5 minutes. 6. Cut open the avocado and remove the pit. Scoop out the inside, place it in a medium bowl, and mash it with garlic powder and pepper. Spread onto the cauliflower. Serve immediately.

Per Serving:
Calories: 321 | fat: 22g | protein: 16g | carbs: 19g | net carbs: 9g | fiber: 10g

Flappa Jacks

Prep time: 10 minutes | Cook time: 14 minutes | Serves 6

1 cup blanched almond flour
¼ cup coconut flour
5 large eggs, whisked
3 (1-gram) packets 0g net carb sweetener
1 teaspoon baking powder
⅓ cup unsweetened almond milk
¼ cup vegetable oil
1½ teaspoons pure vanilla extract
⅛ teaspoon salt

1 In a large mixing bowl, mix all ingredients together until smooth. 2 In a large nonstick skillet over medium heat, pour desired-sized pancakes and cook 3–5 minutes until bubbles form. 3 Flip pancakes and cook another 2 minutes until brown. Repeat as needed to use all batter. Serve.

Per Serving:
Calories: 273 | fat: 23g | protein: 10g | carbs: 7g | net carbs: 3g | fiber: 4g

Sausage Stuffed Poblanos

Prep time: 15 minutes | Cook time: 15 minutes | Serves 4

½ pound (227 g) spicy ground pork breakfast sausage
4 large eggs
4 ounces (113 g) full-fat cream cheese, softened
¼ cup canned diced tomatoes
and green chiles, drained
4 large poblano peppers
8 tablespoons shredded Pepper Jack cheese
½ cup full-fat sour cream

1. In a medium skillet over medium heat, crumble and brown the ground sausage until no pink remains. Remove sausage and drain the fat from the pan. Crack eggs into the pan, scramble, and cook until no longer runny. 2. Place cooked sausage in a large bowl and fold in cream cheese. Mix in diced tomatoes and chiles. Gently fold in eggs. 3. Cut a 4-inch to 5-inch slit in the top of each poblano, removing the seeds and white membrane with a small knife. Separate the filling into four servings and spoon carefully into each pepper. Top each with 2 tablespoons pepper jack cheese. 4. Place each pepper into the air fryer basket. 5. Adjust the temperature to 350ºF (177ºC) and set the timer for 15 minutes. 6. Peppers will be soft and cheese will be browned when ready. Serve immediately with sour cream on top.

Per Serving:
Calories: 429 | fat: 36g | protein: 21g | carbs: 5g | net carbs: 4g | fiber: 1g

Cheesy Turkey Sausage Egg Muffins

Prep time: 10 minutes | Cook time: 15 minutes | Serves 3

1 teaspoon butter
6 eggs
Salt and black pepper, to taste
½ teaspoon dried rosemary

1 cup pecorino romano cheese, grated
3 turkey sausages, chopped

1. Preheat oven to 400ºF and grease muffin cups with cooking spray. 2. In a skillet over medium heat add the butter and cook the turkey sausages for 4-5 minutes. 3. Beat 3 eggs with a fork. Add in sausages, cheese, and seasonings. Divide between the muffin cups and bake for 4 minutes. Crack in an egg to each of the cups. Bake for an additional 4 minutes. Allow cooling before serving.

Per Serving:
Calories: 329 | fat: 21g | protein: 30g | carbs: 2g | net carbs: 2g | fiber: 0g

Home-Fried Bacon Radishes

Prep time: 10 minutes | Cook time: 25 minutes | serves 4

1 (16-ounce) bag radishes
6 slices bacon
Salt and ground black pepper

Chopped fresh flat-leaf parsley, for garnish (optional)

1. Trim the tops off the radishes and chop the radishes into small pieces. 2. In a large skillet over medium heat, cook the bacon until crispy, about 5 minutes. Remove the bacon from the skillet, leaving the drippings in the pan. Crumble the bacon and set aside. 3. Place the radishes in the skillet and cook over medium-high heat for 10 minutes, then reduce the heat to medium. Add the cooked bacon and continue cooking for about 10 more minutes, stirring every couple of minutes, until the radishes are slightly crispy and caramelized around the edges. 4. Season to taste with salt and pepper and serve immediately. Garnish with parsley, if desired.

Per Serving:
Calories: 100 | fat: 7g | protein: 6g | carbs: 4g | net carbs: 2g | fiber: 2g

Keto English Muffins

Prep time: 2 minutes | Cook time: 1 or 12 minutes | Serves 1

1 teaspoon coconut oil, for greasing the ramekin
1 large egg

2 teaspoons coconut flour
Pinch of baking soda
Pinch of fine sea salt

1. Grease a 4-ounce (113-g) ramekin with the coconut oil. If using the toaster oven method, preheat the toaster oven to 400ºF (205ºC). 2. In a small mixing bowl, combine the egg and coconut flour with a fork until well combined, then add the rest of the ingredients and stir to combine. 3. Place the dough in the greased ramekin. To cook in a microwave, cook on high for 1 minute, until a toothpick inserted in the middle comes out clean. To cook in a toaster oven, bake for 12 minutes, until a toothpick inserted in the middle comes out clean. 4. Allow to cool in the ramekin for 5 minutes. Remove the muffin from the ramekin and allow to cool completely. Slice in half and serve.

Per Serving:
Calories: 130 | fat: 7g | protein: 8g | carbs: 8g | net carbs: 3g | fiber: 5g

Sausage and Cauliflower Breakfast Casserole

Prep time: 5 minutes | Cook time: 10 minutes | Serves 6

1 cup water
½ head cauliflower, chopped into bite-sized pieces
4 slices bacon
1 pound (454 g) breakfast sausage
4 tablespoons melted butter
10 eggs

⅓ cup heavy cream
2 teaspoons salt
1 teaspoon pepper
2 tablespoons hot sauce
2 stalks green onion
1 cup shredded sharp Cheddar cheese

1. Pour water into Instant Pot and place steamer basket in bottom. Add cauliflower. Click lid closed. 2. Press the Steam button and adjust time for 1 minute. When timer beeps, quick-release the pressure and place cauliflower to the side in medium bowl. 3. Drain water from Instant Pot, clean, and replace. Press the Sauté button. Press the Adjust button to set heat to Less. Cook bacon until crispy. Once fully cooked, set aside on paper towels. Add breakfast sausage to pot and brown (still using the Sauté function). 4. While sausage is cooking, whisk butter, eggs, heavy cream, salt, pepper, and hot sauce. 5. When sausage is fully cooked, pour egg mixture into Instant Pot. Gently stir using silicone spatula until eggs are completely cooked and fluffy. Press the Cancel button. Slice green onions. Sprinkle green onions, bacon, and cheese over mixture and let melt. Serve warm.

Per Serving:
Calories: 620 | fat: 50g | protein: 30g | carbs: 5g | net carbs: 4g | fiber: 1g

Egg-Stuffed Avocados

Prep time: 5 minutes | Cook time: 35 minutes | Serves 2

1 large avocado, halved and pitted
2 small eggs
Pink Himalayan sea salt

Freshly ground black pepper
1 bacon slice, cooked until crispy and crumbled

1. Preheat the oven to 375ºF (190ºC). 2. Using a small spoon, enlarge the hole of the avocado left by the pit so it is roughly 2 inches in diameter. 3. Place the avocado halves cut-side up on a baking sheet. 4. Crack an egg into the well of each half. Season with salt and pepper. 5. Bake for 30 to 35 minutes, until the yolk reaches your preferred texture, 30 minutes for soft and 35 minutes for hard. 6. Sprinkle the bacon crumbles on top and enjoy!

Per Serving:
Calories: 264 | fat: 21g | protein: 10g | carbs: 12g | net carbs: 3g | fiber: 9g

Nutty "Oatmeal"

Prep time: 5 minutes | Cook time: 4 minutes | Serves 4

2 tablespoons coconut oil	¼ cup unsweetened coconut
1 cup full-fat coconut milk	flakes
1 cup heavy whipping cream	2 tablespoons chopped
½ cup macadamia nuts	hazelnuts
½ cup chopped pecans	2 tablespoons chia seeds
⅓ cup Swerve, or more to taste	½ teaspoon ground cinnamon

1. Before you get started, soak the chia seeds for about 5 to 10 minutes (can be up to 20, if desired) in 1 cup of filtered water. After soaking, set the Instant Pot to Sauté and add the coconut oil. Once melted, pour in the milk, whipping cream, and 1 cup of filtered water. Then add the macadamia nuts, pecans, Swerve, coconut flakes, hazelnuts, chia seeds, and cinnamon. Mix thoroughly inside the Instant Pot. 2. Close the lid, set the pressure release to Sealing, and hit Cancel to stop the current program. Select Manual, set the Instant Pot to 4 minutes on High Pressure, and let cook. 3. Once cooked, carefully switch the pressure release to Venting. 4. Open the Instant Pot, serve, and enjoy!

Per Serving:

Calories: 506 | fat: 53g | protein: 6g | carbs: 11g | net carbs: 5g | fiber: 6g

Herb Chicken Sausages with Braised Bok Choy

Prep time: 5 minutes | Cook time: 25 minutes | Serves 5

1 pound (455 g) ground chicken	1 clove garlic, minced
¾ teaspoon finely ground sea salt	½ teaspoon ground black pepper
2 tablespoons diced white onions	½ teaspoon fresh thyme leaves
2 leaves fresh sage, chopped	⅛ teaspoon red pepper flakes
1 tablespoon chopped fresh chives	3 tablespoons coconut oil, avocado oil, or ghee, for the pan
1 tablespoon chopped fresh parsley	5 cups (350 g) chopped bok choy

1. Place all the ingredients for the sausages in a large mixing bowl and mix until fully incorporated. 2. Heat the oil in a large frying pan over medium-low heat. 3. While the oil is heating, form the chicken mixture into patties: Using a ¼-cup (60-ml) scoop, scoop up and shape the mixture with your hands to form 10 balls about 1¾ inches (4.5 cm) in diameter. Place the balls in the hot pan and press down until the patties are ¼ inch (6 mm) thick. 4. Cook the sausages for 10 minutes per side, or until golden on the outside and cooked through. 5. Transfer the cooked sausages to a serving plate. If you wish, place them in a 180°F (82°C) oven to keep warm. 6. Place the bok choy in the same pan, cover, and cook over medium heat for 5 minutes, or until fork-tender. 7. Transfer the cooked bok choy to the serving plate with the sausages and enjoy.

Per Serving:

Calories: 246 | fat: 14g | protein: 27g | carbs: 2g | net carbs: 1g | fiber: 1g

Ham & Egg Broccoli Bake

Prep time: 15 minutes | Cook time: 20 minutes | Serves 4

2 heads broccoli, cut into small florets	2 teaspoons ghee
2 red bell peppers, seeded and chopped	1 teaspoon dried oregano + extra to garnish
¼ cup chopped ham	Salt and black pepper to taste
	8 fresh eggs

1. Preheat oven to 425°F. 2. Melt the ghee in a frying pan over medium heat; brown the ham, stirring frequently, about 3 minutes. 3. Arrange the broccoli, bell peppers, and ham on a foil-lined baking sheet in a single layer, toss to combine; season with salt, oregano, and black pepper. Bake for 10 minutes until the vegetables have softened. 4. Remove, create eight indentations with a spoon, and crack an egg into each. Return to the oven and continue to bake for an additional 5 to 7 minutes until the egg whites are firm. 5. Season with salt, black pepper, and extra oregano, share the bake into four plates and serve with strawberry lemonade (optional).

Per Serving:

Calories: 240 | fat: 12g | protein: 22g | carbs: 13g | net carbs: 4g | fiber: 9g

Not Your Average Boiled Eggs

Prep time: 10 minutes | Cook time: 10 minutes | Serves 5

Boiled Eggs:	2 tablespoons coconut vinegar
10 eggs	or apple cider vinegar
1 tablespoon coconut vinegar or	1 teaspoon minced fresh garlic
apple cider vinegar	or garlic powder
Sauce:	1 teaspoon minced fresh ginger
1½ cups water	or ground ginger
2 tablespoons liquid aminos or	1 teaspoon sea salt
tamari	½ teaspoon freshly ground
2 tablespoons coconut aminos	black pepper

Make the Boiled Eggs 1. Place the eggs in a medium pot and add enough cold water to cover them. Add a splash of vinegar (this makes the eggs easier to peel) and bring to a boil. When the water boils, remove the pot from the heat, cover, and let sit for 10 minutes. 2. Meanwhile, fill a large bowl with water and ice. When the eggs are done, transfer them to the ice bath for another 10 minutes. 3. Peel the eggs and set them aside. Make the Sauce 4. In a large storage bowl with a lid, whisk together the water, liquid aminos, coconut aminos, vinegar, garlic, ginger, salt, and pepper. Alternatively, you can divide the ingredients in half and add to two large mason jars with lids. 5. Place the peeled eggs in the sauce. Cover and refrigerate. The longer the eggs soak up the sauce, the more flavorful they will be.

Per Serving (2 eggs):

Calories: 144 | fat: 10g | protein: 12g | carbs: 2g | net carbs: 2g | fiber: 0g

Kale, Bacon and Goat Cheese Frittata

Prep time: 15 minutes | Cook time: 45 minutes | Serves 4

½ pound (227 g) bacon, chopped

1 tablespoon cooking fat of choice (optional)

2 cups chopped fresh kale

8 large eggs

¼ cup full-fat coconut, nut, or

dairy milk

½ teaspoon sea salt

½ teaspoon ground black pepper

4 ounces (113 g) goat cheese, crumbled

1. Preheat the oven to 375°F (190°C). 2. Heat an ovenproof 12-inch skillet over medium heat. Place the bacon in the pan and cook for 5 to 10 minutes, until crispy. Taste the cooked bacon—if it's fairly salty, use less salt later in the recipe. If the pan is looking a little dry, add the cooking fat. 3. Add the kale to the skillet and cook until softened, 3 to 4 minutes. 4. While the bacon and kale are cooking, in a large mixing bowl whisk together the eggs, coconut milk, salt, and pepper. 5. Pour the egg mixture into the skillet, over the bacon and kale. Top with the goat cheese (if using). 6. Transfer the skillet to the oven and bake for 25 to 30 minutes, until the eggs are no longer runny, the frittata puffs up a bit, and the edges are golden brown.

Per Serving:
Calories: 549 | fat: 48g | protein: 26g | carbs: 5g | net carbs: 4g | fiber: 1g

Bacon Lovers' Quiche

Prep time: 20 minutes | Cook time: 45 minutes | Serves 8

Crust:

2 cups (220 g) blanched almond flour

1 large egg

2 tablespoons melted lard, plus more for the pans

⅛ teaspoon finely ground gray sea salt

Filling:

6 strips bacon (about 6 ounces/170 g)

1⅓ cups (315 ml) full-fat coconut milk

4 large eggs

¼ cup plus 2 tablespoons (25 g) nutritional yeast

¼ teaspoon finely ground gray sea salt

¼ teaspoon ground black pepper

⅛ teaspoon ground nutmeg

For Garnish (Optional):

Cooked chopped bacon (reserved from above)

Sliced fresh chives

1. Preheat the oven to 350°F (177°C) and lightly grease four 4-inch (10-cm) tart pans with lard. 2. Make the crusts: In a large bowl, combine the almond flour, egg, lard, and salt. Mix with a fork until completely incorporated. 3. Divide the dough into 4 pieces and place each piece in a prepared tart pan. Press the dough into the pans, pushing it evenly up the sides. It should be about ⅛ inch (3 mm) thick. 4. Place the tart pans on a rimmed baking sheet and par-bake for 13 to 15 minutes, until the crusts are lightly golden. 5. Meanwhile, prepare the filling: Cook the bacon in a frying pan over medium heat until crispy, then roughly chop or crumble it; reserve the bacon grease. Put the coconut milk, eggs, nutritional yeast,

salt, pepper, and nutmeg in a bowl. Add the bacon pieces (setting a small amount aside for garnish if you wish) and still-warm reserved bacon grease and whisk to combine. 6. Remove the par-baked crusts from the oven and reduce the temperature to 325°F (163°C). Leaving the crusts on the baking sheet, fill them all the way to the brim with the egg filling. 7. Return the quiches to the oven and bake for 30 minutes, or until the tops are lightly golden. Allow to cool for 30 minutes before serving. Garnish each quiche with the reserved bacon pieces and/or sliced chives, if desired.

Per Serving:
Calories: 404 | fat: 31g | protein: 23g | carbs: 9g | net carbs: 4g | fiber: 5g

Pork and Quill Egg Cups

Prep time: 15 minutes | Cook time: 15 minutes | Serves 4

10 ounces (283 g) ground pork

1 jalapeño pepper, chopped

1 tablespoon butter, softened

1 teaspoon dried dill

½ teaspoon salt

1 cup water

4 quill eggs

1. In a bowl, stir together all the ingredients, except for the quill eggs and water. Transfer the meat mixture to the silicone muffin molds and press the surface gently. 2. Pour the water and insert the trivet in the Instant Pot. Put the meat cups on the trivet. 3. Crack the eggs over the meat mixture. 4. Set the lid in place. Select the Manual mode and set the cooking time for 15 minutes on High Pressure. When the timer goes off, do a quick pressure release. Carefully open the lid. 5. Serve warm.

Per Serving:
Calories: 142 | fat: 6g | protein: 20g | carbs: 0.3g | net carbs: 0.1g | fiber: 0.2g

Smoked Ham and Egg Muffins

Prep time: 5 minutes | Cook time: 25 minutes | Serves 9

2 cups chopped smoked ham

⅓ cup grated Parmesan cheese

¼ cup almond flour

9 eggs

⅓ cup mayonnaise, sugar-free

¼ teaspoon garlic powder

¼ cup chopped onion

Sea salt to taste

1. Preheat your oven to 370°F. 2. Lightly grease nine muffin pans with cooking spray and set aside. Place the onion, ham, garlic powder, and salt, in a food processor, and pulse until ground. Stir in the mayonnaise, almond flour, and Parmesan cheese. Press this mixture into the muffin cups. 3. Make sure it goes all the way up the muffin sides so that there will be room for the egg. Bake for 5 minutes. Crack an egg into each muffin cup. Return to the oven and bake for 20 more minutes or until the tops are firm to the touch and eggs are cooked. Leave to cool slightly before serving.

Per Serving:
Calories: 165 | fat: 11g | protein: 14g | carbs: 2g | net carbs: 1g | fiber: 1g

Streusel Pumpkin Cake

Prep time: 10 minutes | Cook time: 30 minutes | Serves 8

Streusel Topping:	1 cup pumpkin purée
¼ cup Swerve	¾ cup Swerve
¼ cup almond flour	2 teaspoons pumpkin pie spice
2 tablespoons coconut oil or	2 teaspoons vanilla extract
unsalted butter, softened	½ teaspoon fine sea salt
½ teaspoon ground cinnamon	Glaze:
Cake:	½ cup Swerve
2 large eggs, beaten	3 tablespoons unsweetened
2 cups almond flour	almond milk

1. Set a trivet in the Instant Pot and pour in 1 cup water. Line a baking pan with parchment paper. 2. In a small bowl, whisk together all the ingredients for the streusel topping with a fork. 3. In a medium-sized bowl, stir together all the ingredients for the cake until thoroughly combined. 4. Scoop half of the batter into the prepared baking pan and sprinkle half of the streusel topping on top. Repeat with the remaining batter and topping. 5. Place the baking pan on the trivet in the Instant Pot. 6. Lock the lid, select the Manual mode and set the cooking time for 30 minutes on High Pressure. 7. Meanwhile, whisk together the Swerve and almond milk in a small bowl until it reaches a runny consistency. 8. When the timer goes off, do a natural pressure release for 10 minutes, then release any remaining pressure. Open the lid. 9. Remove the baking pan from the pot. Let cool in the pan for 10 minutes. Transfer the cake onto a plate and peel off the parchment paper. 10. Transfer the cake onto a serving platter. Spoon the glaze over the top of the cake. Serve immediately.

Per Serving:

Calories: 238 | fat: 20g | protein: 9g | carbs: 9g | net carbs: 5g | fiber: 4g

Ham and Vegetable Frittata

Prep time: 10 minutes | Cook time: 27 minutes | Serves 4

2 tablespoons butter, at room	1 carrot, chopped
temperature	8 ham slices
½ cup green onions, chopped	8 eggs, whisked
2 garlic cloves, minced	Salt and black pepper, to taste
1 jalapeño pepper, chopped	½ teaspoon dried thyme

1.Set a pan over medium heat and warm the butter. Stir in green onions and sauté for 4 minutes. 2. Place in garlic and cook for 1 minute. Stir in carrot and jalapeño pepper, and cook for 4 more minutes. Remove the mixture to a lightly greased baking pan, with cooking spray, and top with ham slices. 3. Place in the eggs over vegetables and ham; add thyme, black pepper, and salt for seasoning. Bake in the oven for about 18 minutes at 360ºF. Serve warm alongside a dollop of full-fat natural yogurt.

Per Serving:

Calories: 239 | fat: 16g | protein: 19g | carbs: 5g | net carbs: 4g | fiber: 1g

Eggs Benedict on Grilled Portobello Mushroom Caps

Prep time: 5 minutes | Cook time: 10 to 15 minutes | Serves 1

2 portobello mushroom caps	1½ tablespoons olive oil
1 tablespoon avocado oil	Pinch salt
2 large spinach leaves	1 teaspoon paprika
2 slices bacon	Chopped fresh parsley, for
2 eggs	serving
1 egg yolk	Sugar-free hot sauce, for
¼ teaspoon freshly squeezed	serving (optional)
lemon juice	

1. Preheat the oven to broil or to 400ºF (205ºC), or heat a grill. 2. Take a damp paper towel and wipe off the mushroom caps, removing any stem. Rub them all over with the avocado oil, place on a baking sheet, and broil or roast in the oven for 10 minutes, flipping them halfway through. Alternatively, you can grill the mushroom caps for about 5 minutes on each side. 3. In a skillet while the mushrooms are baking, fry the bacon (which doesn't need any added fat) to your desired doneness. Remove from skillet and set aside. 4. Remove the mushrooms from the oven or grill, transfer to a plate, and place the spinach leaves and bacon on top. 5. To poach the eggs, fill a saucepan with water and bring to a boil, then lower the heat to a simmer. 6. Crack the eggs into a small bowl and carefully pour them into the simmering water. Turn off the heat, cover the pan, and let the eggs cook for about 5 minutes. 7. Carefully remove the eggs from the pan with a slotted spoon, straining over the pan, and place on top of the crispy bacon, spinach, and mushroom caps. 8. In a blender, combine the egg yolk, lemon juice, olive oil, and salt. Turn on the blender to its lowest setting and let the mixture whip together. 9. When the hollandaise sauce looks creamy, turn off the blender and pour the sauce over your mushrooms topped with spinach, bacon, and eggs. 10. Sprinkle with the paprika, chopped parsley, and a dash or two of hot sauce, if desired.

Per Serving:

Calories: 841 | fat: 76g | protein: 32g | carbs: 14g | net carbs: 9g | fiber: 5g

Overnight Protein Oats

Prep time: 5 minutes | Cook time: 0 minutes | Makes 1

¼ cup heavy whipping cream	1 scoop flavored protein powder
3 tablespoons hemp hearts	of choice
1 tablespoon chia seeds	

1. Put all the ingredients in a bowl and stir to combine. Cover with plastic wrap and place in the refrigerator for at least 4 hours or overnight. 2. Serve cold, straight out of the refrigerator, or microwave on high for 20 to 30 seconds before serving.

Per Serving:

Calories: 439 | fat: 28g | protein: 39g | carbs: 9g | net carbs: 1g | fiber: 8g

Sausage Egg Cup

Prep time: 10 minutes | Cook time: 15 minutes | Serves 6

12 ounces (340 g) ground pork breakfast sausage	¼ teaspoon ground black pepper
6 large eggs	½ teaspoon crushed red pepper flakes
½ teaspoon salt	

1. Place sausage in six 4-inch ramekins (about 2 ounces / 57 g per ramekin) greased with cooking oil. Press sausage down to cover bottom and about ½-inch up the sides of ramekins. Crack one egg into each ramekin and sprinkle evenly with salt, black pepper, and red pepper flakes. 2. Place ramekins into air fryer basket. Adjust the temperature to 350°F (177°C) and set the timer for 15 minutes. Egg cups will be done when sausage is fully cooked to at least 145°F (63°C) and the egg is firm. Serve warm.

Per Serving:
Calories: 268 | fat: 23g | protein: 14g | carbs: 1g | net carbs: 1g | fiber: 0g

Spinach and Feta Egg Bake

Prep time: 7 minutes | Cook time: 23 to 25 minutes | Serves 2

Avocado oil spray	Sea salt and freshly ground black pepper, to taste
⅓ cup diced red onion	¼ teaspoon cayenne pepper
1 cup frozen chopped spinach, thawed and drained	½ cup crumbled feta cheese
4 large eggs	¼ cup shredded Parmesan cheese
¼ cup heavy (whipping) cream	

1. Spray a deep pan with oil. Put the onion in the pan, and place the pan in the air fryer basket. Set the air fryer to 350°F (177°C) and bake for 7 minutes. 2. Sprinkle the spinach over the onion. 3. In a medium bowl, beat the eggs, heavy cream, salt, black pepper, and cayenne. Pour this mixture over the vegetables. 4. Top with the feta and Parmesan cheese. Bake for 16 to 18 minutes, until the eggs are set and lightly brown.

Per Serving:
Calories: 366 | fat: 26g | protein: 25g | carbs: 8g | net carbs: 5g | fiber: 3g

Greek Yogurt Crunch Bowl

Prep time: 5 minutes | Cook time: 10 minutes | Serves 2

¼ cup unsweetened coconut flakes	Keto-friendly sweetener to taste (optional)
2 tablespoons sliced almonds	2 tablespoons raw almond butter (no added sugar)
1 cup plain full-fat Greek yogurt	2 tablespoons cacao nibs
⅓ cup full-fat coconut milk	Sprinkle of ground cinnamon

1. In a small, dry skillet set over medium-low heat, toast the coconut flakes until lightly brown. Repeat for the sliced almonds. 2. Stir together the yogurt, coconut milk, and sweetener, if using. Divide the mixture between two bowls. Add 1 tablespoon almond butter to each, and stir to swirl together (don't worry about combining entirely). Top each with some toasted coconut, sliced almonds, and cacao nibs, and sprinkle with cinnamon.

Per Serving:
Calories: 481 | fat: 37g | protein: 19g | carbs: 18g | net carbs: 16g | fiber: 2g

Cinnamon-Nut Cottage Cheese

Prep time: 5 minutes | Cook time: 0 minutes | Serves 1

½ cup cottage cheese	2 teaspoons to 1 tablespoon cinnamon
1 stevia packet or a few squirts liquid stevia or substitute	¼ cup chopped pecans

1. In a bowl, combine the cottage cheese and stevia, mixing well. 2. Add the cinnamon and mix just to incorporate. Add more cinnamon or stevia to taste. 3. Sprinkle the pecans on top and enjoy!

Per Serving:
Calories: 324 | fat: 27g | protein: 15g | carbs: 10g | net carbs: 6g | fiber: 4g

Market Veggie Tofu Scramble

Prep time: 10 minutes | Cook time: 10 minutes | serves 4

1 (14-ounce) block firm sprouted organic tofu, pressed and drained	coconut oil
	⅓ cup diced yellow onion
2 tablespoons tahini	⅓ cup diced green bell pepper
2 tablespoons nutritional yeast	¼ teaspoon garlic powder
1 tablespoon chia seeds	¼ cup olives
¼ teaspoon turmeric powder	2 cups coarsely chopped fresh spinach
⅛ teaspoon kala namak salt	1 teaspoon hot sauce (optional)
2 tablespoons cold-pressed	

1. Blot the tofu with a paper towel to remove as much water as possible, then crumble it by hand into a large mixing bowl. 2. Add the tahini, nutritional yeast, chia seeds, turmeric, and kala namak salt to the bowl. Toss the ingredients together and set aside. 3. Heat the coconut oil in a large skillet over medium heat. 4. Add the onion, bell pepper, and garlic powder to the skillet. 5. Once the vegetables are tender and caramelized, toss in the olives and tofu mixture. 6. Allow the tofu to cook undisturbed for about 4 minutes to create a toasted, hash-like texture, then toss once to toast it a bit more. 7. Once the tofu is toasty, remove the skillet from the heat and stir in the spinach until it wilts. 8. Serve with your favorite hot sauce (if using).

Per Serving:
Calories: 253 | fat: 18g | protein: 15g | carbs: 11g | net carbs: 7g | fiber: 4g

Butter Coffee Latte

Prep time: 5 minutes | Cook time: 0 minutes | Serves 1

1 cup (8 ounces / 227 g) brewed coffee	½ tablespoon MCT oil
½ tablespoon unsalted butter	3 tablespoons unsweetened vanilla almond milk

1. In a blender, combine coffee, butter, MCT oil, and almond milk and blend until frothy. (Do not just stir the ingredients together. This will make your coffee oily, not frothy-yuck.) 2. Pour into a mug to serve.

Per Serving:

Calories: 119 | fat: 13g | protein: 0g | carbs: 0g | net carbs: 0g | fiber: 0g

Mini Spinach Quiche

Prep time: 5 minutes | Cook time: 15 minutes | Serves 1

2 eggs	¼ cup chopped fresh spinach
1 tablespoon heavy cream	½ teaspoon salt
1 tablespoon diced green pepper	¼ teaspoon pepper
1 tablespoon diced red onion	1 cup water

1. In medium bowl whisk together all ingredients except water. Pour into 4-inch ramekin. Generally, if the ramekin is oven-safe, it is also safe to use in pressure cooking. 2. Pour water into Instant Pot. Place steam rack into pot. Carefully place ramekin onto steam rack. Click lid closed. Press the Manual button and set time for 15 minutes. When timer beeps, quick-release the pressure. Serve warm.

Per Serving:

Calories: 201 | fat: 14g | protein: 13g | carbs: 3g | net carbs: 2g | fiber: 1g

Spiced Antioxidant Granola Clusters

Prep time: 10 minutes | Cook time: 1 hour 10 minutes | Serves 10

1 cup unsweetened fine coconut flakes	½ teaspoon ground cloves
1 cup unsweetened large coconut flakes	1 tablespoon fresh lemon zest
¼ cup packed flax meal	¼ teaspoon black pepper
¼ cup chia seeds	¼ teaspoon salt
½ cup pecans, chopped	⅓ cup light tahini
1 cup blanched almonds, roughly chopped, or flaked almonds	¼ cup virgin coconut oil
2 teaspoons cinnamon	2 large egg whites
1 teaspoon ground anise seed	Optional:
½ teaspoon ground nutmeg	Unsweetened almond milk, coconut cream, coconut yogurt, or full-fat goat's yogurt, to serve

1. Preheat the oven to 265°F (130°C) conventional or 230°F (110°C)

fan assisted convection. Line a baking tray with parchment paper. 2. Place all of the dry ingredients, including the lemon zest, in a large bowl. Stir to combine. In a small bowl, mix the tahini with the coconut oil, then add to the dry ingredients. Add the egg whites and mix to combine. 3. Spoon onto the lined baking tray and crumble all over. Bake for 1 hour and 10 minutes to 1 hour and 20 minutes, until golden. Remove from the oven and let cool completely; it will crisp up as it cools. Serve on its own or with almond milk, coconut cream or coconut yogurt, or full-fat goat's yogurt. Store in a jar at room temperature for up to 2 weeks or freeze for up to 3 months.

Per Serving:

Calories: 291 | fat: 25g | protein: 6g | carbs: 15g | net carbs: 9g | fiber: 6g

Salmon Bacon Rolls with Dipping Sauce

Prep time: 10 minutes | Cook time: 10 minutes | Makes 16 rolls

8 strips bacon (about 8 ounces/225 g)	½ cup (105 g) mayonnaise
8 ounces (225 g) smoked salmon, cut into 16 squares	2 tablespoons sugar-free barbecue sauce
Dipping Sauce:	Special Equipmnt:
	Toothpicks

1. Cook the bacon in a large frying pan over medium heat until much of the fat is rendered and the bacon is lightly browned but not crispy, 8 to 10 minutes. (You want the bacon to remain pliable so that you can bend it.) 2. Cut the cooked bacon in half lengthwise to create 16 narrow strips. Place a square of salmon on one end of a bacon strip. Roll the salmon in the bacon, secure with a toothpick, and place on a clean plate. Repeat with the remaining bacon and salmon, making a total of 16 rolls. 3. Make the dipping sauce: Place the mayonnaise and barbecue sauce in a small bowl and stir to combine. Serve alongside the salmon rolls.

Per Serving:

Calories: 324 | fat: 29g | protein: 14g | carbs: 3g | net carbs: 2g | fiber: 1g

Mixed Berry Smoothie

Prep time: 5 minutes | Cook time: 0 minutes | Serves 2

½ cup fresh or frozen strawberries	1 cup ice cubes
½ cup fresh or frozen blueberries	½ cup heavy (whipping) cream
½ cup fresh or frozen raspberries	½ cup Two Good vanilla yogurt
	2 tablespoons MCT oil
	¼ to ½ cup water, as needed

1. Fill a high-speed blender with the berries, ice cubes, cream, yogurt, and MCT oil. 2. Blend until smooth. If your blender struggles with the thickness, slowly add the water until it begins to blend. 3. Divide the mixture between 2 glasses and enjoy!

Per Serving:

Calories: 408 | fat: 38g | protein: 4g | carbs: 16g | net carbs: 12g | fiber: 4g

Brussels Sprouts, Bacon, and Eggs

Prep time: 5 minutes | Cook time: 20 minutes | Serves 2

½ pound Brussels sprouts, cleaned, trimmed, and halved
1 tablespoon olive oil
Pink Himalayan salt
Freshly ground black pepper
Nonstick cooking spray

6 bacon slices, diced
4 large eggs
Pinch red pepper flakes
2 tablespoons grated Parmesan cheese

1. Preheat the oven to 400°F. 2. In a medium bowl, toss the halved Brussels sprouts in the olive oil, and season with pink Himalayan salt and pepper. 3. Coat a 9-by-13-inch baking pan with cooking spray. 4. Put the Brussels sprouts and bacon in the pan, and roast for 12 minutes. 5. Take the pan out of the oven, and stir the Brussels sprouts and bacon. Using a spoon, create 4 wells in the mixture. 6. Carefully crack an egg into each well. 7. Season the eggs with pink Himalayan salt, black pepper, and red pepper flakes. 8. Sprinkle the Parmesan cheese over the Brussels sprouts and eggs. 9. Cook in the oven for 8 more minutes, or until the eggs are cooked to your preference, and serve.

Per Serving:
Calories: 401 | fat: 29g | protein: 27g | carbs: 12g | net carbs: 7g | fiber: 5g

Herb & Cheese Fritters

Prep time: 10 minutes | Cook time: 15 minutes | Serves 5

3 medium zucchini
8 ounces (227 g) frozen spinach, thawed and squeezed dry (weight excludes water squeezed out)
4 large eggs
½ teaspoon salt
¼ teaspoon black pepper
3 tablespoons flax meal or

coconut flour
¼ cup grated Pecorino Romano
2 cloves garlic, minced
¼ cup chopped fresh herbs, such as parsley, basil, oregano, mint, chives, and/or thyme
¼ cup extra-virgin avocado oil or ghee

1. Grate the zucchini and place in a bowl lined with cheesecloth. Set aside for 5 minutes, then twist the cheesecloth around the zucchini and squeeze out as much liquid as you can. You should end up with about 13 ounces (370 g) of drained zucchini. 2. In a mixing bowl, combine the zucchini, spinach, eggs, salt, and pepper. Add the flax meal and Pecorino and stir again. Add the garlic and herbs and mix through. 3. Heat a large pan greased with 1 tablespoon of ghee over medium heat. Once hot, use a ¼-cup measuring cup to make the fritters (about 57 g/2 ounces each). Place in the hot pan and shape with a spatula. Cook in batches for 3 to 4 minutes per side, until crisp and golden. Grease the pan between each batch until all the ghee has been used. 4. Eat warm or cold, as a breakfast, side, or snack. Store in the fridge for up to 4 days or freeze for up to 3 months.

Per Serving:
Calories: 239 | fat: 20g | protein: 10g | carbs: 8g | net carbs: 5g | fiber: 3g

Rocket Fuel Hot Chocolate

Prep time: 5 minutes | Cook time: 0 minutes | Makes 2

2 cups (475 ml) milk (nondairy or regular), hot
2 tablespoons cocoa powder
2 tablespoons collagen peptides or protein powder
2 tablespoons coconut oil, MCT oil, unflavored MCT oil

powder, or ghee
1 tablespoon coconut butter
1 tablespoon erythritol, or 4 drops liquid stevia
Pinch of ground cinnamon (optional)

1. Place all the ingredients in a blender and blend for 10 seconds, or until the ingredients are fully incorporated. 2. Divide between 2 mugs, sprinkle with cinnamon if you'd like, and enjoy!

Per Serving:
Calories: 357 | fat: 29g | protein: 13g | carbs: 11g | net carbs: 7g | fiber: 4g

Jelly-Filled Breakfast Strudels

Prep time: 10 minutes | Cook time: 25 minutes | Serves 2

Pastry:
¾ cup shredded low-moisture mozzarella cheese
2 ounces (57 g) full-fat cream cheese, at room temperature
1 cup almond flour
1 large egg
4 tablespoons stevia-sweetened jelly

Frosting:
¼ cup powdered erythritol
2 ounces (57 g) full-fat cream cheese, at room temperature
1 tablespoon butter, at room temperature
2 teaspoons heavy (whipping) cream
¼ teaspoon vanilla extract

1. Preheat the oven to 325°F (163°C). Have a silicone-lined baking sheet nearby. 2. To make the dough: In a large, microwave-safe bowl, combine the mozzarella and cream cheese. 3. Microwave for 1 minute, until the cheese is melted. Then stir to combine. 4. Add the almond flour and egg to the melted cheese. Combine using a rubber scraper, working quickly so the cheese does not cool and harden. (If it starts to harden, reheat in the microwave for 20 seconds, being careful not to cook the egg.) 5. Roll out the dough between 2 pieces of parchment paper to a large rectangle that is between ¼ and ⅛ inch thick. 6. Make 3 even cuts widthwise to form 4 long rectangles of dough. 7. Place 1 tablespoon of jelly in the top half of each rectangle, leaving a little room on the sides. 8. Puncture the non-jellied bottom of each rectangle with a fork. Then, fold this bottom half over the top jellied half. 9. Seal the edges all the way around the square by pressing down with a fork. Transfer the squares to the baking sheet. 10. Bake for 20 to 25 minutes, until the pastry is golden brown. 11. Remove from the oven, and allow to cool for 10 minutes. 12. To make the frosting: In a small bowl, combine the erythritol, cream cheese, butter, cream, and vanilla and mix until smooth. 13. With a knife or the back of a spoon, coat the strudels with frosting and enjoy.

Per Serving:
Calories: 702 | fat: 61g | protein: 27g | carbs: 16g | net carbs: 10g | fiber: 6g

Cheesy Bacon Grab-and-Go Egg Muffins

Prep time: 10 minutes | Cook time: 20 minutes | Makes 12 muffins

Butter, ghee, or coconut oil, for greasing	½ teaspoon sea salt
12 bacon slices	¼ teaspoon freshly ground black pepper
12 eggs	1 cup shredded sharp Cheddar cheese
1 teaspoon garlic powder	

1. Preheat the oven to 350ºF (180ºC). Grease a muffin pan very well with butter, ghee, or coconut oil. Alternatively, you can use silicone cups or parchment paper muffin liners. 2. In a large skillet over medium-high heat, cook the bacon in batches until crisp, 5 to 7 minutes, and let drain on a paper towel. 3. Crack the eggs into a large bowl. Add the garlic powder, salt, and pepper and whisk to combine. 4. Divide the egg mixture equally among the muffin cups. Crumble one slice of bacon over the top of each muffin cup. Sprinkle the cheese on top, dividing equally. 5. Bake for 12 to 15 minutes or until the eggs are firm and slightly golden brown along the edges. 6. Divide the muffins into glass containers or plastic bags and store in the refrigerator for the week or freeze for up to 2 months. 7. To serve, reheat in the microwave for 30 to 45 seconds.

Per Serving (2 muffins):
Calories: 324 | fat: 24g | protein: 25g | carbs: 2g | net carbs: 2g | fiber: 0g

Pancakes

Prep time: 10 minutes | Cook time: 40 minutes | Makes 4 pancakes

Pancakes:	milk
2.8 ounces (80 g) unseasoned pork rinds	¼ scant teaspoon liquid stevia
2 teaspoons ground cinnamon, plus more for garnish (optional)	2 tablespoons coconut oil, divided, for the pan
½ teaspoon baking powder	Sauce:
4 large eggs	2 tablespoons coconut oil
½ cup (120 ml) full-fat coconut	2 tablespoons unsweetened smooth almond butter

1. Place the pork rinds in a spice grinder or blender. Grind to a very fine but clumping powder (it will clump together when pinched because of the fat content in the pork rinds). 2. Transfer the ground pork rinds to a small bowl and add the cinnamon and baking powder. Stir to combine. 3. In a larger bowl, whisk together the eggs, coconut milk, and stevia. Add the pork rind mixture and stir to incorporate. 4. In an 8-inch (20-cm) nonstick frying pan, melt ½ tablespoon of coconut oil over medium-low heat. 5. Preheat your oven to the lowest temperature possible. 6. Pour a quarter of the batter into the hot oiled pan and spread the batter evenly into a circle with the back of a spoon or by rotating the pan. Do not allow the batter to migrate too far up the sides of the pan, or it will burn. Cook the pancake for 4 to 5 minutes, until bubbles form all over. Flip carefully and cook for another 4 to 5 minutes. 7. Transfer the completed pancake to a clean oven-safe plate and place in the preheated oven. 8. Add another ½ tablespoon of coconut oil to the pan. The batter may have thickened while sitting. If so, add water, a splash at a time, and mix until the batter returns to its original consistency, being careful not to add too much water. 9. Pour another quarter of the batter into the pan, form it into a circle, and cook, following Step 6. Repeat with the remaining coconut oil and batter. 10. While the last pancake is cooking, prepare the sauce: Melt the 2 tablespoons of coconut oil and put it in a small bowl along with the almond butter. Stir to combine. 11. When the pancakes are ready, divide between 2 plates and drizzle with the almond butter sauce. Sprinkle with additional cinnamon, if desired.

Per Serving:
Calories: 885 | fat: 71g | protein: 53g | carbs: 8g | net carbs: 5g | fiber: 3g

Pecan and Walnut Granola

Prep time: 10 minutes | Cook time: 2 minutes | Serves 12

2 cups chopped raw pecans	½ cup chopped raw walnuts
1¾ cups vanilla-flavored egg white protein powder	½ cup slivered almonds
	½ cup sesame seeds
1¼ cups unsalted butter, softened	½ cup Swerve
	1 teaspoon ground cinnamon
1 cup sunflower seeds	½ teaspoon sea salt

1. Add all the ingredients to the Instant Pot and stir to combine. 2. Lock the lid, select the Manual mode and set the cooking time for 2 minutes on High Pressure. When the timer goes off, do a natural pressure release for 10 minutes, then release any remaining pressure. Open the lid. 3. Stir well and pour the granola onto a sheet of parchment paper to cool. It will become crispy when completely cool. Serve the granola in bowls.

Per Serving:
Calories: 491 | fat: 44g | protein: 17g | carbs: 9g | net carbs: 4g | fiber: 5g

Scrambled Egg Cups

Prep time: 10 minutes | Cook time: 18 minutes | Serves 4

Coconut oil cooking spray	¼ cup sliced fresh mushrooms
4 large eggs	¼ cup chopped fresh spinach
1 tablespoon heavy (whipping) cream	2 bacon slices, cooked until crisp and crumbled
Pink Himalayan sea salt	2 tablespoons chopped onion
Freshly ground black pepper	¼ cup shredded Cheddar cheese

1. Preheat the oven to 350ºF (180ºC). Spray 4 cups of a muffin pan with the cooking spray. 2. In a medium bowl, whisk the eggs and cream, then season with salt and pepper. 3. In another medium bowl, mix the mushrooms, spinach, bacon, and onion. 4. Spoon the egg mixture evenly into the 4 muffin cups. 5. Top each with some of the bacon mixture. Finally, top the cups with an even sprinkling of Cheddar cheese. 6. Bake for 16 to 18 minutes, until the eggs are set.

Per Serving (1 egg muffin) :
Calories: 146 | fat: 11g | protein: 10g | carbs: 1g | net carbs: 1g | fiber: 0g

Bacon Cheddar Bites

Prep time: 15 minutes | Cook time: 3 minutes | Serves 2

2 tablespoons coconut flour	2 bacon slices, cooked
½ cup shredded Cheddar cheese	½ teaspoon dried parsley
2 teaspoons coconut cream	1 cup water, for cooking

1. In the mixing bowl, mix up coconut flour, Cheddar cheese, coconut cream, and dried parsley. 2. Then chop the cooked bacon and add it in the mixture. 3. Stir it well. 4. Pour water and insert the trivet in the instant pot. 5. Line the trivet with baking paper. 6. After this, make the small balls (bites) from the cheese mixture and put them on the prepared trivet. 7. Cook the meal for 3 minutes on Manual mode (High Pressure). 8. Then make a quick pressure release and cool the cooked meal well.

Per Serving:
Calories: 260 | fat: 19g | protein: 15g | carbs: 6g | net carbs: 3g | fiber: 3g

Mexican Breakfast Pepper Rings

Prep time: 5 minutes | Cook time: 10 minutes | Serves 4

Olive oil	4 eggs
1 large red, yellow, or orange bell pepper, cut into four ¾-inch rings	Salt and freshly ground black pepper, to taste
	2 teaspoons salsa

1. Preheat the air fryer to 350ºF (177ºC). Lightly spray a baking pan with olive oil. 2. Place 2 bell pepper rings on the pan. Crack one egg into each bell pepper ring. Season with salt and black pepper. 3. Spoon ½ teaspoon of salsa on top of each egg. 4. Place the pan in the air fryer basket. Air fry until the yolk is slightly runny, 5 to 6 minutes or until the yolk is fully cooked, 8 to 10 minutes. 5. Repeat with the remaining 2 pepper rings. Serve hot.

Per Serving:
Calories: 76 | fat: 4g | protein: 6g | carbs: 3g | net carbs: 2g | fiber: 1g

Chunky Cobb-Style Egg Salad

Prep time: 5 minutes | Cook time: 10 minutes | Serves 6

8 cups water	2 tablespoons minced shallots or red onions
1 dozen large eggs, room temperature	12 slices cooked bacon, chopped
¼ cup mayonnaise, homemade or store-bought	Sea salt and ground black pepper, to taste
2 tablespoons chopped fresh chives	Microgreens, for serving
2 tablespoons chopped fresh dill	Sliced cucumbers, for serving (optional)

1. Fill a large pot with the water and bring to a boil. Fill a large bowl with ice water. 2. Place the eggs in the boiling water and cook for 10 minutes. Transfer the eggs to the ice water and chill for 10 minutes. This will keep them from turning green around the yolks. 3. Peel the eggs, place them in a large bowl, and mash them with a potato masher or large fork. Mix in the mayonnaise, chives, dill, and shallots. Stir in the bacon so it is evenly distributed. 4. Season with salt and pepper to taste and serve over microgreens and with sliced cucumbers on the side, if desired.

Per Serving:
Calories: 498 | fat: 46g | protein: 20g | carbs: 2g | net carbs: 2g | fiber: 0g

Buffalo Egg Cups

Prep time: 10 minutes | Cook time: 15 minutes | Serves 2

4 large eggs	2 tablespoons buffalo sauce
2 ounces (57 g) full-fat cream cheese	½ cup shredded sharp Cheddar cheese

1. Crack eggs into two ramekins. 2. In a small microwave-safe bowl, mix cream cheese, buffalo sauce, and Cheddar. Microwave for 20 seconds and then stir. Place a spoonful into each ramekin on top of the eggs. 3. Place ramekins into the air fryer basket. 4. Adjust the temperature to 320ºF (160ºC) and bake for 15 minutes. 5. Serve warm.

Per Serving:
Calories: 354 | fat: 29g | protein: 21g | carbs: 3g | net carbs: 3g | fiber: 0g

Low-Carb Egg Curry

Prep time: 15 minutes | Cook time: 20 minutes | Serves 4

½ onion, finely diced	2 teaspoons chili powder
1 small (1-inch) knob fresh ginger	2 teaspoons ground coriander
2 garlic cloves	2 teaspoons garam masala
1 small green chile pepper	½ cup water
1 large Roma tomato	Salt and freshly ground black pepper, to taste
1 tablespoon ghee	4 hardboiled eggs, peeled
2 teaspoons ground turmeric	

1. In a food processor or blender, combine the onion, ginger, garlic, and chile pepper. Process until a paste forms. Transfer to a small bowl and set aside. 2. Rinse out the blender then purée the tomato in it. Set aside. 3. In a small saucepan over medium heat, melt the ghee. Add the onion-ginger-garlic-chile paste to the pan. Stir and let it cook for 3 to 4 minutes or until fragrant. 4. Stir in the turmeric, chili powder, coriander, and garam masala. 5. Stir in the puréed tomato. Cook for 1 to 2 minutes then add the water, stirring to thoroughly combine. Season with salt and pepper, cover the pan, and cook for about 10 minutes over low heat. 6. Add the peeled eggs to the curry and gently stir to get all sides coated with the sauce. Cook for 3 to 5 minutes over low heat and serve.

Per Serving:
Calories: 128 | fat: 8g | protein: 7g | carbs: 7g | net carbs: 5g | fiber: 2g

Bacon, Spinach, and Avocado Egg Wrap

Prep time: 10 minutes | Cook time: 10 minutes | Serves 2

6 bacon slices	Freshly ground black pepper
2 large eggs	1 tablespoon butter, if needed
2 tablespoons heavy (whipping) cream	1 cup fresh spinach (or other greens of your choice)
Pink Himalayan salt	½ avocado, sliced

1. In a medium skillet over medium-high heat, cook the bacon on both sides until crispy, about 8 minutes. Transfer the bacon to a paper towel–lined plate. 2. In a medium bowl, whisk the eggs and cream, and season with pink Himalayan salt and pepper. Whisk again to combine. 3. Add half the egg mixture to the skillet with the bacon grease. 4. Cook the egg mixture for about 1 minute, or until set, then flip with a spatula and cook the other side for 1 minute. 5. Transfer the cooked-egg mixture to a paper towel–lined plate to soak up extra grease. 6. Repeat steps 4 and 5 for the other half of the egg mixture. If the pan gets dry, add the butter. 7. Place a cooked egg mixture on each of two warmed plates. Top each with half of the spinach, bacon, and avocado slices. 8. Season with pink Himalayan salt and pepper, and roll the wraps. Serve hot.

Per Serving:

Calories: 336 | fat: 29g | protein: 17g | carbs: 5g | net carbs: 2g | fiber: 3g

Creamy Cinnamon Porridge

Prep time: 10 minutes | Cook time: 10 minutes | Serves 2

¼ cup coconut milk	¼ cup macadamia nuts
¾ cup unsweetened almond milk or water	¼ cup hazelnuts
	4 Brazil nuts
¼ cup almond butter or hazelnut butter	Optional: low-carb sweetener, to taste
1 tablespoon virgin coconut oil	¼ cup unsweetened large coconut flakes
2 tablespoons chia seeds	
1 tablespoon flax meal	1 tablespoon cacao nibs
1 teaspoon cinnamon	

1. In a small saucepan, mix the coconut milk and almond milk and heat over medium heat. Once hot (not boiling), take off the heat. Add the almond butter and coconut oil. Stir until well combined. If needed, use an immersion blender and process until smooth. 2. Add the chia seeds, flax meal, and cinnamon, and leave to rest for 5 to 10 minutes. Roughly chop the macadamias, hazelnuts, and Brazil nuts and stir in. Add sweetener, if using, and stir. Transfer to serving bowls. In a small skillet, dry-roast the coconut flakes over medium-high heat for 1 to 2 minutes, until lightly toasted and fragrant. Top the porridge with the toasted coconut flakes and cacao nibs (or you can use chopped 100% chocolate). Serve immediately or store in the fridge for up to 3 days.

Per Serving:

Calories: 646 | fat: 61g | protein: 13g | carbs: 23g | net carbs: 13g | fiber: 10g

Creamiest Keto Scrambled Eggs

Prep time: 3 minutes | Cook time: 25 minutes | Serves 2

2 (2-inch) cross-cut beef or veal marrow bones, split lengthwise	5 large eggs
1 teaspoon fine sea salt, divided	1 teaspoon fresh herbs of choice (whole or chopped leaves, depending on size), for garnish (optional)
½ teaspoon freshly ground black pepper, divided	

1. Preheat the oven to 450°F (235°C). 2. Rinse and drain the bones and pat dry. Season them with ½ teaspoon of the salt and ¼ teaspoon of the pepper and place them cut side up in a roasting pan. 3. Roast for 15 to 25 minutes (the exact timing will depend on the diameter of the bones; if they are 2 inches in diameter, it will take closer to 15 minutes), until the marrow in the center has puffed slightly and is warm. To test for doneness, insert a metal skewer into the center of the bone; there should be no resistance when it is inserted, and some of the marrow will have started to leak from the bones. 4. Heat a cast-iron skillet over medium heat. Place some of the liquid from the roasting pan in the skillet. Using a small spoon, scoop the marrow out of the bones into a bowl, then add the eggs and the remaining ½ teaspoon of salt and ¼ teaspoon of pepper and whisk until well combined. Pour the egg mixture into the skillet. Gently scramble the eggs until they are set and creamy. Garnish with fresh herbs. 5. Best served fresh. Store extras in an airtight container in the fridge for up to 3 days.

Per Serving:

Calories: 398 | fat: 35g | protein: 18g | carbs: 2g | net carbs: 2g | fiber: 0g

Bacon Spaghetti Squash Fritters

Prep time: 20 minutes | Cook time: 15 minutes | Serves 4

½ cooked spaghetti squash	¼ teaspoon pepper
2 tablespoons cream cheese	1 stalk green onion, sliced
½ cup shredded whole-milk Mozzarella cheese	4 slices cooked bacon, crumbled
1 egg	2 tablespoons coconut oil
½ teaspoon salt	

1. Remove seeds from cooked squash and use fork to scrape strands out of shell. Place strands into cheesecloth or kitchen towel and squeeze to remove as much excess moisture as possible. 2. Place cream cheese and Mozzarella in small bowl and microwave for 45 seconds to melt together. Mix with spoon and place in large bowl. Add all ingredients except coconut oil to bowl. Mixture will be wet like batter. 3. Press the Sauté button and then press the Adjust button to set heat to Less. Add coconut oil to Instant Pot. When fully preheated, add 2 to 3 tablespoons of batter to pot to make a fritter. Let fry until firm and completely cooked through.

Per Serving:

Calories: 202 | fat: 16g | protein: 9g | carbs: 2g | net carbs: 1g | fiber: 1g

Ground Pork Breakfast Patties

Prep time: 5 minutes | Cook time: 15 minutes | Serves 4

1 pound (454 g) 84% lean ground pork	½ teaspoon garlic powder
1 teaspoon dried thyme	½ teaspoon salt
½ teaspoon dried sage	¼ teaspoon pepper
	¼ teaspoon red pepper flakes

1. Mix all ingredients in large bowl. Form into 4 patties based on preference. Press the Sauté button and press the Adjust button to lower heat to Less. 2. Place patties in Instant Pot and allow fat to render while patties begin browning. After 5 minutes, or when a few tablespoons of fat have rendered from meat, press the Cancel button. 3. Press the Sauté button and press the Adjust button to set heat to Normal. Sear each side of patties and allow them to cook fully until no pink remains in centers, approximately 10 additional minutes, depending on thickness.

Per Serving:

Calories: 249 | fat: 16g | protein: 20g | carbs: 1g | net carbs: 1g | fiber: 0g

Breakfast Almond Muffins

Prep time: 5 minutes | Cook time: 20 minutes | Serves 4

2 drops liquid stevia	softened
2 cups almond flour	¼ cup melted butter
2 teaspoons baking powder	1 egg
½ teaspoon salt	1 cup unsweetened almond
8 ounces cream cheese,	milk

1. Preheat oven to 400°F and grease a 12-cup muffin tray with cooking spray. Mix the flour, baking powder, and salt in a large bowl. 2. In a separate bowl, beat the cream cheese, stevia, and butter using a hand mixer and whisk in the egg and milk. Fold in the flour, and spoon the batter into the muffin cups two-thirds way up. 3. Bake for 20 minutes until puffy at the top and golden brown, remove to a wire rack to cool slightly for 5 minutes before serving. Serve with tea.

Per Serving:

Calories: 546 | fat: 50g | protein: 13g | carbs: 11g | net carbs: 6g | fiber: 5g

Bacon Tomato Cups

Prep time: 10 minutes | Cook time: 25 minutes | Serves 6

12 bacon slices	1 cup mayonnaise
2 tomatoes, diced	12 low carb crepes/pancakes
1 onion, diced	1 teaspoon dried basil
1 cup shredded cheddar cheese	Chopped chives to garnish

1. Fry the bacon in a skillet over medium heat for 5 minutes. Remove and chop with a knife. Transfer to a bowl. Add in cheddar cheese, tomatoes, onion, mayonnaise, and basil. Mix well set aside. 2. Place the crepes on a flat surface and use egg rings to cut a circle out of each crepe. Grease the muffin cups with cooking spray and fit the circled crepes into them to make a cup. 3. Now, fill the cups with 3 tablespoons of bacon-tomato mixture. Place the muffin cups on a baking sheet, and bake for 18 minutes. Garnish with the chives, and serve with a tomato or cheese sauce.

Per Serving:

Calories: 474 | fat: 42g | protein: 18g | carbs: 6g | net carbs: 4g | fiber: 2g

Sausage, Egg, and Cheese Breakfast Bake

Prep time: 15 minutes | Cook time: 35 minutes | Serves 6

1 tablespoon unsalted butter	1 clove garlic, pressed
⅓ cup chopped yellow onions	1 teaspoon salt
1 pound bulk breakfast sausage	½ teaspoon ground black
8 large eggs	pepper
⅓ cup heavy whipping cream	1 cup shredded cheddar cheese

1 Preheat the oven to 350°F. Lightly coat an 8-inch deep-dish pie dish or baking dish with coconut oil or nonstick cooking spray. 2 Heat the butter in a large skillet over medium heat. Add the onions and sauté until soft, 3 to 4 minutes. 3 Add the sausage and cook until evenly browned, 4 to 5 minutes. Drain and set aside. 4 In a large bowl, whisk the eggs, cream, garlic, salt, and pepper. 5 Spread the sausage evenly on the bottom of the prepared dish and top with the cheese. Pour the egg mixture over the cheese. 6 Bake for 35 minutes, until the eggs are set and the top is lightly golden brown. 7 Allow to cool for 3 to 5 minutes before serving. Leftovers can be covered and stored in the refrigerator for up to 4 days.

Per Serving:

Calories: 394 | fat: 33g | protein: 22g | carbs: 3g | net carbs: 3g | fiber: 0g

Creamy Almond Coffee Smoothie

Prep time: 5 minutes | Cook time: 0 minutes | Serves 2

2 cups unsweetened strong-brewed coffee	2 tablespoons chia seeds
1 cup unsweetened almond milk	2 tablespoons flaxseed meal
	2 tablespoons coconut oil
1 cup unsweetened coconut milk	⅛ teaspoon ground cinnamon
	Monk fruit sweetener, granulated, to taste

1. Make coffee ice cubes. Pour the coffee into an ice cube tray and freeze for 4 hours minimum. 2. Blend the smoothie. Put all of the coffee ice cubes (2 cups worth), almond milk, coconut milk, chia seeds, flaxseed meal, coconut oil, and cinnamon in a blender and blend until smooth and creamy. 3. Add a sweetener. Add in as much (or as little) sweetener as you like and blend again. 4. Serve. Pour into two tall glasses and serve immediately.

Per Serving:

Calories: 444 | fat: 44g | protein: 6g | carbs: 6g | net carbs: 2g | fiber: 4g

Egg Baked in Avocado

Prep time: 5 minutes | Cook time: 15 minutes | Serves 2

1 ripe large avocado	serving
2 large eggs	2 tablespoons chopped tomato,
Salt	for serving
Freshly ground black pepper	2 tablespoons crumbled feta,
4 tablespoons jarred pesto, for	for serving (optional)

1. Preheat the oven to 425°F(220°C). 2. Slice the avocado in half and remove the pit. Scoop out about 1 to 2 tablespoons from each half to create a hole large enough to fit an egg. Place the avocado halves on a baking sheet, cut-side up. 3. Crack 1 egg in each avocado half and season with salt and pepper. 4. Bake until the eggs are set and cooked to desired level of doneness, 10 to 15 minutes. 5. Remove from oven and top each avocado with 2 tablespoons pesto, 1 tablespoon chopped tomato, and 1 tablespoon crumbled feta (if using).

Per Serving:
Calories: 248 | fat: 23g | protein: 10g | carbs: 2g | net carbs: 1g | fiber: 1g

Heart-Healthy Hazelnut-Collagen Shake

Prep time: 5 minutes | Cook time: 0 minutes | Serves 1

1½ cups unsweetened almond	⅛ teaspoon LoSalt or pink
milk	Himalayan salt
2 tablespoons hazelnut butter	⅛ teaspoon sugar-free almond
2 tablespoons grass-fed	extract
collagen powder	1 tablespoon macadamia oil or
½–1 teaspoon cinnamon	hazelnut oil

1. Place all of the ingredients in a blender and pulse until smooth and frothy. Serve immediately.

Per Serving:
Calories: 507 | fat: 41g | protein: 3g | carbs: 35g | net carbs: 23g | fiber: 12g

Almond Flour Pancakes

Prep time: 5 minutes | Cook time: 10 minutes | Serves 6

2 cups (8 ounces / 227 g)	⅔ cup unsweetened almond
blanched almond flour	milk
¼ cup erythritol	¼ cup avocado oil, plus more
1 tablespoon baking powder	for frying
¼ teaspoon sea salt	2 teaspoons vanilla extract
4 large eggs	

1. In a blender, combine all ingredients and blend until smooth. Let the batter rest for 5 to 10 minutes. 2. Preheat a large, very lightly oiled skillet over medium-low heat. (Keep oil very minimal for perfectly round pancakes.) Working in batches, pour circles of batter onto the pan, 2 tablespoons (⅛ cup) at a time for 3-inch pancakes. Cook 1½ to 2 minutes, until bubbles start to form on the edges. Flip and cook another minute or two, until browned on the other side. 3. Repeat with the remaining batter.

Per Serving:
Calories: 355 | fat: 31g | protein: 12g | carbs: 12g | net carbs: 5g | fiber: 7g

Cheesy Cauliflower "Hash Browns"

Prep time: 30 minutes | Cook time: 24 minutes |
Makes 6 hash browns

2 ounces (57 g) 100% cheese	instructions
crisps	1 large egg
1 (12-ounce / 340-g) steamer	½ cup shredded sharp Cheddar
bag cauliflower, cooked	cheese
according to package	½ teaspoon salt

1. Let cooked cauliflower cool 10 minutes. 2. Place cheese crisps into food processor and pulse on low 30 seconds until crisps are finely ground. 3. Using a kitchen towel, wring out excess moisture from cauliflower and place into food processor. 4. Add egg to food processor and sprinkle with Cheddar and salt. Pulse five times until mixture is mostly smooth. 5. Cut two pieces of parchment to fit air fryer basket. Separate mixture into six even scoops and place three on each piece of ungreased parchment, keeping at least 2 inch of space between each scoop. Press each into a hash brown shape, about ¼ inch thick. 6. Place one batch on parchment into air fryer basket. Adjust the temperature to 375°F (191°C) and air fry for 12 minutes, turning hash browns halfway through cooking. Hash browns will be golden brown when done. Repeat with second batch. 7. Allow 5 minutes to cool. Serve warm.

Per Serving:
Calories: 100 | fat: 7g | protein: 7g | carbs: 3g | net carbs: 2g | fiber: 1g

Pizza Eggs

Prep time: 5 minutes | Cook time: 10 minutes | Serves 2

1 cup shredded Mozzarella	¼ teaspoon dried oregano
cheese	¼ teaspoon dried parsley
7 slices pepperoni, chopped	¼ teaspoon garlic powder
1 large egg, whisked	¼ teaspoon salt

1. Place Mozzarella in a single layer on the bottom of an ungreased round nonstick baking dish. Scatter pepperoni over cheese, then pour egg evenly around baking dish. 2. Sprinkle with remaining ingredients and place into air fryer basket. Adjust the temperature to 330°F (166°C) and bake for 10 minutes. When cheese is brown and egg is set, dish will be done. 3. Let cool in dish 5 minutes before serving.

Per Serving:
Calories: 240 | fat: 18g | protein: 17g | carbs: 2g | net carbs: 2g | fiber: 0g

Spicy Mediterranean Shakshuka

Prep time: 5 minutes | Cook time: 30 minutes | Serves 3

1 tablespoon avocado oil
½ cup (2 ounces / 57 g) diced onion
2 cloves garlic, minced
1 (10-ounce / 283-g) can no-salt-added diced tomatoes with green chilies
½ cup tomato sauce
1 teaspoon paprika
1 teaspoon ground cumin
½ teaspoon sea salt, plus more for taste
6 large eggs
2 tablespoons chopped fresh parsley

1. In a 12-inch sauté pan, heat the oil over medium-low heat. Add the diced onion and cook for about 10 minutes, until browned. Add the minced garlic and sauté for about 1 minute, until fragrant. 2. Add the diced tomatoes (with juices), tomato sauce, paprika, and cumin and mix. Add the sea salt. Cover and simmer 12 to 15 minutes, until the tomato mixture has thickened and most of the liquid is gone. If needed, cook for a couple of minutes uncovered to reduce. 3. Crack the eggs into the pan so that each egg is surrounded by tomato sauce. If desired, you can create a little well for each egg first. Sprinkle the eggs lightly with more sea salt. 4. Cover and cook for 4 to 6 minutes, until the egg whites are opaque, but the yolks are still runny. If you prefer them more done, continue cooking the eggs to your liking. 5. Sprinkle with parsley to serve.

Per Serving:
Calories: 248 | fat: 15g | protein: 16g | carbs: 10g | net carbs: 8g | fiber: 2g

Veggie Frittata

Prep time: 7 minutes | Cook time: 21 to 23 minutes | Serves 2

Avocado oil spray
¼ cup diced red onion
¼ cup diced red bell pepper
¼ cup finely chopped broccoli
4 large eggs
3 ounces (85 g) shredded sharp Cheddar cheese, divided
½ teaspoon dried thyme
Sea salt and freshly ground black pepper, to taste

1. Spray a pan well with oil. Put the onion, pepper, and broccoli in the pan, place the pan in the air fryer, and set to 350ºF (177ºC). Bake for 5 minutes. 2. While the vegetables cook, beat the eggs in a medium bowl. Stir in half of the cheese, and season with the thyme, salt, and pepper. 3. Add the eggs to the pan and top with the remaining cheese. Set the air fryer to 350ºF (177ºC). Bake for 16 to 18 minutes, until cooked through.

Per Serving:
Calories: 326 | fat: 23g | protein: 24g | carbs: 4g | net carbs: 3g | fiber: 1g

Golden Egg Skillet

Prep time: 15 minutes | Cook time: 20 minutes | Serves 2

2 tablespoons extra-virgin avocado oil or ghee
2 medium spring onions, white and green parts separated, sliced
1 clove garlic, minced
3½ ounces (99 g) Swiss chard or collard greens, stalks and leaves separated, chopped
1 medium zucchini, sliced into coins
2 tablespoons water
1 teaspoon Dijon or yellow mustard
½ teaspoon ground turmeric
¼ teaspoon black pepper
Salt, to taste
4 large eggs
¾ cup grated Manchego or Pecorino Romano cheese
2 tablespoons (30 ml) extra-virgin olive oil

1. Preheat the oven to 360°F (182ºC) fan assisted or 400°F (205ºC) conventional. 2. Grease a large, ovenproof skillet (with a lid) with the avocado oil. Cook the white parts of the spring onions and the garlic for about 1 minute, until just fragrant. Add the chard stalks, zucchini, and water. Stir, then cover with a lid. Cook over medium-low heat for about 10 minutes or until the zucchini is tender. Add the mustard, turmeric, pepper, and salt. Add the chard leaves and cook until just wilted. 3. Use a spatula to make 4 wells in the mixture. Crack an egg into each well and cook until the egg whites start to set while the yolks are still runny. Top with the cheese, transfer to the oven, and bake for 5 to 7 minutes. Remove from the oven and sprinkle with the reserved spring onions. Drizzle with the olive oil and serve warm.

Per Serving:
Calories: 600 | fat: 49g | protein: 31g | carbs: 10g | net carbs: 6g | fiber: 4g

Chapter 3 Fish and Seafood

Turmeric Salmon

Prep time: 10 minutes | Cook time: 4 minutes | Serves 3

1 pound (454 g) salmon fillet
1 teaspoon ground black pepper
½ teaspoon salt
1 teaspoon ground turmeric
1 teaspoon lemon juice
1 cup water

1. In the shallow bowl, mix up salt, ground black pepper, and ground turmeric. 2. Sprinkle the salmon fillet with lemon juice and rub with the spice mixture. 3. Then pour water in the instant pot and insert the steamer rack. 4. Wrap the salmon fillet in the foil and place it on the rack. 5. Close and seal the lid. 6. Cook the fish on Manual mode (High Pressure) for 4 minutes. 7. Make a quick pressure release and cut the fish on servings.

Per Serving:
Calories: 205 | fat: 9g | protein: 30g | carbs: 1g | net carbs: 1g | fiber: 0g

Basil Cod Fillets

Prep time: 5 minutes | Cook time: 12 minutes | Serves 4

½ cup water
4 frozen cod fillets (about 6 ounces / 170 g each)
1 teaspoon dried basil
Pinch of salt
Pinch of black pepper
4 lemon slices
¼ cup heavy cream
2 tablespoons butter, softened
1 ounce (28 g) cream cheese, softened
2 teaspoons lemon juice
1½ teaspoons chopped fresh basil, plus more for garnish (optional)
Lemon wedges, for garnish (optional)

1. Place the trivet inside the pot and add the water. Lay a piece of aluminum foil on top of the trivet and place the cod on top. 2. Sprinkle the fish with the dried basil, salt, and pepper. Set a lemon slice on top of each fillet. 3. Close the lid and seal the vent. Cook on High Pressure for 9 minutes. Quick release the steam. Press Cancel. 4. Remove the trivet and fish from the pot. Rinse the pot if needed and turn to Sauté mode. 5. Add the cream and butter and whisk as the butter melts and the cream warms up. Add the cream cheese and whisk until thickened, 2 to 3 minutes. Add the lemon juice and another pinch of salt and pepper. Once the sauce is thickened and well combined, 1 to 2 minutes, press Cancel and add the fresh basil. 6. Pour the sauce over the fish. Garnish with fresh basil or a lemon wedge, if desired.

Per Serving:
Calories: 221 | fat: 11g | protein: 27g | carbs: 1g | net carbs: 1g | fiber: 0g

Shrimp Zoodle Alfredo

Prep time: 10 minutes | Cook time: 10 minutes | Serves 4

10 ounces (283 g) salmon fillet (2 fillets)
4 ounces (113 g) Mozzarella, sliced
4 cherry tomatoes, sliced
1 teaspoon erythritol
1 teaspoon dried basil
½ teaspoon ground black pepper
1 tablespoon apple cider vinegar
1 tablespoon butter
1 cup water, for cooking

1. Melt the butter on Sauté mode and add shrimp. 2. Sprinkle them with seafood seasoning and sauté then for 2 minutes. 3. After this, spiralizer the zucchini with the help of the spiralizer and add in the shrimp. 4. Add coconut cream and close the lid. Cook the meal on Sauté mode for 8 minutes.

Per Serving:
Calories: 213 | fat: 16g | protein: 12g | carbs: 7g | net carbs: 5g | fiber: 2g

Spicy Tuna Hand Rolls

Prep time: 10 minutes | Cook time: 0 minutes | Serves 6

Tuna:
12 ounces sushi-grade ahi tuna, finely chopped
2 tablespoons Sriracha sauce
1 tablespoon mayonnaise, homemade or store-bought
1 teaspoon toasted sesame oil
Hand Rolls:
3 sheets nori
1 medium-sized avocado, thinly sliced
½ cucumber, julienned
Black and white sesame seeds, for garnish (optional)
Soy sauce, for serving

1. Put the tuna, Sriracha, mayonnaise, and sesame oil in a small bowl and mix with a spoon. 2. Cut the nori sheets in half lengthwise to create 6 rectangular wrappers. 3. Place a wrapper on the palm of one of your hands. Put 2 ounces of tuna and 3 or 4 slices each of avocado and cucumber on the left end of the wrapper, on a diagonal to make rolling easier. Starting from the bottom-left corner, tightly roll into a cone shape, moistening the edge of the nori to create a seal. Garnish the top of the roll with sesame seeds, if desired. Repeat with the remaining ingredients. 4. Serve the rolls with soy sauce. These are best eaten immediately, as they don't store well.

Per Serving:
Calories: 133 | fat: 6g | protein: 15g | carbs: 4g | net carbs: 2g | fiber: 2g

Creamy Shrimp and Bacon Skillet

Prep time: 5 minutes | Cook time: 20 minutes | Serves 4

10 ounces (283 g) thick-cut bacon, diced

½ onion, diced

2 garlic cloves, minced

1 pound (454 g) shrimp, peeled, deveined, tails removed

Salt, to taste

Freshly ground black pepper, to taste

4 ounces (113 g) cream cheese

Dash chicken broth (optional)

¼ cup grated Parmesan cheese

1. Preheat the broiler. 2. In a large ovenproof skillet over medium-high heat, cook the bacon in its own fat for about 5 minutes until it starts to get crispy. 3. Add the onion and garlic. Sauté for 5 to 7 minutes until the onion is softened and translucent. 4. Add the shrimp. Season with salt and pepper. Cook for 2 to 3 minutes, stirring, or until the shrimp start to turn pink. 5. Add the cream cheese and stir well to combine as it melts. If necessary, add a splash of chicken broth to thin it out. 6. Top with the Parmesan and transfer the skillet to the oven. Broil for 4 to 5 minutes until the Parmesan is lightly browned. Refrigerate leftovers in an airtight container for up to 5 days.

Per Serving:

Calories: 574 | fat: 45g | protein: 36g | carbs: 5g | net carbs: 5g | fiber: 0g

Seafood Fideo

Prep time: 15 minutes | Cook time: 20 minutes | Serves 6 to 8

2 tablespoons extra-virgin olive oil, plus ½ cup, divided

6 cups zucchini noodles, roughly chopped (2 to 3 medium zucchini)

1 pound (454 g) shrimp, peeled, deveined and roughly chopped

6 to 8 ounces (170 to 227 g) canned chopped clams, drained

4 ounces (113 g) crabmeat

½ cup crumbled goat cheese

½ cup crumbled feta cheese

1 (28-ounce / 794-g) can chopped tomatoes, with their juices

1 teaspoon salt

1 teaspoon garlic powder

½ teaspoon smoked paprika

½ cup shredded Parmesan cheese

¼ cup chopped fresh flat-leaf Italian parsley, for garnish

1. Preheat the oven to 375°F(190°C). 2. Pour 2 tablespoons olive oil in the bottom of a 9-by-13-inch baking dish and swirl to coat the bottom. 3. In a large bowl, combine the zucchini noodles, shrimp, clams, and crabmeat. 4. In another bowl, combine the goat cheese, feta, and ¼ cup olive oil and stir to combine well. Add the canned tomatoes and their juices, salt, garlic powder, and paprika and combine well. Add the mixture to the zucchini and seafood mixture and stir to combine. 5. Pour the mixture into the prepared baking dish, spreading evenly. Spread shredded Parmesan over top and drizzle with the remaining ¼ cup olive oil. Bake until bubbly, 20 to 25 minutes. Serve warm, garnished with chopped parsley.

Per Serving:

Calories: 302 | fat: 21g | protein: 22g | carbs: 9g | net carbs: 6g | fiber: 3g

Tilapia with Pecans

Prep time: 20 minutes | Cook time: 16 minutes | Serves 5

2 tablespoons ground flaxseeds

1 teaspoon paprika

Sea salt and white pepper, to taste

1 teaspoon garlic paste

2 tablespoons extra-virgin olive oil

½ cup pecans, ground

5 tilapia fillets, sliced into halves

1. Combine the ground flaxseeds, paprika, salt, white pepper, garlic paste, olive oil, and ground pecans in a Ziploc bag. Add the fish fillets and shake to coat well. 2. Spritz the air fryer basket with cooking spray. Cook in the preheated air fryer at 400°F (204°C) for 10 minutes; turn them over and cook for 6 minutes more. Work in batches. 3. Serve with lemon wedges, if desired. Enjoy!

Per Serving:

Calories: 252 | fat: 17g | protein: 25g | carbs: 3g | net carbs: 1g | fiber: 2g

Dill Salmon Cakes

Prep time: 15 minutes | Cook time: 10 minutes | Serves 4

1 pound (454 g) salmon fillet, chopped

1 tablespoon chopped dill

2 eggs, beaten

½ cup almond flour

1 tablespoon coconut oil

1. Put the chopped salmon, dill, eggs, and almond flour in the food processor. 2. Blend the mixture until it is smooth. 3. Then make the small balls (cakes) from the salmon mixture. 4. After this, heat up the coconut oil on Sauté mode for 3 minutes. 5. Put the salmon cakes in the instant pot in one layer and cook them on Sauté mode for 2 minutes from each side or until they are light brown.

Per Serving:

Calories: 297 | fat: 19g | protein: 28g | carbs: 4g | net carbs: 2g | fiber: 2g

Cajun Salmon

Prep time: 5 minutes | Cook time: 7 minutes | Serves 2

2 (4-ounce / 113-g) salmon fillets, skin removed

2 tablespoons unsalted butter, melted

⅛ teaspoon ground cayenne

pepper

½ teaspoon garlic powder

1 teaspoon paprika

¼ teaspoon ground black pepper

1. Brush each fillet with butter. 2. Combine remaining ingredients in a small bowl and then rub onto fish. Place fillets into the air fryer basket. 3. Adjust the temperature to 390ºF (199ºC) and air fry for 7 minutes. 4. When fully cooked, internal temperature will be 145ºF (63ºC). Serve immediately.

Per Serving:

Calories: 213 | fat: 12g | protein: 24g | carbs: 1g | net carbs: 0g | fiber: 1g

Quick Shrimp Skewers

Prep time: 10 minutes | Cook time: 5 minutes | Serves 5

4 pounds (1.8 kg) shrimp, peeled

1 tablespoon dried rosemary

1 tablespoon avocado oil

1 teaspoon apple cider vinegar

1. Mix the shrimps with dried rosemary, avocado oil, and apple cider vinegar. 2. Then sting the shrimps into skewers and put in the air fryer. 3. Cook the shrimps at 400ºF (204ºC) for 5 minutes.

Per Serving:

Calories: 336 | fat: 5g | protein: 73g | carbs: 0g | net carbs: 0g | fiber: 0g

Lemon Pepper Shrimp

Prep time: 15 minutes | Cook time: 8 minutes | Serves 2

Oil, for spraying

12 ounces (340 g) medium raw shrimp, peeled and deveined

3 tablespoons lemon juice

1 tablespoon olive oil

1 teaspoon lemon pepper

¼ teaspoon paprika

¼ teaspoon granulated garlic

1. Preheat the air fryer to 400ºF (204ºC). Line the air fryer basket with parchment and spray lightly with oil. 2. In a medium bowl, toss together the shrimp, lemon juice, olive oil, lemon pepper, paprika, and garlic until evenly coated. 3. Place the shrimp in the prepared basket. 4. Cook for 6 to 8 minutes, or until pink and firm. Serve immediately.

Per Serving:

Calories: 211 | fat: 8g | protein: 34g | carbs: 2g | net carbs: 2g | fiber: 0g

Parmesan-Crusted Salmon

Prep time: 5 minutes | Cook time: 20 minutes | Serves 2

2 tablespoons mayonnaise

1 tablespoon grated Parmesan cheese

1 tablespoon shredded Parmesan cheese

1 teaspoon freshly squeezed lemon juice

½ teaspoon dried parsley

½ teaspoon minced garlic

Pink Himalayan sea salt

Freshly ground black pepper

2 (8-ounce / 227-g) salmon fillets, skin on

1. Preheat the oven to 400ºF (205ºC). Line a baking sheet with aluminum foil. 2. In a small bowl, combine the mayonnaise, both types of Parmesan, lemon juice, parsley, and garlic. Season with salt and pepper. 3. Place the salmon skin-side down on the baking sheet. Spread the sauce evenly across both fillets. 4. Bake for 15 to 17 minutes, until the salmon flakes easily with a fork. Serve immediately.

Per Serving:

Calories: 584 | fat: 40g | protein: 53g | carbs: 1g | net carbs: 1g | fiber: 0g

Lemon Salmon with Tomatoes

Prep time: 7 minutes | Cook time: 21 minutes | Serves 4

1 tablespoon unsalted butter

3 cloves garlic, minced

¼ cup lemon juice

1¼ cups fresh or canned diced tomatoes

1 tablespoon chopped fresh flat-leaf parsley, plus more for

garnish

¼ teaspoon ground black pepper

4 (6-ounce / 170-g) skinless salmon fillets

1 teaspoon fine sea salt

Lemon wedges, for garnish

1. Add the butter to your Instant Pot and select the Sauté mode. Once melted, add the garlic (if using) and sauté for 1 minute. 2. Add the roasted garlic, lemon juice, tomatoes, parsley, and pepper. Let simmer for 5 minutes, or until the liquid has reduced a bit. 3. Meanwhile, rinse the salmon and pat dry with a paper towel. Sprinkle on all sides with the salt. 4. Using a spatula, push the reduced sauce to one side of the pot and place the salmon on the other side. Spoon the sauce over the salmon. 5. Sauté uncovered for another 15 minutes, or until the salmon flakes easily with a fork. The timing will depend on the thickness of the fillets. 6. Transfer the salmon to a serving plate. Serve with the sauce and garnish with the parsley and lemon wedges.

Per Serving:

Calories: 248 | fat: 10g | protein: 35g | carbs: 5g | net carbs: 4g | fiber: 1g

Shrimp Scampi with Zucchini Noodles

Prep time: 5 minutes | Cook time: 10 minutes | Serves 4

½ cup extra-virgin olive oil, divided

1 pound (454 g) shrimp, peeled and deveined

1 teaspoon salt

¼ teaspoon freshly ground black pepper

2 tablespoons unsalted butter

6 garlic cloves, minced

2 tablespoons dry white wine or chicken broth

½ teaspoon red pepper flakes

Zest and juice of 1 lemon

¼ cup chopped fresh Italian parsley

4 cups spiralized zucchini noodles (about 2 medium zucchini)

1. In a large skillet, heat ¼ cup of olive oil over medium-high heat. Add the shrimp, sprinkle with salt and pepper, and sauté for 2 to 3 minutes, or until the shrimp is just pink. Using a slotted spoon, transfer the shrimp to a bowl and cover to keep warm. 2. Reduce heat to low and add the remaining ¼ cup of olive oil, butter, and garlic. Cook the garlic, stirring frequently, until very fragrant, 3 to 4 minutes. 3. Whisk in the wine, red pepper flakes, and lemon zest and juice. Increase the heat to medium-high and bring to a simmer. Remove the skillet from the heat as soon as the liquid simmers. Return the shrimp to the skillet, add the parsley, and toss. 4. To serve, place the raw zucchini noodles in a large bowl. Add the shrimp and sauce and toss to coat.

Per Serving:

Calories: 414 | fat: 34g | protein: 25g | carbs: 5g | net carbs: 3g | fiber: 2g

Sardine Fritter Wraps

Prep time: 5 minutes | Cook time: 8 minutes | Serves 4

⅓ cup (80 ml) refined avocado oil, for frying
FRITTERS:
2 (4.375-ounce/125-g) cans sardines, drained
½ cup (55 g) blanched almond flour
2 large eggs
2 tablespoons finely chopped fresh parsley
2 tablespoons finely diced red bell pepper
2 cloves garlic, minced
½ teaspoon finely ground gray sea salt
¼ teaspoon ground black pepper
FOR SERVING:
8 romaine lettuce leaves
1 small English cucumber, sliced thin
8 tablespoons (105 g) mayonnaise
Thinly sliced green onions

1. Pour the avocado oil into a large frying pan. Heat on medium for a couple of minutes. 2. Meanwhile, prepare the fritters: Place the fritter ingredients in a medium-sized bowl and stir to combine, being careful not to mash the heck out of the sardines. Spoon about 1 tablespoon of the mixture into the palm of your hand and roll it into a ball, then flatten it like a burger patty. Repeat with the remaining fritter mixture, making a total of 16 small patties. 3. Fry the fritters in the hot oil for 2 minutes per side, then transfer to a cooling rack. You may have to fry the fritters in batches if your pan isn't large enough to fit them all without overcrowding. 4. Meanwhile, divide the lettuce leaves among 4 dinner plates. Top with the sliced cucumber. When the fritters are done, place 2 fritters on each leaf. Top with a dollop of mayonnaise, sprinkle with sliced green onions, and serve!

Per Serving:
Calories: 612 | fat: 56g | protein: 23g | carbs: 6g | net carbs: 4g | fiber: 2g

Red Cabbage Tilapia Taco Bowl

Prep time: 15 minutes | Cook time: 10 minutes | Serves 4

2 cups cauli rice
2 teaspoons ghee
4 tilapia fillets, cut into cubes
¼ teaspoon taco seasoning
Salt and chili pepper to taste
¼ head red cabbage, shredded
1 ripe avocado, pitted and chopped

1. Sprinkle cauli rice in a bowl with a little water and microwave for 3 minutes. Fluff after with a fork and set aside. Melt ghee in a skillet over medium heat, rub the tilapia with the taco seasoning, salt, and chili pepper, and fry until brown on all sides, for about 8 minutes in total. 2. Transfer to a plate and set aside. In 4 serving bowls, share the cauli rice, cabbage, fish, and avocado. Serve with chipotle lime sour cream dressing.

Per Serving:
Calories: 315 | fat: 23g | protein: 21g | carbs: 6g | net carbs: 3g | fiber: 3g

Tilapia Bake

Prep time: 5 minutes | Cook time: 30 minutes | Serves 4

3 medium or 4 small tilapia fillets (approximately 1 pound / 454 g total)
1 teaspoon kosher salt
1 teaspoon black pepper
2 tablespoons plus 1 teaspoon butter
1 medium leek, white part
thinly sliced (¾ cup)
10 ounces (283 g) baby spinach
¼ cup heavy cream
½ teaspoon dried parsley
½ teaspoon dried oregano
¼ teaspoon red pepper flakes
1 cup crumbled feta cheese

1. Preheat the oven to 425ºF (220ºC). Season the tilapia fillets with ½ teaspoon each of the salt and pepper. 2. In a large skillet, melt 2 tablespoons of the butter over medium-high heat. Add the leeks and sauté a few minutes, until soft but not brown. Add the spinach a handful at a time; the spinach will reduce in volume by a lot. Add the cream and the parsley, oregano, and red pepper flakes, as well as the remaining ½ teaspoon each salt and pepper. Reduce the heat to medium low and simmer, stirring frequently, until the mixture thickens a bit. 3. Use the remaining 1 teaspoon butter to lightly grease a small glass baking dish. Transfer three-fourths of the spinach mixture to the baking dish and arrange the fish in a single layer on top. Layer the rest of the spinach on top. Sprinkle the feta evenly over and bake for 20 to 25 minutes, or until the fish is cooked through.

Per Serving:
Calories: 318 | fat: 20g | protein: 27g | carbs: 5g | net carbs: 3g | fiber: 2g

Fish Gratin

Prep time: 30 minutes | Cook time: 17 minutes | Serves 4

1 tablespoon avocado oil
1 pound (454 g) hake fillets
1 teaspoon garlic powder
Sea salt and ground white pepper, to taste
2 tablespoons shallots, chopped
1 bell pepper, seeded and
chopped
½ cup Cottage cheese
½ cup sour cream
1 egg, well whisked
1 teaspoon yellow mustard
1 tablespoon lime juice
½ cup Swiss cheese, shredded

1. Brush the bottom and sides of a casserole dish with avocado oil. Add the hake fillets to the casserole dish and sprinkle with garlic powder, salt, and pepper. 2. Add the chopped shallots and bell peppers. 3. In a mixing bowl, thoroughly combine the Cottage cheese, sour cream, egg, mustard, and lime juice. Pour the mixture over fish and spread evenly. 4. Cook in the preheated air fryer at 370ºF (188ºC) for 10 minutes. 5. Top with the Swiss cheese and cook an additional 7 minutes. Let it rest for 10 minutes before slicing and serving. Bon appétit!

Per Serving:
Calories: 256 | fat: 12g | protein: 28g | carbs: 8g | net carbs: 7g | fiber: 1g

Coconut Cream Mackerel

Prep time: 10 minutes | Cook time: 6 minutes | Serves 4

2 pounds (907 g) mackerel fillet
1 cup coconut cream
1 teaspoon ground coriander

1 teaspoon cumin seeds
1 garlic clove, peeled, chopped

1. Chop the mackerel roughly and sprinkle it with coconut cream, ground coriander, cumin seeds, and garlic. 2. Then put the fish in the air fryer and cook at 400ºF (204ºC) for 6 minutes.

Per Serving:
Calories: 439 | fat: 25g | protein: 48g | carbs: 4g | net carbs: 3g | fiber: 1g

Almond Pesto Salmon

Prep time: 5 minutes | Cook time: 12 minutes | Serves 2

¼ cup pesto
¼ cup sliced almonds, roughly chopped
2 (1½-inch-thick) salmon fillets

(about 4 ounces / 113 g each)
2 tablespoons unsalted butter, melted

1. In a small bowl, mix pesto and almonds. Set aside. 2. Place fillets into a round baking dish. 3. Brush each fillet with butter and place half of the pesto mixture on the top of each fillet. Place dish into the air fryer basket. 4. Adjust the temperature to 390ºF (199ºC) and set the timer for 12 minutes. 5. Salmon will easily flake when fully cooked and reach an internal temperature of at least 145ºF (63ºC). Serve warm.

Per Serving:
Calories: 478 | fat: 39g | protein: 29g | carbs: 4g | net carbs: 2g | fiber: 2g

Breaded Shrimp Tacos

Prep time: 10 minutes | Cook time: 9 minutes | Makes 8 tacos

2 large eggs
1 teaspoon prepared yellow mustard
1 pound (454 g) small shrimp, peeled, deveined, and tails removed
½ cup finely shredded Gouda or Parmesan cheese

½ cup pork dust
For Serving:
8 large Boston lettuce leaves
¼ cup pico de gallo
¼ cup shredded purple cabbage
1 lemon, sliced
Guacamole (optional)

1. Preheat the air fryer to 400ºF (204ºC). 2. Crack the eggs into a large bowl, add the mustard, and whisk until well combined. Add the shrimp and stir well to coat. 3. In a medium-sized bowl, mix together the cheese and pork dust until well combined. 4. One at a time, roll the coated shrimp in the pork dust mixture and use your hands to press it onto each shrimp. Spray the coated shrimp with avocado oil and place them in the air fryer basket, leaving space between them. 5. Air fry the shrimp for 9 minutes, or until cooked through and no longer translucent, flipping after 4 minutes. 6. To serve, place a lettuce leaf on a serving plate, place several shrimp on top, and top with 1½ teaspoons each of pico de gallo and purple cabbage. Squeeze some lemon juice on top and serve with guacamole, if desired. 7. Store leftover shrimp in an airtight container in the refrigerator for up to 3 days. Reheat in a preheated 400ºF (204ºC) air fryer for 5 minutes, or until warmed through.

Per Serving:
Calories: 115 | fat: 4g | protein: 18g | carbs: 2g | net carbs: 1g | fiber: 1g

Low-Carb Lowcountry Seafood Boil

Prep time: 30 minutes | Cook time: 1 hour | Serves 8

4 gallons water
6 bay leaves
2 onions, quartered
2 lemons, halved
3 tablespoons salt
2½ tablespoons paprika
1½ tablespoons ground coriander
1 tablespoon ground allspice
1 tablespoon red pepper flakes
1 tablespoon chili powder
1 tablespoon dried marjoram
1 tablespoon onion powder
1 tablespoon garlic powder
1 tablespoon dry mustard
1 tablespoon dried tarragon

1 tablespoon dried thyme
1 tablespoon dried rosemary
2½ teaspoons peppercorns
1 teaspoon ground cumin
½ teaspoon ground cayenne pepper
2 pounds (907 g) Italian sausage, each link cut into thirds
1½ pounds (680 g) mussels
2½ pounds (1.1 kg) cod fillets
3½ pounds (1.6 kg) snow crab legs
1½ pounds (680 g) large raw shrimp, shells on

1. Fill a large stockpot over high heat about three-fourths full with the water. Bring to a boil. Add the bay leaves, onions, lemons, salt, paprika, coriander, allspice, red pepper flakes, chili powder, marjoram, onion powder, garlic powder, mustard, tarragon, thyme, rosemary, peppercorns, cumin, and cayenne. 2. In a large skillet over medium heat, cook the sausage for about 3 minutes per side, turning to brown all sides. They don't have to be fully cooked because they'll finish cooking in the stockpot. Remove from the heat and set aside. 3. Remove any excess fat from the skillet and place it back over medium heat. Add the mussels and 1 cup of seasoned water from the stockpot. Cover the skillet and steam the mussels for 5 to 7 minutes. Discard any that don't open. 4. Add the sausage to the stockpot, followed by the cod. Keep the water at a low boil and cook for 5 minutes. 5. Add the mussels and crab legs. Cook for 5 minutes more. 6. About 5 minutes before you're ready to serve, add the shrimp. Cook for 4 to 5 minutes until completely pink and opaque. 7. Carefully drain the contents of the stockpot and transfer everything to a large serving bowl. Serve immediately. Go traditional and pour the contents of the bowl onto a newspaper-lined table and dig in with your hands!

Per Serving:
Calories: 805 | fat: 40g | protein: 96g | carbs: 7g | net carbs: 7g | fiber: 0g

Parmesan-Garlic Salmon with Asparagus

Prep time: 10 minutes | Cook time: 15 minutes | Serves 2

2 (6-ounce) salmon fillets, skin on
Pink Himalayan salt
Freshly ground black pepper
1 pound fresh asparagus, ends
snapped off
3 tablespoons butter
2 garlic cloves, minced
¼ cup grated Parmesan cheese

1. Preheat the oven to 400°F. Line a baking sheet with aluminum foil or a silicone baking mat. 2. Pat the salmon dry with a paper towel, and season both sides with pink Himalayan salt and pepper. 3. Place the salmon in the middle of the prepared pan, and arrange the asparagus around the salmon. 4. In a small saucepan over medium heat, melt the butter. Add the minced garlic and stir until the garlic just begins to brown, about 3 minutes. 5. Drizzle the garlic-butter sauce over the salmon and asparagus, and top both with the Parmesan cheese. 6. Bake until the salmon is cooked and the asparagus is crisp-tender, about 12 minutes. You can switch the oven to broil at the end of cooking time for about 3 minutes to get a nice char on the asparagus. 7. Serve hot.

Per Serving:
Calories: 434 | fat: 26g | protein: 42g | carbs: 10g | net carbs: 6g | fiber: 5g

Escabeche

Prep time: 10 minutes | Cook time: 20 minutes | Serves 4

1 pound (454 g) wild-caught Spanish mackerel fillets, cut into four pieces
1 teaspoon salt
½ teaspoon freshly ground black pepper
8 tablespoons extra-virgin olive oil, divided
1 bunch asparagus, trimmed
and cut into 2-inch pieces
1 (13¾-ounce / 390-g) can artichoke hearts, drained and quartered
4 large garlic cloves, peeled and crushed
2 bay leaves
¼ cup red wine vinegar
½ teaspoon smoked paprika

1. Sprinkle the fillets with salt and pepper and let sit at room temperature for 5 minutes. 2. In a large skillet, heat 2 tablespoons olive oil over medium-high heat. Add the fish, skin-side up, and cook 5 minutes. Flip and cook 5 minutes on the other side, until browned and cooked through. Transfer to a serving dish, pour the cooking oil over the fish, and cover to keep warm. 3. Heat the remaining 6 tablespoons olive oil in the same skillet over medium heat. Add the asparagus, artichokes, garlic, and bay leaves and sauté until the vegetables are tender, 6 to 8 minutes. 4. Using a slotted spoon, top the fish with the cooked vegetables, reserving the oil in the skillet. Add the vinegar and paprika to the oil and whisk to combine well. Pour the vinaigrette over the fish and vegetables and let sit at room temperature for at least 15 minutes, or marinate in the refrigerator up to 24 hours for a deeper flavor. Remove the bay leaf before serving.

Per Serving:
Calories: 459 | fat: 34g | protein: 26g | carbs: 13g | net carbs: 7g | fiber: 6g

Creamy Hoki with Almond Bread Crust

Prep time: 10 minutes | Cook time: 35 minutes | Serves 4

1 cup flaked smoked hoki, bones removed
1 cup cubed hoki fillets, cubed
4 eggs
1 cup water
3 tablespoons almond flour
1 onion, sliced
2 cups sour cream
1 tablespoon chopped parsley
1 cup pork rinds, crushed
1 cup grated cheddar cheese
Salt and black pepper to taste
2 tablespoons butter

1. Preheat the oven to 360°F and lightly grease a baking dish with cooking spray. 2. Then, boil the eggs in water in a pot over medium heat to be well done for 10 minutes, run the eggs under cold water and peel the shells. After, place on a cutting board and chop them. 3. Melt the butter in a saucepan over medium heat and sauté the onion for 4 minutes. Turn the heat off and stir in the almond flour to form a roux. Turn the heat back on and cook the roux to be golden brown and stir in the cream until the mixture is smooth. Season with salt and black pepper, and stir in the parsley. 4. Spread the smoked and cubed fish in the baking dish, sprinkle the eggs on top, and spoon the sauce over. In a bowl, mix the pork rinds with the cheddar cheese, and sprinkle it over the sauce. 5. Bake the casserole in the oven for 20 minutes until the top is golden and the sauce and cheese are bubbly. Remove the bake after and serve with a steamed green vegetable mix.

Per Serving:
Calories: 411 | fat: 31g | protein: 27g | carbs: 6g | net carbs: 4g | fiber: 2g

Mahi-Mahi Fillets with Peppers

Prep time: 10 minutes | Cook time: 3 minutes | Serves 3

2 sprigs fresh rosemary
2 sprigs dill, tarragon
1 sprig fresh thyme
1 cup water
1 lemon, sliced
3 mahi-mahi fillets
2 tablespoons coconut oil,
melted
Sea salt and ground black pepper, to taste
1 serrano pepper, seeded and sliced
1 green bell pepper, sliced
1 red bell pepper, sliced

1. Add the herbs, water, and lemon slices to the Instant Pot and insert a steamer basket. 2. Arrange the mahi-mahi fillets in the steamer basket. 3. Drizzle the melted coconut oil over the top and season with the salt and black pepper. 4. Lock the lid. Select the Manual mode and set the cooking time for 3 minutes at Low Pressure. 5. When the timer beeps, perform a natural pressure release for 10 minutes, then release any remaining pressure. Carefully remove the lid. 6. Place the peppers on top. Select the Sauté mode and let it simmer for another 1 minute. 7. Serve immediately.

Per Serving:
Calories: 454 | fat: 15g | protein: 76g | carbs: 4g | net carbs: 3 | fiber: 1g

Coconut Milk-Braised Squid

Prep time: 10 minutes | Cook time: 20 minutes | Serves 3

1 pound (454 g) squid, sliced	1 cup coconut milk
1 teaspoon sugar-free tomato paste	1 teaspoon cayenne pepper
	½ teaspoon salt

1. Put all ingredients from the list above in the instant pot. 2. Close and seal the lid and cook the squid on Manual (High Pressure) for 20 minutes. 3. When the cooking time is finished, do the quick pressure release. 4. Serve the squid with coconut milk gravy.

Per Serving:

Calories: 326 | fat: 21g | protein: 25g | carbs: 10g | net carbs: 8g | fiber: 2g

Shrimp Fry

Prep time: 5 minutes | Cook time: 20 minutes | Serves 4

¼ cup (55 g) coconut oil	1 tablespoon paprika
1 pound (455 g) medium shrimp, peeled, deveined, and tails removed	2 teaspoons garlic powder
	1 teaspoon onion powder
	1 teaspoon dried thyme leaves
12 ounces (340 g) smoked sausage (chicken, pork, beef—anything goes), cubed	½ teaspoon finely ground sea salt
	¼ teaspoon ground black pepper
5 asparagus spears, woody ends snapped off, thinly sliced	Pinch of cayenne pepper (optional)
4 ounces (115 g) cremini mushrooms, sliced	Handful of fresh parsley leaves, chopped, for serving
1 medium zucchini, cubed	

1. Melt the oil in a large frying pan over medium heat. 2. Add the remaining ingredients, except the parsley. Toss to coat in the oil, then cover and cook for 15 to 20 minutes, until the asparagus is tender and the shrimp has turned pink. 3. Divide the mixture among 4 serving plates, sprinkle with parsley, and serve.

Per Serving:

Calories: 574 | fat: 40g | protein: 45g | carbs: 8g | net carbs: 6g | fiber: 2g

Simple Nut-Crusted Mahi Mahi

Prep time: 5 minutes | Cook time: 15 minutes | Serves 4

Coconut oil, for greasing	macadamia nuts, coarsely chopped
4 (4-ounce / 113-g) mahi mahi fillets, rinsed and patted dry	2 tablespoons almond flour (or crushed pork rinds)
1 teaspoon sea salt, plus a pinch	½ teaspoon garlic powder
½ teaspoon freshly ground black pepper, plus a pinch	½ teaspoon onion powder
½ cup roasted and salted	4 tablespoons mayonnaise

1. Preheat the oven to 400°F (205°C). Grease an 8-inch square baking dish with coconut oil. 2. Place the mahi mahi in the prepared baking dish. 3. Sprinkle each fillet with salt and pepper on both sides. 4. In small bowl, mix together the macadamia nuts, almond flour, garlic powder, onion powder, and a pinch salt and pepper. 5. Spread 1 tablespoon of mayonnaise on each fillet. Divide the nut mixture among the tops of the 4 fillets, gently patting it down so it adheres to the mayonnaise. 6. Bake for about 15 minutes until golden brown and cooked through.

Per Serving (1 fillet):

Calories: 364 | fat: 28g | protein: 24g | carbs: 4g | net carbs: 2g | fiber: 2g

Chili and Turmeric Haddock

Prep time: 10 minutes | Cook time: 5 minutes | Serves 4

1 chili pepper, minced	½ teaspoon ground turmeric
1 pound (454 g) haddock, chopped	½ cup fish stock
	1 cup water

1. In the mixing bowl mix up chili pepper, ground turmeric, and fish stock. 2. Then add chopped haddock and transfer the mixture in the baking mold. 3. Pour water in the instant pot and insert the trivet. 4. Place the baking mold with fish on the trivet and close the lid. 5. Cook the meal on Manual (High Pressure) for 5 minutes. Make a quick pressure release.

Per Serving:

Calories: 130 | fat: 1g | protein: 28g | carbs: 0g | net carbs: 0g | fiber: 0g

Rainbow Trout with Mixed Greens

Prep time: 5 minutes | Cook time: 12 minutes | Serves 4

1 cup water	1 pound (454 g) mixed greens, trimmed and torn into pieces
1½ (680 g) pounds rainbow trout fillets	1 bunch of scallions
4 tablespoons melted butter, divided	½ cup chicken broth
	1 tablespoon apple cider vinegar
Sea salt and ground black pepper, to taste	1 teaspoon cayenne pepper

1. Pour the water into your Instant Pot and insert a steamer basket. 2. Add the fish to the basket. Drizzle with 1 tablespoon of the melted butter and season with the salt and black pepper. 3. Lock the lid. Select the Manual mode and set the cooking time for 12 minutes at Low pressure. 4. When the timer beeps, perform a quick pressure release. Carefully remove the lid. 5. Wipe down the Instant Pot with a damp cloth. 6. Add and warm the remaining 3 tablespoons of butter. Once hot, add the greens, scallions, broth, vinegar, and cayenne pepper and cook until the greens are wilted, stirring occasionally. 7. Serve the prepared trout fillets with the greens on the side.

Per Serving:

Calories: 349 | fat: 18.1g | protein: 39g | carbs: 7g | net carbs: 3g | fiber: 4g

Sheet-Pan Shrimp

Prep time: 15 minutes | Cook time: 10 minutes | Serves 4

8 tablespoons (1 stick) butter, melted

4 ounces (113 g) cream cheese, at room temperature

1 teaspoon garlic salt

1 pound (454 g) shrimp, any size, peeled, deveined, tails off, patted dry

Juice of 1 lemon

2 scallions, thinly sliced

1. Preheat the oven to 400°F (205°C). Line a rimmed baking sheet with parchment paper and set aside. 2. In a medium bowl, mix together the melted butter, cream cheese, and garlic salt until well combined. 3. Drop the shrimp into the butter mixture and fold gently to coat all the shrimp. 4. Pour the shrimp mixture onto the prepared baking sheet and spread out the shrimp so none overlap. 5. Bake for 8 to 10 minutes. 6. Squeeze the lemon juice across the top of the shrimp, garnish with the scallions, and serve immediately.

Per Serving (¼ recipe):

Calories: 420 | fat: 35g | protein: 25g | carbs: 3g | net carbs: 3g | fiber: 0g

Salmon with Provolone Cheese

Prep time: 5 minutes | Cook time: 15 minutes | Serves 4

1 pound (454 g) salmon fillet, chopped

2 ounces (57 g) Provolone,

grated

1 teaspoon avocado oil

¼ teaspoon ground paprika

1. Sprinkle the salmon fillets with avocado oil and put in the air fryer. 2. Then sprinkle the fish with ground paprika and top with Provolone cheese. 3. Cook the fish at 360°F (182°C) for 15 minutes.

Per Serving:

Calories: 204 | fat: 10g | protein: 27g | carbs: 0g | net carbs: 0g | fiber: 0g

White Fish with Cauliflower

Prep time: 30 minutes | Cook time: 13 minutes | Serves 4

½ pound (227 g) cauliflower florets

½ teaspoon English mustard

2 tablespoons butter, room temperature

½ tablespoon cilantro, minced

2 tablespoons sour cream

2 ½ cups cooked white fish

Salt and freshly cracked black pepper, to taste

1. Boil the cauliflower until tender. Then, purée the cauliflower in your blender. Transfer to a mixing dish. 2. Now, stir in the fish, cilantro, salt, and black pepper. 3. Add the sour cream, English mustard, and butter; mix until everything's well incorporated. Using your hands, shape into patties. 4. Place in the refrigerator for about 2 hours. Cook for 13 minutes at 395°F (202°C). Serve with some extra English mustard.

Per Serving:

Calories: 297 | fat: 16g | protein: 33g | carbs: 5g | net carbs: 4g | fiber: 1g

Thai Coconut Fish

Prep time: 10 minutes | Cook time: 25 to 45 minutes | Serves 4

1 tablespoon avocado oil, MCT oil, or extra-virgin olive oil

3 shallots, chopped

1½ tablespoons red curry paste

1½ cups chicken bone broth, homemade or store-bought

1 (13½-ounce / 383-g) can full-fat coconut milk

¼ teaspoon fine sea salt, plus more for the fish

1 pound (454 g) halibut fillets, cut into 2-inch pieces

¼ cup fresh cilantro leaves, chopped, plus more for garnish

2 green onions, cut into ½-inch pieces, plus more for garnish

Juice of 1 lime

2 cups zoodles, for serving (optional)

1. Heat the oil in a cast-iron skillet over medium heat. Add the shallots and sauté until tender, about 2 minutes. Reduce the heat to low. Whisk in the curry paste, broth, coconut milk, and salt. Simmer, uncovered, until thickened a bit, 20 to 40 minutes, depending on exactly how thick you would like the soup to be. 2. Sprinkle salt all over the fish pieces and add to the soup. Cover the skillet and poach the fish until it is cooked through and opaque and flakes easily, 4 to 5 minutes, depending on how thick your pieces are. 3. Once the fish is cooked through, stir in the cilantro, green onions, and lime juice. Immediately remove from the heat and place in serving bowls over zoodles, if desired. Garnish with additional sliced green onions and cilantro leaves. 4. Store extras in an airtight container in the fridge for up to 3 days. Store any leftover zoodles separately to keep them from getting soggy. Reheat in a saucepan over medium heat for a few minutes or until warmed to your liking, then spoon over warmed zoodles.

Per Serving:

Calories: 360 | fat: 22g | protein: 32g | carbs: 7g | net carbs: 6g | fiber: 1g

Rosemary Catfish

Prep time: 10 minutes | Cook time: 20 minutes | Serves 4

16 ounces (454 g) catfish fillet

1 tablespoon dried rosemary

1 teaspoon garlic powder

1 tablespoon avocado oil

1 teaspoon salt

1 cup water, for cooking

1. Cut the catfish fillet into 4 steaks. 2. Then sprinkle them with dried rosemary, garlic powder, avocado oil, and salt. 3. Place the fish steak in the baking mold in one layer. 4. After this, pour water and insert the steamer rack in the instant pot. 5. Put the baking mold with fish on the rack. Close and seal the lid. 6. Cook the meal on Manual (High Pressure) for 20 minutes. Make a quick pressure release.

Per Serving:

Calories: 163 | fat: 9g | protein: 18g | carbs: 1g | net carbs: 1g | fiber: 0g

Cheesy Garlic Salmon

Prep time: 10 minutes | Cook time: 12 minutes | Serves 4

½ cup Asiago cheese	1 teaspoon chopped fresh basil
2 tablespoons freshly squeezed lemon juice	1 teaspoon chopped fresh oregano
2 tablespoons butter, at room temperature	4 (5-ounce) salmon fillets
2 teaspoons minced garlic	1 tablespoon olive oil

1. Preheat the oven to 350°F. Line a baking sheet with parchment paper and set aside. 2. In a small bowl, stir together the Asiago cheese, lemon juice, butter, garlic, basil, and oregano. 3. Pat the salmon dry with paper towels and place the fillets on the baking sheet skin-side down. Divide the topping evenly between the fillets and spread it across the fish using a knife or the back of a spoon. 4. Drizzle the fish with the olive oil and bake until the topping is golden and the fish is just cooked through, about 12 minutes. 5. Serve.

Per Serving:

Calories: 357 | fat: 28g | protein: 24g | carbs: 2g | net carbs: 2g | fiber: 0g

Foil-Pack Haddock with Spinach

Prep time: 15 minutes | Cook time: 15 minutes | Serves 4

12 ounces (340 g) haddock fillet	1 teaspoon minced garlic
1 cup spinach	½ teaspoon ground coriander
1 tablespoon avocado oil	1 cup water, for cooking

1. Blend the spinach until smooth and mix up with avocado oil, ground coriander, and minced garlic. 2. Then cut the haddock into 4 fillets and place on the foil. 3. Top the fish fillets with spinach mixture and place them on the rack. 4. Pour water and insert the rack in the instant pot. 5. Close and seal the lid and cook the haddock on Manual (High Pressure) for 15 minutes. 6. Do a quick pressure release.

Per Serving:

Calories: 103 | fat: 1g | protein: 21g | carbs: 1g | net carbs: 1g | fiber: 0g

Trout Casserole

Prep time: 5 minutes | Cook time: 10 minutes | Serves 3

1½ cups water	more to taste
1½ tablespoons olive oil	⅓ teaspoon black pepper
3 plum tomatoes, sliced	Salt, to taste
½ teaspoon dried oregano	1 bay leaf
1 teaspoon dried basil	1 cup shredded Pepper Jack cheese
3 trout fillets	
½ teaspoon cayenne pepper, or	

1. Pour the water into your Instant Pot and insert a trivet. 2. Grease a baking dish with the olive oil. Add the tomatoes slices to the baking dish and sprinkle with the oregano and basil. 3. Add the fish fillets and season with the cayenne pepper, black pepper, and salt. Add the bay leaf. Lower the baking dish onto the trivet. 4. Lock the lid. Select the Manual mode and set the cooking time for 10 minutes at High Pressure. 5. When the timer beeps, perform a quick pressure release. Carefully remove the lid. 6. Scatter the Pepper Jack cheese on top, lock the lid, and allow the cheese to melt. 7. Serve warm.

Per Serving:

Calories: 361 | fat: 24g | protein: 25g | carbs: 12g | net carbs: 11g | fiber: 1g

Zoodles in Clam Sauce

Prep time: 5 minutes | Cook time: 7 minutes | Serves 2

¼ cup MCT oil, duck fat, or bacon fat	¼ teaspoon fine sea salt
2 tablespoons minced onions	⅛ teaspoon freshly ground black pepper
2 cloves garlic, minced	2 cups zoodles
1 (6½-ounce / 184-g) can whole clams, drained and chopped	Fresh basil leaves, for garnish (optional)

1. Heat the oil in a cast-iron skillet over medium heat. Add the onions and garlic and cook until the onions are translucent, about 4 minutes. Add the chopped clams and heat for 3 minutes. Season with the salt and pepper. 2. Serve over zoodles, garnished with basil, if desired. 3. Store extra sauce and zoodles separately in airtight containers in the fridge for up to 3 days. Reheat in a skillet over medium heat until warmed.

Per Serving:

Calories: 355 | fat: 29g | protein: 16g | carbs: 8g | net carbs: 7g | fiber: 1g

Mayo-Less Tuna Salad

Prep time: 5 minutes | Cook time: 0 minutes | Serves 1

1 can tuna packed in olive oil	1 teaspoon dried basil (optional)
5 olives, pitted and chopped	Salt and freshly ground black pepper, to taste
4 sun-dried tomatoes, chopped	
2 tablespoons chopped jicama	1 cup fresh spinach leaves
1 tablespoon olive oil	Sugar-free hot sauce, for serving (optional)
1 teaspoon mustard	

1. In a mixing bowl, combine the tuna and its oil with the olives, sun-dried tomatoes, jicama, olive oil, and mustard. Season with the basil (if using), salt, and pepper. Stir everything together until well combined. 2. Arrange the spinach leaves on a plate or in a bowl and top with the tuna salad. Or simply toss the spinach with the tuna salad to save yourself a little bit of cleanup! If you'd like, sprinkle with some hot sauce.

Per Serving:

Calories: 450 | fat: 38g | protein: 18g | carbs: 9g | net carbs: 5g | fiber: 4g

Rosemary-Lemon Snapper Baked in Parchment

Prep time: 15 minutes | Cook time: 15 minutes | Serves 4

1¼ pounds (567 g) fresh red snapper fillet, cut into two equal pieces	tablespoons dried rosemary
	½ cup extra-virgin olive oil
2 lemons, thinly sliced	6 garlic cloves, thinly sliced
6 to 8 sprigs fresh rosemary, stems removed or 1 to 2	1 teaspoon salt
	½ teaspoon freshly ground black pepper

1. Preheat the oven to 425°F(220°C). 2. Place two large sheets of parchment (about twice the size of each piece of fish) on the counter. Place 1 piece of fish in the center of each sheet. 3. Top the fish pieces with lemon slices and rosemary leaves. 4. In a small bowl, combine the olive oil, garlic, salt, and pepper. Drizzle the oil over each piece of fish. 5. Top each piece of fish with a second large sheet of parchment and starting on a long side, fold the paper up to about 1 inch from the fish. Repeat on the remaining sides, going in a clockwise direction. Fold in each corner once to secure. 6. Place both parchment pouches on a baking sheet and bake until the fish is cooked through, 10 to 12 minutes.

Per Serving:
Calories: 399 | fat: 29g | protein: 30g | carbs: 5g | net carbs: 4g | fiber: 1g

Cod Cakes

Prep time: 5 minutes | Cook time: 20 minutes | Serves 2

2 tablespoons plus 1 teaspoon extra-virgin olive oil, divided	2 tablespoons ground flaxseed
¼ medium onion, chopped	1 tablespoon freshly squeezed lemon juice
1 garlic clove, minced	1 teaspoon dried dill
1 cup cauliflower rice, fresh or thawed frozen	½ teaspoon ground cumin
1 pound (454 g) cod fillets	½ teaspoon pink Himalayan sea salt
½ cup almond flour	¼ teaspoon freshly ground black pepper
1 large egg	Tartar sauce
2 tablespoons chopped fresh parsley	

1. In a medium sauté pan or skillet, heat 1 tablespoon of olive oil over medium heat. Add the onion and garlic and cook for about 7 minutes, until tender. 2. Add the cauliflower rice and continue to stir for 5 to 7 minutes, until warmed through and tender. Transfer to a large bowl. 3. In the same skillet, heat 1 teaspoon of olive oil over medium-high heat. Cook the cod for 4 to 5 minutes on each side, until cooked through. Let the cod cool for a couple of minutes. 4. Add the almond flour, egg, parsley, flaxseed, lemon juice, dill, cumin, salt, and pepper to the bowl with the cauliflower rice. Using your hands, mix until the ingredients are well combined. 5. Add the fish to the bowl and mix well. I like to use a fluffing motion to keep the fish in chunks, rather than smashing it all. 6. In the skillet, heat the remaining 1 tablespoon of olive oil over medium heat. 7. Using a ½ cup measuring cup, form the fish cakes by packing the mixture into the cup, then slipping the cake out of the cup onto a plate. You

should be able to shape 4 cakes. 8. Place the fish cakes in the hot oil and cook for about 5 minutes per side, flipping once, until golden brown on both sides. 9. Place the cod cakes on serving plates, and serve with tartar sauce.

Per Serving:
Calories: 531 | fat: 34g | protein: 45g | carbs: 12g | net carbs: 6g | fiber: 6g

Tuna Salad with Tomatoes and Peppers

Prep time: 10 minutes | Cook time: 4 minutes | Serves 4

1½ cups water	2 tablespoons Kalamata olives, pitted and halved
1 pound (454 g) tuna steaks	
1 green bell pepper, sliced	2 tablespoons extra-virgin olive oil
1 red bell pepper, sliced	
2 Roma tomatoes, sliced	2 tablespoons balsamic vinegar
1 head lettuce	½ teaspoon chili flakes
1 red onion, chopped	Sea salt, to taste

1. Add the water to the Instant Pot and insert a steamer basket. 2. Arrange the tuna steaks in the basket. Put the bell peppers and tomato slices on top. 3. Lock the lid. Select the Manual mode and set the cooking time for 4 minutes at High Pressure. 4. When the timer beeps, perform a quick pressure release. Carefully remove the lid. 5. Flake the fish with a fork. 6. Divide the lettuce leaves among 4 serving plates to make a bed for your salad. Add the onion and olives. Drizzle with the olive oil and balsamic vinegar. 7. Season with the chili flakes and salt. Place the prepared fish, tomatoes, and bell peppers on top. 8. Serve immediately.

Per Serving:
Calories: 170 | fat: 5g | protein: 24g | carbs: 8g | net carbs: 6g | fiber: 2g

Paprika Crab Burgers

Prep time: 30 minutes | Cook time: 14 minutes | Serves 3

2 eggs, beaten	10 ounces (283 g) crab meat
1 shallot, chopped	1 teaspoon smoked paprika
2 garlic cloves, crushed	½ teaspoon ground black pepper
1 tablespoon olive oil	
1 teaspoon yellow mustard	Sea salt, to taste
1 teaspoon fresh cilantro, chopped	¾ cup Parmesan cheese

1. In a mixing bowl, thoroughly combine the eggs, shallot, garlic, olive oil, mustard, cilantro, crab meat, paprika, black pepper, and salt. Mix until well combined. 2. Shape the mixture into 6 patties. Roll the crab patties over grated Parmesan cheese, coating well on all sides. Place in your refrigerator for 2 hours. 3. Spritz the crab patties with cooking oil on both sides. Cook in the preheated air fryer at 360°F (182°C) for 14 minutes. Serve on dinner rolls if desired. Bon appétit!

Per Serving:
Calories: 288 | fat: 16g | protein: 32g | carbs: 4g | net carbs: 3g | fiber: 1g

Curried Fish Stew

Prep time: 10 minutes | Cook time: 20 minutes | Serves 6

1 tablespoon olive oil	cubed
1 medium onion, chopped	1 teaspoon ground cayenne
3 garlic cloves, minced	pepper (more or less depending
1 tablespoon tomato paste	on your taste)
2 tablespoons curry powder	Salt, to taste
1 head cauliflower, chopped	Freshly ground black pepper, to
2 cups fish broth, or vegetable	taste
broth	1 (13½-ounce / 383-g) can full-
1½ pounds (680 g) firm	fat coconut milk
whitefish (cod or halibut),	

1. In a large saucepan over medium heat, heat the olive oil. 2. Add the onion and garlic. Sauté for 5 to 7 minutes until the onion is softened and translucent. 3. Stir in the tomato paste, curry powder, and cauliflower. Cook for 1 to 2 minutes. 4. While stirring, slowly add the broth. Bring to a simmer and add the fish. Cook for 10 to 15 minutes or until the fish is opaque. Season with the cayenne and some salt and pepper. 5. Stir in the coconut milk. Simmer on low until ready to serve. Refrigerate leftovers in an airtight container for up to 4 days.

Per Serving:

Calories: 373 | fat: 21g | protein: 33g | carbs: 13g | net carbs: 8g | fiber: 5g

Garam Masala Fish

Prep time: 10 minutes | Cook time: 10 minutes | Serves 4

2 tablespoons sesame oil	1 tablespoon chopped fresh dill
½ teaspoon cumin seeds	leaves
½ cup chopped leeks	1 tablespoon chopped fresh
1 teaspoon ginger-garlic paste	curry leaves
1 pound (454 g) cod fillets,	1 tablespoon chopped fresh
boneless and sliced	parsley leaves
2 ripe tomatoes, chopped	Coarse sea salt, to taste
1½ tablespoons fresh lemon	½ teaspoon smoked cayenne
juice	pepper
½ teaspoon garam masala	¼ teaspoon ground black
½ teaspoon turmeric powder	pepper, or more to taste

1. Set the Instant Pot to Sauté. Add and heat the sesame oil until hot. Sauté the cumin seeds for 30 seconds. 2. Add the leeks and cook for another 2 minutes until translucent. Add the ginger-garlic paste and cook for an additional 40 seconds. 3. Stir in the remaining ingredients. 4. Lock the lid. Select the Manual mode and set the cooking time for 6 minutes at Low Pressure. 5. When the timer beeps, perform a quick pressure release. Carefully remove the lid. 6. Serve immediately.

Per Serving:

Calories: 166 | fat: 8g | protein: 18g | carbs: 6g | net carbs: 4g | fiber: 2g

Seared-Salmon Shirataki Rice Bowls

Prep time: 10 minutes | Cook time: 10 minutes | Serves 2

2 (6-ounce) salmon fillets, skin	1 tablespoon ghee
on	1 (8-ounce) pack Miracle
4 tablespoons soy sauce (or	Shirataki Rice
coconut aminos), divided	1 avocado, diced
2 small Persian cucumbers or ½	Pink Himalayan salt
large English cucumber	Freshly ground black pepper

1. Place the salmon in an 8-inch baking dish, and add 3 tablespoons of soy sauce. Cover and marinate in the refrigerator for 30 minutes. 2. Meanwhile, slice the cucumbers thin, put them in a small bowl, and add the remaining 1 tablespoon of soy sauce. Set aside to marinate. 3. In a medium skillet over medium heat, melt the ghee. Add the salmon fillets skin-side down. Pour some of the soy sauce marinade over the salmon, and sear the fish for 3 to 4 minutes on each side. 4. Meanwhile, in a large saucepan, cook the shirataki rice per package instructions: 1. Rinse the shirataki rice in cold water in a colander. 2. In a saucepan filled with boiling water, cook the rice for 2 minutes. 3. Pour the rice into the colander. Dry out the pan. 4. Transfer the rice to the dry pan and dry roast over medium heat until dry and opaque. 5. Season the avocado with pink Himalayan salt and pepper. 6. Place the salmon fillets on a plate, and remove the skin. Cut the salmon into bite-size pieces. 7. Assemble the rice bowls: In two bowls, make a layer of the cooked Miracle Rice. Top each with the cucumbers, avocado, and salmon, and serve.

Per Serving:

Calories: 328 | fat: 18g | protein: 36g | carbs: 8g | net carbs: 5g | fiber: 3g

Ahi Tuna and Cherry Tomato Salad

Prep time: 5 minutes | Cook time: 4 minutes | Serves 4

1 cup water	1 head lettuce
2 sprigs thyme	1 cup cherry tomatoes, halved
2 sprigs rosemary	1 red bell pepper, julienned
2 sprigs parsley	2 tablespoons extra-virgin olive
1 lemon, sliced	oil
1 pound (454 g) ahi tuna	1 teaspoon Dijon mustard
⅓ teaspoon ground black	Sea salt, to taste
pepper	

1. Pour the water into your Instant Pot. Add the thyme, rosemary, parsley, and lemon and insert a trivet. 2. Lay the fish on the trivet and season with the ground black pepper. 3. Lock the lid. Select the Manual mode and set the cooking time for 4 minutes at High Pressure. 4. When the timer beeps, perform a quick pressure release. Carefully remove the lid. 5. In a salad bowl, place the remaining ingredients and toss well. Add the flaked tuna and toss again. 6. Serve chilled.

Per Serving:

Calories: 253 | fat: 14g | protein: 28g | carbs: 5g | net carbs: 4g | fiber: 1g

Cod with Parsley Pistou

Prep time: 15 minutes | Cook time: 10 minutes | Serves 4

1 cup packed roughly chopped fresh flat-leaf Italian parsley

1 to 2 small garlic cloves, minced

Zest and juice of 1 lemon

1 teaspoon salt

½ teaspoon freshly ground black pepper

1 cup extra-virgin olive oil, divided

1 pound (454 g) cod fillets, cut into 4 equal-sized pieces

1. In a food processor, combine the parsley, garlic, lemon zest and juice, salt, and pepper. Pulse to chop well. 2. While the food processor is running, slowly stream in ¾ cup olive oil until well combined. Set aside. 3. In a large skillet, heat the remaining ¼ cup olive oil over medium-high heat. Add the cod fillets, cover, and cook 4 to 5 minutes on each side, or until cooked through. Thicker fillets may require a bit more cooking time. Remove from the heat and keep warm. 4. Add the pistou to the skillet and heat over medium-low heat. Return the cooked fish to the skillet, flipping to coat in the sauce. Serve warm, covered with pistou.

Per Serving:
Calories: 580 | fat: 55g | protein: 21g | carbs: 2g | net carbs: 1g | fiber: 1g

Fish and Scallop Ceviche

Prep time: 10 minutes | Cook time: 0 minutes | Serves 3

4 ounces (113 g) shrimp, peeled and chopped

1 (4-ounce / 113-g) white fish fillet, chopped into bite-size pieces

4 ounces (113 g) bay or other small scallops

¼ small red onion, chopped

½ jalapeño pepper, seeded and finely chopped

1 garlic clove, minced

½ teaspoon pink Himalayan sea salt

¼ teaspoon freshly ground black pepper

3 or 4 limes

½ medium cucumber, peeled and chopped

½ avocado, slightly firm, chopped

⅓ cup grape tomatoes, halved

3 tablespoons chopped fresh cilantro

2 teaspoons extra-virgin olive oil

Firm lettuce leaves, for wraps

1. In a large bowl, combine the shrimp, fish, and scallops. 2. Add the red onion, jalapeño, garlic, salt, and pepper. Using a wooden spoon, stir to mix the ingredients. 3. Roll the limes on the countertop, pressing firmly down with your hand to soften. Slice the limes in half crosswise, then squeeze the juice into the bowl and stir well. 4. Cover the bowl with plastic wrap, and place in the refrigerator for 45 minutes to 1 hour. 5. Add the cucumber, avocado, tomatoes, and cilantro to the bowl. Gently mix, trying not to smash the avocado. 6. Drizzle the ceviche with the olive oil, then serve with the lettuce to make wraps.

Per Serving:
Calories: 211 | fat: 9g | protein: 21g | carbs: 13g | net carbs: 9g | fiber: 4g

Thai Soup with Shrimp

Prep time: 20 minutes | Cook time: 15 minutes | Serves 4

1 teaspoon kosher salt

1 teaspoon black pepper

1 teaspoon ground turmeric

½ teaspoon ground cumin

¼ teaspoon ground cinnamon

2 tablespoons coconut oil

4 green onions, trimmed and chopped

1 tablespoon grated or finely minced fresh ginger

3 cups chicken broth, preferably homemade

2 tablespoons tamari (gluten-

free soy sauce)

1 teaspoon Thai or Vietnamese fish sauce

½ teaspoon red pepper flakes

1 can (14 ounces / 397 g) full-fat coconut milk

12 medium shrimp, peeled and deveined

Juice of 1 lime

¼ cup fresh cilantro leaves (optional)

1 large avocado, diced

1. In a small bowl, combine the salt, pepper, turmeric, cumin, and cinnamon. 2. In a stockpot, melt the coconut oil. Add the green onions and ginger and sauté until fragrant, about 2 minutes. Add the spice mix and stir. Cook about 30 seconds. 3. Slowly pour in the chicken broth, stirring continuously. Add the tamari, fish sauce, and red pepper flakes. Bring to a boil, then reduce to a simmer. Simmer for 5 minutes. 4. Whisk in the coconut milk. Bring to simmer again, then add the shrimp and simmer approximately 5 minutes, or until the shrimp is just cooked through. 5. Remove from the heat. Stir in the lime juice and cilantro. Ladle into 4 individual bowls and top each bowl with one-fourth of the diced avocado.

Per Serving:
Calories: 464 | fat: 40g | protein: 11g | carbs: 15g | net carbs: 10g | fiber: 5g

Simple Lemon-Herb Whitefish

Prep time: 5 minutes | Cook time: 14 minutes | Serves 6

6 white fish fillets (5 ounces / 142 g each), preferably lake whitefish, grouper, or halibut

1 teaspoon sea salt

½ teaspoon black pepper

3 tablespoons olive oil

2 teaspoons lemon zest

2 teaspoons lemon juice

2 cloves garlic, minced

1 teaspoon minced capers (optional)

3 tablespoons minced fresh parsley

3 tablespoons minced fresh dill

1. Preheat the oven to 400°F (205°C). Line a sheet pan with foil or parchment paper and grease lightly. 2. Place the fish fillets in a single layer on the pan. Season the fish on both sides with the sea salt and black pepper. 3. In a small bowl, whisk together the oil, lemon zest, lemon juice, garlic, capers (if using), parsley, and dill. Spoon about 1 tablespoon of the lemon-herb oil over each piece of fish, then use a brush to spread it. 4. Bake for 10 to 14 minutes, depending on the thickness of the fish, until the fish flakes easily with a fork.

Per Serving:
Calories: 325 | fat: 17g | protein: 37g | carbs: 0g | net carbs: 0g | fiber: 0g

Coconut Shrimp

Prep time: 5 minutes | Cook time: 6 minutes | Serves 2

8 ounces (227 g) medium shelled and deveined shrimp
2 tablespoons salted butter, melted

½ teaspoon Old Bay seasoning
¼ cup unsweetened shredded coconut

1. In a large bowl, toss the shrimp in butter and Old Bay seasoning. 2. Place shredded coconut in bowl. Coat each piece of shrimp in the coconut and place into the air fryer basket. 3. Adjust the temperature to 400°F (204°C) and air fry for 6 minutes. 4. Gently turn the shrimp halfway through the cooking time. Serve immediately.

Per Serving:
Calories: 197 | fat: 13g | protein: 16g | carbs: 2g | net carbs: 1g | fiber: 1g

Friday Night Fish Fry

Prep time: 10 minutes | Cook time: 10 minutes | Serves 4

1 large egg
½ cup powdered Parmesan cheese (about 1½ ounces / 43 g)
1 teaspoon smoked paprika
¼ teaspoon celery salt
¼ teaspoon ground black

pepper
4 (4-ounce / 113-g) cod fillets
Chopped fresh oregano or parsley, for garnish (optional)
Lemon slices, for serving (optional)

1. Spray the air fryer basket with avocado oil. Preheat the air fryer to 400°F (204°C). 2. Crack the egg in a shallow bowl and beat it lightly with a fork. Combine the Parmesan cheese, paprika, celery salt, and pepper in a separate shallow bowl. 3. One at a time, dip the fillets into the egg, then dredge them in the Parmesan mixture. Using your hands, press the Parmesan onto the fillets to form a nice crust. As you finish, place the fish in the air fryer basket. 4. Air fry the fish in the air fryer for 10 minutes, or until it is cooked through and flakes easily with a fork. Garnish with fresh oregano or parsley and serve with lemon slices, if desired. 5. Store leftovers in an airtight container in the refrigerator for up to 3 days. Reheat in a preheated 400°F (204°C) air fryer for 5 minutes, or until warmed through.

Per Serving:
Calories: 165 | fat: 6g | protein: 25g | carbs: 2g | fiber: 0g | sodium: 392mg

Scallops & Mozza Broccoli Mash

Prep time: 5 minutes | Cook time: 35 minutes | Serves 4

MOZZA BROCCOLI MASH:
¼ cup (55 g) coconut oil or ghee, or ¼ cup (60 ml) avocado oil
6 cups (570 g) broccoli florets
4 cloves garlic, minced

1 (2-in/5-cm) piece fresh ginger root, grated
⅔ cup (160 ml) chicken bone broth
½ cup (70 g) shredded mozzarella cheese (dairy-free

or regular)
SCALLOPS:
1 pound (455 g) sea scallops
¼ teaspoon finely ground sea salt

¼ teaspoon ground black pepper
2 tablespoons coconut oil, avocado oil, or ghee
Lemon wedges, for serving

1. Prepare the mash: Heat the oil in a large frying pan over low heat. Add the broccoli, garlic, and ginger and cook, uncovered, for 5 minutes, or until the garlic is fragrant. 2. Pour in the broth, then cover and cook on low for 25 minutes, or until the broccoli is easily mashed. 3. About 5 minutes before the broccoli is ready, prepare the scallops: Pat the scallops dry and season them on both sides with the salt and pepper. Heat the oil in a medium-sized frying pan over medium heat. When the oil is hot, add the scallops. Cook for 2 minutes per side, or until lightly golden. 4. When the broccoli is done, add the cheese and mash with a fork. Divide the mash among 4 dinner plates and top with the scallops. Serve with lemon wedges and enjoy!

Per Serving:
Calories: 353 | fat: 25g | protein: 19g | carbs: 12g | net carbs: 5g | fiber: 7g

Parchment-Baked Cod and Asparagus with Beurre Blanc

Prep time: 15 minutes | Cook time: 15 minutes | Serves 4

1 pound (454 g) skinless cod, halibut, or other white flaky fish
1 teaspoon salt, divided
½ teaspoon freshly ground black pepper, divided
2 garlic cloves, thinly sliced
1 lemon, thinly sliced
½ pound (227 g) asparagus spears, rough ends trimmed

4 tablespoons extra-virgin olive oil, divided
1 tablespoon finely chopped red onion
¼ cup white wine vinegar
¼ cup heavy cream
½ cup (1 stick) chilled unsalted butter, cut into tablespoon-size pieces

1. Preheat the oven to 375°F (190°C). 2. Place 1 large sheet of parchment paper (about twice the size of the fish fillet) on a rimmed baking sheet. Place the fish in the center of the parchment and sprinkle with ½ teaspoon of the salt and ¼ teaspoon of the pepper. 3. Top the fish with the garlic and lemon slices. Top with the asparagus spears and drizzle with 2 tablespoons of olive oil. 4. Top the fish with a second large piece of parchment. Starting on a long side, fold the paper up to about 1 inch from the fish and vegetables. Repeat on the remaining sides, going in a clockwise direction. Fold in each corner once to secure. 5. Bake for 10 to 12 minutes, until the fish is cooked through and flakes easily when poked with a paring knife. 6. Meanwhile, prepare the sauce. Heat the remaining 2 tablespoons of olive oil over medium heat. Add the red onion and sauté until tender, 3 to 4 minutes. Add the vinegar, cream, remaining ½ teaspoon of salt, and ¼ teaspoon of pepper. Bring to a simmer and reduce heat to low. 7. Whisking constantly, add the butter, a couple tablespoons at a time, until melted and creamy. Remove the sauce from the heat and serve warm, poured over the fish and asparagus.

Per Serving:
Calories: 472 | fat: 43g | protein: 19g | carbs: 4g | net carbs: 3g | fiber: 1g

Baked Lemon-Butter Fish

Prep time: 10 minutes | Cook time: 20 minutes | Serves 2

4 tablespoons butter, plus more for coating

2 (5-ounce) tilapia fillets

Pink Himalayan salt

Freshly ground black pepper

2 garlic cloves, minced

1 lemon, zested and juiced

2 tablespoons capers, rinsed and chopped

1. Preheat the oven to 400°F. Coat an 8-inch baking dish with butter. 2. Pat dry the tilapia with paper towels, and season on both sides with pink Himalayan salt and pepper. Place in the prepared baking dish. 3. In a medium skillet over medium heat, melt the butter. Add the garlic and cook for 3 to 5 minutes, until slightly browned but not burned. 4. Remove the garlic butter from the heat, and mix in the lemon zest and 2 tablespoons of lemon juice. 5. Pour the lemon-butter sauce over the fish, and sprinkle the capers around the baking pan. 6. Bake for 12 to 15 minutes, until the fish is just cooked through, and serve.

Per Serving:

Calories: 299 | fat: 26g | protein: 16g | carbs: 5g | net carbs: 3g | fiber: 1g

Sheet-Pan Cajun Crab Legs and Veggies

Prep time: 15 minutes | Cook time: 30 minutes | Serves 6

Coconut oil, for greasing

2 zucchini, halved lengthwise and sliced

3 cups roughly chopped cauliflower

10 tablespoons butter or ghee, melted, divided

2 tablespoons Cajun seasoning

1 tablespoon minced garlic

6 ounces (170 g) Polish

sausages or bratwurst, cut into rounds ½-inch thick

2 pounds (907 g) frozen snow crab legs (about two clusters), thawed in the refrigerator overnight or for a few minutes under cold running water

½ lemon

Chopped fresh parsley, for garnish

1. Preheat the oven to 450ºF (235ºC). Line a large baking sheet with aluminum foil and grease the foil with oil. 2. Arrange the zucchini halves cut-side up on the prepared baking sheet. Add the cauliflower and spread it out in an even layer. 3. In a small bowl, stir together 5 tablespoons of melted butter, Cajun seasoning, and garlic until well mixed. Pour half of the butter mixture over the veggies, making sure to cover the cauliflower. 4. Bake for 15 to 20 minutes until the veggies are tender. 5. Place the sausage slices among the vegetables. Break up the crab legs and add them to the pan. Drizzle with the remaining butter mixture. Bake for an additional 10 minutes. 6. Squeeze the lemon half over the top, garnish with parsley, and serve immediately with the remaining 5 tablespoons of butter for dipping.

Per Serving:

Calories: 415 | fat: 29g | protein: 33g | carbs: 5g | net carbs: 3g | fiber: 2g

Clam Chowder

Prep time: 5 minutes | Cook time: 15 minutes | Serves 4

4 slices bacon, chopped into ½-inch squares

2 tablespoons unsalted butter

½ small yellow onion, chopped

4 ribs celery, cut into ¼-inch-thick half-moons

1 cup chopped cauliflower florets, cut to about ½ inch thick

4 ounces (113 g) chopped mushrooms

4 cloves garlic, minced

1 teaspoon dried tarragon

1 teaspoon salt

¼ teaspoon freshly ground black pepper

8 ounces (227 g) bottled clam juice

1 cup vegetable stock or broth

½ cup heavy cream

8 ounces (227 g) cream cheese, room temperature

3 (6½-ounce / 184-g) cans chopped clams, with juice

¼ cup freshly chopped Italian parsley

1. Place the bacon in a medium saucepan over medium heat. Fry until just browned and most of the fat has been rendered, 3 to 4 minutes. Remove the bacon with a slotted spoon, reserving the rendered fat. 2. Add the butter to the pan with the fat and melt over medium heat. Add the onion, celery, cauliflower, and mushrooms and sauté until vegetables are just tender, 4 to 5 minutes. Add the garlic, tarragon, salt, and pepper and sauté for another 30 seconds or until fragrant. 3. Add the clam juice, stock, cream, and cream cheese and whisk until the cheese is melted and creamy, 2 to 3 minutes. Add the clams and their juice, bring to a simmer, and cook for 1 to 2 minutes so the flavors meld. Stir in the parsley and serve warm.

Per Serving:

Calories: 671 | fat: 54g | protein: 34g | carbs: 15g | net carbs: 13g | fiber: 2g

Flounder Meuniere

Prep time: 15 minutes | Cook time: 10 minutes | Serves 4

16 ounces (454 g) flounder fillet

½ teaspoon ground black pepper

½ teaspoon salt

½ cup almond flour

2 tablespoons olive oil

1 tablespoon lemon juice

1 teaspoon chopped fresh parsley

1. Cut the fish fillets into 4 servings and sprinkle with salt, ground black pepper, and lemon juice. 2. Heat up the instant pot on Sauté mode for 2 minutes and add olive oil. 3. Coat the flounder fillets in the almond flour and put them in the hot olive oil. 4. Sauté the fish fillets for 4 minutes and then flip on another side. 5. Cook the meal for 3 minutes more or until it is golden brown. 6. Sprinkle the cooked flounder with the fresh parsley.

Per Serving:

Calories: 214 | fat: 10g | protein: 28g | carbs: 1g | net carbs: 1g | fiber: 0g

Tuna Cakes

Prep time: 10 minutes | Cook time: 10 minutes | Serves 4

4 (3-ounce / 85-g) pouches tuna, drained	2 tablespoons peeled and chopped white onion
1 large egg, whisked	½ teaspoon Old Bay seasoning

1. In a large bowl, mix all ingredients together and form into four patties. 2. Place patties into ungreased air fryer basket. Adjust the temperature to 400°F (204°C) and air fry for 10 minutes. Patties will be browned and crispy when done. Let cool 5 minutes before serving.

Per Serving:

Calories: 113 | fat: 2g | protein: 22g | carbs: 1g | fiber: 0g | sodium: 56mg

Clam Chowder with Bacon and Celery

Prep time: 10 minutes | Cook time: 4 minutes | Serves 2

5 ounces (142 g) clams	½ cup water
1 ounce (28 g) bacon, chopped	½ cup heavy cream
3 ounces (85 g) celery, chopped	

1. Cook the bacon on Sauté mode for 1 minute. 2. Then add clams, celery, water, and heavy cream. 3. Close and seal the lid. 4. Cook the seafood on steam mode (High Pressure) for 3 minutes. Make a quick pressure release. 5. Ladle the clams with the heavy cream mixture in the bowls.

Per Serving:

Calories: 221 | fat: 17g | protein: 7g | carbs: 10g | net carbs: 9g | fiber: 1g

Salmon Romesco

Prep time: 10 minutes | Cook time: 30 minutes | Serves 4

½ cup almonds	vinegar
4 garlic cloves, peeled	1 tablespoon smoked paprika
1 tomato	1 teaspoon ground cayenne pepper
4 (6-ounce / 170-g) salmon fillets	Salt, to taste
2 red bell peppers	Freshly ground black pepper, to taste
¼ cup olive oil	
2 tablespoons white wine	

1. Preheat the oven to 375°F (190°C). 2. On a large baking sheet, spread out the almonds and add the garlic and tomato. Roast for 10 minutes or until the almonds are fragrant and just starting to brown. Remove the almonds and continue roasting the garlic and tomato for 15 to 20 minutes more until the garlic is browned and the tomato has softened. 3. While the almonds, garlic, and tomato roast, on a separate baking sheet, bake the salmon for 30 to 35 minutes or until the flesh is opaque and flakes easily with a fork. 4. Meanwhile, roast the red peppers for 3 to 5 minutes over an open flame or on a hot (medium high) grill until the skins are blackened.

Cover with plastic wrap and let sweat until cool enough to handle. Peel off the blackened skin and remove the seeds. 5. In a food processor, combine the almonds, garlic, tomato, bell peppers, olive oil, vinegar, paprika, cayenne, and some salt and pepper. Purée until smooth. Serve over the salmon and enjoy immediately.

Per Serving:

Calories: 513 | fat: 37g | protein: 37g | carbs: 8g | net carbs: 4g | fiber: 4g

Italian Salmon

Prep time: 10 minutes | Cook time: 4 minutes | Serves 2

10 ounces (283 g) salmon fillet	1 cup water
1 teaspoon Italian seasoning	

1. Pour water and insert the trivet in the instant pot. 2. Then rub the salmon fillet with Italian seasoning and wrap in the foil. 3. Place the wrapped fish on the trivet and close the lid. 4. Cook the meal on Manual mode (High Pressure) for 4 minutes. 5. Make a quick pressure release and remove the fish from the foil. 6. Cut it into servings.

Per Serving:

Calories: 195 | fat: 10g | protein: 27g | carbs: 0g | net carbs: 0g | fiber: 0g

Simple Flounder in Brown Butter Lemon Sauce

Prep time: 10 minutes | Cook time: 10 minutes | Serves 4

For the Sauce:	fillets
½ cup unsalted grass-fed butter, cut into pieces	Sea salt, for seasoning
Juice of 1 lemon	Freshly ground black pepper, for seasoning
Sea salt, for seasoning	¼ cup almond flour
Freshly ground black pepper, for seasoning	2 tablespoons good-quality olive oil
For the Fish:	1 tablespoon chopped fresh parsley
4 (4-ounce) boneless flounder	

To Make The Sauce: 1. Brown the butter. In a medium saucepan over medium heat, cook the butter, stirring it once in a while, until it is golden brown, about 4 minutes. 2. Finish the sauce. Remove the saucepan from the heat and stir in the lemon juice. Season the sauce with salt and pepper and set it aside. To Make The Fish: 1. Season the fish. Pat the fish fillets dry and season them lightly with salt and pepper. Spoon the almond flour onto a plate, then roll the fish fillets through the flour until they're lightly coated. 2. Cook the fish. In a large skillet over medium-high heat, warm the olive oil. Add the fish fillets and fry them until they're crispy and golden on both sides, 2 to 3 minutes per side. 3. Serve. Transfer the fish to a serving plate and drizzle with the sauce. Top with the parsley and serve it hot.

Per Serving:

Calories: 389 | fat: 33g | protein: 22g | carbs: 1g | net carbs: 1g | fiber: 0g

Tuna Slow-Cooked in Olive Oil

Prep time: 5 minutes | Cook time: 45 minutes | Serves 4

1 cup extra-virgin olive oil, plus more if needed

4 (3- to 4-inch) sprigs fresh rosemary

8 (3- to 4-inch) sprigs fresh thyme

2 large garlic cloves, thinly sliced

2 (2-inch) strips lemon zest

1 teaspoon salt

½ teaspoon freshly ground black pepper

1 pound (454 g) fresh tuna steaks (about 1 inch thick)

1. Select a thick pot just large enough to fit the tuna in a single layer on the bottom. The larger the pot, the more olive oil you will need to use. Combine the olive oil, rosemary, thyme, garlic, lemon zest, salt, and pepper over medium-low heat and cook until warm and fragrant, 20 to 25 minutes, lowering the heat if it begins to smoke. 2. Remove from the heat and allow to cool for 25 to 30 minutes, until warm but not hot. 3. Add the tuna to the bottom of the pan, adding additional oil if needed so that tuna is fully submerged, and return to medium-low heat. Cook for 5 to 10 minutes, or until the oil heats back up and is warm and fragrant but not smoking. Lower the heat if it gets too hot. 4. Remove the pot from the heat and let the tuna cook in warm oil 4 to 5 minutes, to your desired level of doneness. For a tuna that is rare in the center, cook for 2 to 3 minutes. 5. Remove from the oil and serve warm, drizzling 2 to 3 tablespoons seasoned oil over the tuna. 6. To store for later use, remove the tuna from the oil and place in a container with a lid. Allow tuna and oil to cool separately. When both have cooled, remove the herb stems with a slotted spoon and pour the cooking oil over the tuna. Cover and store in the refrigerator for up to 1 week. Bring to room temperature to allow the oil to liquify before serving.

Per Serving:

Calories: 606 | fat: 55g | protein: 28g | carbs: 1g | net carbs: 1g | fiber: 0g

Dill Lemon Salmon

Prep time: 10 minutes | Cook time: 4 minutes | Serves 4

1 pound (454 g) salmon fillet

1 tablespoon butter, melted

2 tablespoons lemon juice

1 teaspoon dried dill

1 cup water

1. Cut the salmon fillet on 4 servings. 2. Line the instant pot baking pan with foil and put the salmon fillets inside in one layer. 3. Then sprinkle the fish with dried dill, lemon juice, and butter. 4. Pour water in the instant pot and insert the rack. 5. Place the baking pan with salmon on the rack and close the lid. 6. Cook the meal on Manual mode (High Pressure) for 4 minutes. Allow the natural pressure release for 5 minutes and remove the fish from the instant pot.

Per Serving:

Calories: 178 | fat: 10g | protein: 22g | carbs: 0g | net carbs: 0g | fiber: 0g

Simple Chicken Masala

Prep time: 10 minutes | Cook time: 17 minutes | Serves 3

12 ounces (340 g) chicken fillet
1 tablespoon masala spices
1 tablespoon avocado oil

3 tablespoons organic almond milk

1. Heat up avocado oil in the instant pot on Sauté mode for 2 minutes. 2. Meanwhile, chop the chicken fillet roughly and mix it up with masala spices. 3. Add almond milk and transfer the chicken in the instant pot. 4. Cook the chicken bites on Sauté mode for 15 minutes. Stir the meal occasionally.

Per Serving:
Calories: 211 | fat: 9g | protein: 25g | carbs: 6g | net carbs: 6g | fiber: 0g

Garlic Dill Wings

Prep time: 5 minutes | Cook time: 25 minutes | Serves 4

2 pounds (907 g) bone-in chicken wings, separated at joints
½ teaspoon salt
½ teaspoon ground black

pepper
½ teaspoon onion powder
½ teaspoon garlic powder
1 teaspoon dried dill

1. In a large bowl, toss wings with salt, pepper, onion powder, garlic powder, and dill until evenly coated. Place wings into ungreased air fryer basket in a single layer, working in batches if needed. 2. Adjust the temperature to 400ºF (204ºC) and air fry for 25 minutes, shaking the basket every 7 minutes during cooking. Wings should have an internal temperature of at least 165ºF (74ºC) and be golden brown when done. Serve warm.

Per Serving:
Calories: 290 | fat: 8g | protein: 50g | carbs: 1g | fiber: 0g | sodium: 475mg

Chicken Pesto Parmigiana

Prep time: 10 minutes | Cook time: 23 minutes | Serves 4

2 large eggs
1 tablespoon water
Fine sea salt and ground black pepper, to taste
1 cup powdered Parmesan cheese (about 3 ounces / 85 g)
2 teaspoons Italian seasoning

4 (5-ounce / 142-g) boneless, skinless chicken breasts or thighs, pounded to ¼ inch thick
1 cup pesto
1 cup shredded Mozzarella cheese (about 4 ounces / 113 g)
Finely chopped fresh basil, for

garnish (optional)
Grape tomatoes, halved, for

serving (optional)

1. Spray the air fryer basket with avocado oil. Preheat the air fryer to 400ºF (204ºC). 2. Crack the eggs into a shallow baking dish, add the water and a pinch each of salt and pepper, and whisk to combine. In another shallow baking dish, stir together the Parmesan and Italian seasoning until well combined. 3. Season the chicken breasts well on both sides with salt and pepper. Dip one chicken breast in the eggs and let any excess drip off, then dredge both sides of the breast in the Parmesan mixture. Spray the breast with avocado oil and place it in the air fryer basket. Repeat with the remaining 3 chicken breasts. 4. Air fry the chicken in the air fryer for 20 minutes, or until the internal temperature reaches 165ºF (74ºC) and the breading is golden brown, flipping halfway through. 5. Dollop each chicken breast with ¼ cup of the pesto and top with the Mozzarella. Return the breasts to the air fryer and cook for 3 minutes, or until the cheese is melted. Garnish with basil and serve with halved grape tomatoes on the side, if desired. 6. Store leftovers in an airtight container in the refrigerator for up to 4 days. Reheat in a preheated 400ºF (204ºC) air fryer for 5 minutes, or until warmed through.

Per Serving:
Calories: 631 | fat: 45g | protein: 52g | carbs: 4g | fiber: 0g | sodium: 607mg

Pork Rind Fried Chicken

Prep time: 30 minutes | Cook time: 20 minutes | Serves 4

¼ cup buffalo sauce
4 (4-ounce / 113-g) boneless, skinless chicken breasts
½ teaspoon paprika
½ teaspoon garlic powder

¼ teaspoon ground black pepper
2 ounces (57 g) plain pork rinds, finely crushed

1. Pour buffalo sauce into a large sealable bowl or bag. Add chicken and toss to coat. Place sealed bowl or bag into refrigerator and let marinate at least 30 minutes up to overnight. 2. Remove chicken from marinade but do not shake excess sauce off chicken. Sprinkle both sides of thighs with paprika, garlic powder, and pepper. 3. Place pork rinds into a large bowl and press each chicken breast into pork rinds to coat evenly on both sides. 4. Place chicken into ungreased air fryer basket. Adjust the temperature to 400ºF (204ºC) and roast for 20 minutes, turning chicken halfway through cooking. Chicken will be golden and have an internal temperature of at least 165ºF (74ºC) when done. Serve warm.

Per Serving:
Calories: 217 | fat: 8g | protein: 35g | carbs: 1g | fiber: 0g | sodium: 400mg

Orange-Glazed Roasted Duck

Prep time: 15 minutes | Cook time: 1½ hours | Serves 6

1 (5-pound/2.3-kg) whole duck, giblets removed	broth, divided
1 orange	¼ cup white wine, such as Pinot Grigio, Sauvignon Blanc, or unoaked Chardonnay
4 fresh thyme sprigs	
Handful of fresh parsley	
2¼ teaspoons finely ground gray sea salt, divided	⅓ cup (53 g) confectioners'-style erythritol
1 teaspoon ground coriander	2 tablespoons apple cider vinegar
¾ teaspoon ground black pepper	
½ teaspoon ground cumin	Special Equipment: Cotton twine
¾ cup (180 ml) chicken bone	

1. Preheat the oven to 475°F (245°C). 2. Using a microplane or fine grater, zest the orange, then cut the orange in half. Juice one half and cut the other half into wedges. Set the zest and juice aside. Stuff the orange wedges and thyme and parsley sprigs into the duck cavity. Tie the legs together with cotton twine and set the duck in a cast-iron pan or small roasting pan. 3. Sprinkle 2 teaspoons of the salt, the coriander, pepper, and cumin all over the outside of the duck. Roast for 30 minutes. 4. Put the reserved orange juice in a bowl along with ½ cup (120 ml) of the bone broth and the wine. After the duck has roasted for 30 minutes, lower the heat to 350°F (177°C) and pour the broth mixture into the pan. Bake for an additional 50 to 60 minutes, until the internal temperature reaches 165°F (74°C). If you want crispy skin, set the broiler to high, move the rack to the top position, and broil for 5 minutes, or until the skin has crisped up. Remove from the oven and transfer the roasted duck to a cutting board. 5. Make the glaze: Place the remaining ¼ cup (60 ml) of bone broth, erythritol, vinegar, and remaining ¼ teaspoon salt in the pan with the drippings. Set over medium-low heat and whisk continuously until the erythritol has dissolved. Add the reserved orange zest. Whisk continuously for 5 minutes, until the glaze has thickened. 6. Slice the duck and place on a serving plate. Drizzle with the orange glaze, or serve the glaze on the side in a gravy boat.

Per Serving:
Calories: 458 | fat: 37g | protein: 26g | carbs: 4g | net carbs: 3g | fiber: 1g

Chicken and Zucchini Bake

Prep time: 10 minutes | Cook time: 30 minutes | Serves 4

1 zucchini, chopped	1 tomato, cored and chopped
Salt and black pepper, to taste	½ teaspoon dried oregano
1 teaspoon garlic powder	½ teaspoon dried basil
1 tablespoon avocado oil	½ cup mozzarella cheese, shredded
2 chicken breasts, skinless, boneless, sliced	

1. Apply pepper, garlic powder and salt to the chicken. Set a pan over medium heat and warm avocado oil, add in the chicken slices, cook until golden; remove to a baking dish. To the same pan add the zucchini, tomato, pepper, basil, oregano, and salt, cook for 2 minutes, and spread over chicken. 2. Bake in the oven at 330°F for 20 minutes. Sprinkle the mozzarella over the chicken, return to the oven, and bake for 5 minutes until the cheese is melted and bubbling. Serve with green salad.

Per Serving:
Calories: 279 | fat: 15g | protein: 33g | carbs: 3g | net carbs: 2g | fiber: 1g

Parmesan Wings with Yogurt Sauce

Prep time: 5 minutes | Cook time: 20 minutes | Serves 6

For the Dipping Sauce	Salt and black pepper to taste
1 cup plain yogurt	Cooking spray
1 teaspoon fresh lemon juice	½ cup melted butter
Salt and black pepper to taste	½ cup Hot sauce
For the Wings	¼ cup grated Parmesan cheese
2 pounds (907 g) chicken wings	

1. Mix the yogurt, lemon juice, salt, and black pepper in a bowl. Chill while making the chicken. 2. Preheat oven to 400°F and season wings with salt and black pepper. Line them on a baking sheet and grease lightly with cooking spray. Bake for 20 minutes until golden brown. Mix butter, hot sauce, and Parmesan cheese in a bowl. Toss chicken in the sauce to evenly coat and plate. Serve with yogurt dipping sauce and celery strips.

Per Serving:
Calories: 435 | fat: 31g | protein: 33g | carbs: 6g | net carbs: 4g | fiber: 2g

Alex's "Chick and Brock" Casserole

Prep time: 10 minutes | Cook time: 50 minutes | Serves 8

1 cup heavy whipping cream	½ teaspoon black pepper
1 cup mascarpone cheese, softened	½ teaspoon garlic salt
1 cup grated Parmesan cheese	1 pound cooked, shredded boneless chicken breast
3 cloves garlic, peeled and minced	4 cups raw broccoli florets
2 teaspoons dried parsley	2 cups shredded whole milk mozzarella cheese, divided
½ teaspoon salt	

1. Preheat oven to 375°F. Grease a 9" × 12" casserole dish. 2. In a large bowl, add all ingredients except chicken, broccoli, and mozzarella. Mix until blended to thick sauce. 3. In a separate large bowl, mix shredded chicken, broccoli, and 1 cup mozzarella. Add sauce mixture and mix well. 4. Transfer to casserole dish. Spread remaining 1 cup mozzarella evenly over top. 5. Bake 40–50 minutes or until broccoli is tender and cheese is golden brown.

Per Serving:
Calories: 427 | fat: 23g | protein: 31g | carbs: 9g | net carbs: 8g | fiber: 1g

The Best Grilled Chicken

Prep time: 5 minutes | Cook time: 10 minutes | Serves 4 to 8

4 boneless, skinless chicken breast halves (approximately 2½ pounds / 1.1 kg)	2 tablespoons avocado oil
3 tablespoons kosher salt	2 tablespoons poultry seasoning (make sure there is no added sugar)
Ice cubes	

1. Cut each chicken breast on the diagonal into 3 long portions. 2. Bring 1 cup of water to a boil. Combine the boiling water and salt in a large glass or metal bowl. When the salt is dissolved, pour in a quart of cold water and add enough ice cubes to cool. Add the chicken slices and enough cold water so that the chicken is covered by 1 to 2 inches. Put in the refrigerator for 15 minutes. 3. Drain the chicken. If you don't want the chicken to be salty, rinse it now, but it's not necessary. Mix the oil and poultry seasoning in the empty bowl, then toss the chicken in the oil. Let sit for a few minutes. 4. Heat a grill to medium-high heat. When hot, place the chicken slices on the grill and close the lid. Cook for about 4 minutes, flip, and continue cooking until internal temperature reaches 165°F (74°C), another 3 to 4 minutes. 5. Remove the chicken from the grill and serve.

Per Serving:

Calories: 245 | fat: 6g | protein: 44g | carbs: 0g | net carbs: 0g | fiber: 0g

Braised Chicken with Olives

Prep time: 10 minutes | Cook time: 45 minutes | Serves 6

6 bone-in, skin-on chicken thighs (approximately 2 pounds / 907 g)	2 teaspoons ground cumin
	1 teaspoon smoked paprika
	1 teaspoon ground ginger
2 teaspoons kosher salt	1 teaspoon ground cinnamon,
Freshly ground black pepper, to taste	or 2 cinnamon sticks (optional)
	2 cups chicken broth, preferably
3 tablespoons avocado oil, or more as needed	homemade
	1 dried bay leaf
1 small onion, halved and thinly sliced (approximately ½ cup)	2 lemons, preferably Meyer lemons
4 garlic cloves, chopped	1 cup pitted olives

1. Season the tops of the chicken thighs with 1 teaspoon salt and some pepper. In a large skillet, heat the oil over medium-high heat until quite hot. Place the chicken skin side down in the hot oil and let cook for 3 to 5 minutes without moving. Season the chicken with more salt and pepper, then flip and sear the underside for another 3 minutes or so. 2. Remove the chicken to a plate. Add more oil if the pan is too dry and reduce the heat to medium. Add the onion and sauté for 5 minutes, until soft. Add the garlic and sauté for 1 minute. Add the cumin, paprika, and ginger, as well as the ground cinnamon, if using, and stir well. (If using cinnamon sticks, add them later.) 3. Slowly add the broth, scraping up any browned particles. Turn the heat to medium high, return the chicken to the pan, and pour back in any juice that collected on the plate.

Add the bay leaf and cinnamon sticks, if using, to the broth. 4. Cut one of the lemons into wedges and nestle those wedges among the chicken thighs. Scatter the olives evenly over the top of the chicken. Squeeze the juice from the other lemon over everything. 5. Allow the liquid to come to a boil, then reduce to a low simmer. Cover and simmer 30 minutes. Discard the bay leaf and cinnamon sticks. Serve the chicken thighs with sauce from the pan spooned over.

Per Serving:

Calories: 368 | fat: 26g | protein: 27g | carbs: 7g | net carbs: 5g | fiber: 2g

Chicken Breasts with Cheddar & Pepperoni

Prep time: 10 minutes | Cook time: 35 minutes | Serves 4

12 ounces canned tomato sauce	to taste
1 tablespoon olive oil	1 teaspoon dried oregano
4 chicken breast halves, skinless and boneless	4 ounces cheddar cheese, sliced
	1 teaspoon garlic powder
Salt and ground black pepper,	2 ounces pepperoni, sliced

1. Preheat your oven to 390°F. In a bowl, combine chicken with oregano, salt, garlic, and pepper. 2. Heat a pan with the olive oil over medium heat, add in the chicken, cook each side for 2 minutes, and remove to a baking dish. Top with the cheddar cheese slices spread the sauce, then cover with pepperoni slices. Bake for 30 minutes. Serve warm garnished with fresh oregano if desired.

Per Serving:

Calories: 348 | fat: 24g | protein: 29g | carbs: 4g | net carbs: 4g | fiber: 0g

Keto Chicken Strips

Prep time: 10 minutes | Cook time: 35 minutes | Serves 4

Olive oil, or butter, for preparing the baking sheet	Salt, to taste
	Freshly ground black pepper, to taste
1½ pounds (680 g) boneless skinless chicken breasts, cut into 12 strips	2 eggs
	1 cup almond flour

1. Preheat the oven to 350°F (180°C). 2. Lightly grease a baking sheet with olive oil and set aside. 3. Season the chicken strips with salt and pepper. 4. Break the eggs into a shallow dish and whisk to combine. 5. Place the almond flour in a separate shallow dish and season with more salt and pepper. 6. Dip each piece of chicken first into the eggs and then into the almond flour. Flip the chicken to ensure the whole piece is coated with almond flour. Place the strips on the prepared baking sheet and bake for about 30 minutes until lightly browned and cooked through (the juices will run clear). 7. Turn the oven to broil, and broil the chicken for 1 to 2 minutes to get them nicely browned. Serve immediately. Refrigerate leftovers in an airtight container for up to 5 days. Reheat for 1 minute in the microwave, or in the oven at 350°F (180°C) for 15 to 20 minutes.

Per Serving:

Calories: 253 | fat: 8g | protein: 42g | carbs: 0g | net carbs: 0g | fiber: 0g

Chicken Thighs with Cilantro

Prep time: 15 minutes | Cook time: 25 minutes |
Serves 4

1 tablespoon olive oil	8 bone-in chicken thighs, skin
Juice of ½ lime	on
1 tablespoon coconut aminos	2 tablespoons chopped fresh
1½ teaspoons Montreal chicken	cilantro
seasoning	

1. In a gallon-size resealable bag, combine the olive oil, lime juice, coconut aminos, and chicken seasoning. Add the chicken thighs, seal the bag, and massage the bag to ensure the chicken is thoroughly coated. Refrigerate for at least 2 hours, preferably overnight. 2. Preheat the air fryer to 400°F (204°C). 3. Remove the chicken from the marinade (discard the marinade) and arrange in a single layer in the air fryer basket. Pausing halfway through the cooking time to flip the chicken, air fry for 20 to 25 minutes, until a thermometer inserted into the thickest part registers 165°F (74°C). 4. Transfer the chicken to a serving platter and top with the cilantro before serving.

Per Serving:
Calories: 692 | fat: 53g | protein: 49g | carbs: 2g | fiber: 0g | sodium: 242mg

Mezze Cake

Prep time: 10 minutes | Cook time: 35 minutes |
Serves 2 to 4

Nonstick cooking spray	quartered artichoke hearts
2 coconut wraps (one of them is	½ cup cauliflower rice
optional)	¼ cup black olives, pitted and
1 small eggplant, thinly sliced	coarsely chopped
lengthwise	2 precooked sugar-free chicken
Salt, to taste	sausages, cut into bite-size
1 zucchini, thinly sliced	pieces
lengthwise	1 tablespoon dried oregano or
1 (8-ounce / 227-g) jar sun-	marjoram
dried tomatoes packed in olive	½ tablespoon garlic powder
oil (do not discard oil), chopped	Freshly ground black pepper, to
or whole	taste
½ (14-ounce / 397-g) can	

1. Preheat the oven to 350°F (180°C). Coat a shallow baking dish with nonstick spray and place a coconut wrap in the bottom. 2. Sprinkle the eggplant with ½ teaspoon of salt and let sit for 5 minutes to let the moisture come to the surface. Get a damp towel and wipe off the salt and excess water from the eggplant. 3. Lay the eggplant slices on top of the coconut wrap, then lay the zucchini slices on top of the eggplant. Next add the sun-dried tomatoes and drizzle in the olive oil they're packed in. Sprinkle in the artichoke hearts, then add the cauliflower rice. Scatter the olives on top, then shower the chicken sausage over all the vegetables. Season everything with the oregano, garlic powder, salt, and pepper. 4. Place another coconut wrap over the top of everything, if desired,

and bake this vegetable layer "cake" in the oven for about 25 minutes, or until the vegetables are a bit wilted. 5. Turn the oven to broil and cook for another 5 minutes, or until the top is crisp. 6. Remove from the oven and let cool before slicing and serving.

Per Serving:
Calories: 510 | fat: 38g | protein: 17g | carbs: 25g | net carbs: 13g | fiber: 12g

Paprika Chicken

Prep time: 10 minutes | Cook time: 25 minutes | Serves 4

4 (4-ounce) chicken breasts,	½ cup heavy (whipping) cream
skin-on	2 teaspoons smoked paprika
Sea salt	½ cup sour cream
Freshly ground black pepper	2 tablespoons chopped fresh
1 tablespoon olive oil	parsley
½ cup chopped sweet onion	

1. Lightly season the chicken with salt and pepper. 2. Place a large skillet over medium-high heat and add the olive oil. 3. Sear the chicken on both sides until almost cooked through, about 15 minutes in total. Remove the chicken to a plate. 4. Add the onion to the skillet and sauté until tender, about 4 minutes. 5. Stir in the cream and paprika and bring the liquid to a simmer. 6. Return the chicken and any accumulated juices to the skillet and simmer the chicken for 5 minutes until completely cooked. 7. Stir in the sour cream and remove the skillet from the heat. 8. Serve topped with the parsley.

Per Serving:
Calories: 389 | fat: 30g | protein: 25g | carbs: 4g | net carbs: 4g | fiber: 0g

Zucchini Spaghetti with Turkey Bolognese Sauce

Prep time: 10 minutes | Cook time: 35 minutes |
Serves 6

3 cups sliced mushrooms	1 cup diced onion
2 teaspoonsolive oil	2 cups broccoli florets
1 pound ground turkey	6 cups zucchini, spiralized
3 tablespoons pesto sauce	

1. Heat the oil in a skillet. Add zucchini and cook for 2-3 minutes, stirring continuously; set aside. 2. Add turkey to the skillet and cook until browned, about 7-8 minutes. Transfer to a plate. Add onion and cook until translucent, about 3 minutes. Add broccoli and mushrooms, and cook for 7 more minutes. Return the turkey to the skillet. Stir in the pesto sauce. Cover the pan, lower the heat, and simmer for 15 minutes. Stir in zucchini pasta and serve immediately.

Per Serving:
Calories: 279 | fat: 19g | protein: 22g | carbs: 5g | net carbs: 3g | fiber: 2g

Pesto Chicken

Prep time: 5 minutes | Cook time: 25 minutes | Serves 2

2 (6-ounce / 170-g) boneless, skinless chicken breasts, butterflied	1 cup water
½ teaspoon salt	¼ cup whole-milk ricotta cheese
¼ teaspoon pepper	¼ cup pesto
¼ teaspoon dried parsley	¼ cup shredded whole-milk Mozzarella cheese
¼ teaspoon garlic powder	Chopped parsley, for garnish (optional)
2 tablespoons coconut oil	

1. Sprinkle the chicken breasts with salt, pepper, parsley, and garlic powder. 2. Set your Instant Pot to Sauté and melt the coconut oil. 3. Add the chicken and brown for 3 to 5 minutes. Remove the chicken from the pot to a 7-cup glass bowl. 4. Pour the water into the Instant Pot and use a wooden spoon or rubber spatula to make sure no seasoning is stuck to bottom of pot. 5. Scatter the ricotta cheese on top of the chicken. Pour the pesto over chicken, and sprinkle the Mozzarella cheese over chicken. Cover with aluminum foil. Add the trivet to the Instant Pot and place the bowl on the trivet. 6. Secure the lid. Select the Manual mode and set the cooking time for 20 minutes at High Pressure. 7. Once cooking is complete, do a natural pressure release for 10 minutes, then release any remaining pressure. Carefully open the lid. 8. Serve the chicken garnished with the chopped parsley, if desired.

Per Serving:

Calories: 519 | fat: 32g | protein: 46g | carbs: 4g | net carbs: 3g | fiber: 1g

Cheesy Chicken and Ham Roll-ups

Prep time: 5 minutes | Cook time: 40 minutes | Serves 4

4 boneless, skinless chicken breast halves (approximately 2½ pounds / 1.1 kg)	2 teaspoons dried thyme
	Avocado oil
4 slices prosciutto	1 cup shredded Gruyère cheese
4 slices Swiss cheese	½ cup chicken broth, preferably homemade
1 teaspoon salt, or more as needed	1 tablespoon Dijon mustard
	2 tablespoons butter
1 teaspoon black pepper, or more as needed	½ cup heavy cream
	½ cup grated Parmesan cheese

1. One at a time, place the chicken breasts between two slices of wax paper or parchment paper and use a flat meat hammer or rolling pin to pound the chicken until each piece is ½ inch (13 mm) thick. Try to pound so that the chicken ends up in a long rectangular shape instead of a circle. 2. Cut the sliced prosciutto in half lengthwise. Place ½ slice of prosciutto and 1 slice of Swiss cheese on each piece of chicken, then roll up. Secure with toothpicks. 3. Mix the salt, pepper, and thyme in a small bowl, then use the mixture to generously season the outside of each roll. 4. Heat the oil in a skillet large enough to fit the 4 rolls. Brown the rolls on all sides, starting with the side with the seam. 5. Once browned, place ½ slice of prosciutto on top of each roll and sprinkle with Gruyère. Pour in the broth, cover the pan with a tight-fitting lid, and

cook over medium-low heat for 30 minutes, or until the chicken is cooked through. 6. Use tongs to remove the chicken rolls to a broiler pan or heavy rimmed baking sheet and let rest. Preheat the broiler (on low heat if adjustable). 7. Heat the liquid left over in the skillet over medium heat. Add the mustard, then the butter, then the cream, whisking constantly. Finally, add the Parmesan cheese and whisk until melted. Taste and adjust salt and pepper as needed. 8. Place the chicken under the broiler for a minute to give the cheese a nice golden-brown color. Pour the sauce over the chicken and serve immediately.

Per Serving:

Calories: 507 | fat: 40g | protein: 33g | carbs: 4g | net carbs: 4g | fiber: 0g

Parmesan Carbonara Chicken

Prep time: 15 minutes | Cook time: 25 minutes | Serves 5

1 pound (454 g) chicken, skinless, boneless, chopped	grated
	1 teaspoon ground black pepper
1 cup heavy cream	1 tablespoon coconut oil
1 cup chopped spinach	2 ounces (57 g) bacon, chopped
2 ounces (57 g) Parmesan,	

1. Put the coconut oil and chopped chicken in the instant pot. 2. Sauté the chicken for 10 minutes. Stir it from time to time. 3. Then add ground black pepper, and spinach. Stir the mixture well and sauté for 5 minutes more. 4. Then add heavy cream and Parmesan. Close and seal the lid. 5. Cook the meal on Manual mode (High Pressure) for 10 minutes. Allow the natural pressure release for 10 minutes.

Per Serving:

Calories: 343 | fat: 22g | protein: 35g | carbs: 2g | net carbs: 2g | fiber: 0g

Chicken Thighs with Broccoli & Green Onions

Prep time: 10 minutes | Cook time: 25 minutes | Serves 2

2 chicken thighs, skinless, boneless, cut into strips	½ teaspoon garlic powder
	½ cup water
1 tablespoon olive oil	½ cup erythritol
1 teaspoon red pepper flakes	½ teaspoon xanthan gum
1 teaspoon onion powder	½ cup green onions, chopped
1 tablespoon fresh ginger, grated	1 small head broccoli, cut into florets
¼ cup tamari sauce	

1. Set a pan over medium heat and warm oil, cook in the chicken and ginger for 4 minutes. Stir in the water, onion powder, pepper flakes, garlic powder, tamari sauce, xanthan gum, and erythritol, and cook for 15 minutes. Add in the green onions and broccoli, cook for 6 minutes. Serve hot.

Per Serving:

Calories: 386 | fat: 26g | protein: 32g | carbs: 6g | net carbs: 4g | fiber: 2g

Crunchy Chicken Tacos

Prep time: 5 minutes | Cook time: 30 minutes to 8 hours | Serves 4

1 pound (454 g) frozen boneless, skinless chicken thighs

1 cup chicken broth

1 cup low-carb green salsa

½ medium onion, chopped

2 teaspoons minced garlic

8 slices provolone cheese

1 cup shredded lettuce

¼ cup chopped ripe tomato

½ cup sour cream

1. In a slow cooker or electric pressure cooker, combine the chicken thighs, broth, salsa, onion, and garlic. 2. Place the lid on the pot. If using a slow cooker, cook on the low setting for 7 to 8 hours or on high for 3 to 4 hours. If using a pressure cooker, cook for 20 minutes on high pressure, then quick-release the pressure. 3. Place a slice of the provolone on a piece of parchment paper (not wax paper). Microwave on high power for 45 seconds; the cheese should just begin to turn a brownish orange in a few spots. 4. Quickly and carefully remove the parchment paper from the microwave. Holding opposite edges of the paper, form the melted cheese into a U shape. Hold it in this position for about 10 seconds, until it cools enough to hold its shape. (You can also hang the microwaved cheese slice over a wooden spoon handle to form the shape.) Remove the taco from the parchment paper. Repeat with the remaining 7 cheese slices. 5. Using a slotted spoon, remove the chicken from the cooker. Using 2 forks, shred the chicken, then return it to the cooker. 6. Use tongs or a slotted spoon to fill the tacos with equal portions of the chicken, being careful to drain off some of the liquid so the tacos don't get soggy. 7. Top the chicken filling with shredded lettuce, tomato, and sour cream, then serve.

Per Serving:

Calories: 528 | fat: 40g | protein: 35g | carbs: 8g | net carbs: 6g | fiber: 2g

Lemon-Rosemary Spatchcock Chicken

Prep time: 20 minutes | Cook time: 45 minutes | Serves 6 to 8

½ cup extra-virgin olive oil, divided

1 (3- to 4-pound/ 1.4- to 1.8-kg) roasting chicken

8 garlic cloves, roughly chopped

2 to 4 tablespoons chopped fresh rosemary

2 teaspoons salt, divided

1 teaspoon freshly ground black pepper, divided

2 lemons, thinly sliced

1. Preheat the oven to 425°F(220°C). 2. Pour 2 tablespoons olive oil in the bottom of a 9-by-13-inch baking dish or rimmed baking sheet and swirl to coat the bottom. 3. To spatchcock the bird, place the whole chicken breast-side down on a large work surface. Using a very sharp knife, cut along the backbone, starting at the tail end and working your way up to the neck. Pull apart the two sides, opening up the chicken. Flip it over, breast-side up, pressing down with your hands to flatten the bird. Transfer to the prepared baking dish. 4. Loosen the skin over the breasts and thighs by cutting a small incision and sticking one or two fingers inside to pull the skin away

from the meat without removing it. 5. To prepare the filling, in a small bowl, combine ¼ cup olive oil, garlic, rosemary, 1 teaspoon salt, and ½ teaspoon pepper and whisk together. 6. Rub the garlic-herb oil evenly under the skin of each breast and each thigh. Add the lemon slices evenly to the same areas. 7. Whisk together the remaining 2 tablespoons olive oil, 1 teaspoon salt, and ½ teaspoon pepper and rub over the outside of the chicken. 8. Place in the oven, uncovered, and roast for 45 minutes, or until cooked through and golden brown. Allow to rest 5 minutes before carving to serve.

Per Serving:

Calories: 317 | fat: 18g | protein: 35g | carbs: 2g | fiber: 1g | sodium: 710mg

Bruschetta and Cheese Stuffed Chicken

Prep time: 10 minutes | Cook time: 10 minutes | Serves 4

6 ounces (170 g) diced Roma tomatoes

2 tablespoons avocado oil

1 tablespoon thinly sliced fresh basil, plus more for garnish

1½ teaspoons balsamic vinegar

Pinch of salt

Pinch of black pepper

4 boneless, skinless chicken breasts (about 2 pounds / 907 g)

12 ounces (340 g) goat cheese, divided

2 teaspoons Italian seasoning, divided

1 cup water

1. Prepare the bruschetta by mixing the tomatoes, avocado oil, basil, vinegar, salt, and pepper in a small bowl. Let it marinate until the chicken is done. 2. Pat the chicken dry with a paper towel. Butterfly the breast open but do not cut all the way through. Stuff each breast with 3 ounces (85 g) of the goat cheese. Use toothpicks to close the edges. 3. Sprinkle ½ teaspoon of the Italian seasoning on top of each breast. 4. Pour the water into the pot. Place the trivet inside. Lay a piece of aluminum foil on top of the trivet and place the chicken breasts on top. It is okay if they overlap. 5. Close the lid and seal the vent. Cook on High Pressure for 10 minutes. Quick release the steam. 6. Remove the toothpicks and top each breast with one-fourth of the bruschetta.

Per Serving:

Calories: 581 | fat: 34g | protein: 64g | carbs: 5g | net carbs: 4g | fiber: 1g

Poblano Chicken

Prep time: 10 minutes | Cook time: 29 minutes | Serves 4

2 Poblano peppers, sliced

16 ounces (454 g) chicken fillet

½ teaspoon salt

½ cup coconut cream

1 tablespoon butter

½ teaspoon chili powder

1. Heat up the butter on Sauté mode for 3 minutes. 2. Add Poblano and cook them for 3 minutes. 3. Meanwhile, cut the chicken fillet into the strips and sprinkle with salt and chili powder. 4. Add the chicken strips to the instant pot. 5. Then add coconut cream and close the lid. Cook the meal on Sauté mode for 20 minutes.

Per Serving:

Calories: 320 | fat: 18g | protein: 34g | carbs: 4g | net carbs: 3g | fiber: 1g

Stuffed Mushrooms with Chicken

Prep time: 10 minutes | Cook time: 38 minutes | Serves 5

3 cups cauliflower florets	2 tablespoons butter
Salt and black pepper, to taste	10 portobello mushrooms,
1 onion, chopped	stems removed
1½ pounds ground chicken	½ cup vegetable broth
3 teaspoons fajita seasoning	

1. In a food processor, add the cauliflower florets, pepper and salt, blend for a few times, and transfer to a plate. Set a pan over medium heat and warm butter, stir in onion and cook for 3 minutes. Add in the cauliflower rice, and cook for 3 minutes. 2. Stir in the seasoning, pepper, chicken, broth, and salt and cook for a further 2 minutes. Arrange the mushrooms on a lined baking sheet, stuff each one with chicken mixture, put in the oven at 350°F, and bake for 30 minutes. Serve in serving plates and enjoy.

Per Serving:

Calories: 269 | fat: 16g | protein: 26g | carbs: 7g | net carbs: 5g | fiber: 2g

Greek Chicken with Gravy and Asparagus

Prep time: 15 minutes | Cook time: 1½ hours | Serves 6

1 (3½-pound/1.6-kg) whole chicken, giblets removed and reserved	Handful of fresh parsley
	6 sprigs fresh oregano
	6 sprigs fresh thyme
3 tablespoons refined avocado oil or melted coconut oil	4 small cloves garlic
	GRAVY:
1½ tablespoons Greek seasoning	Giblets (from above)
	3 tablespoons melted duck fat
1 apple, roughly chopped	1 teaspoon tapioca starch

1. pound (455 g) asparagus, tough ends removed, for serving 1. Preheat the oven to 350°F (177°C). Set the chicken in a roasting pan or large cast-iron frying pan. Coat all sides of the bird with the oil, then top with the Greek seasoning. Stuff the bird with the apple, parsley, oregano, thyme, and garlic. Roast for 1 hour 15 minutes, or until the internal temperature in the thigh reaches 165°F (74°C) and the juices run clear. 2. While the bird is cooking, cook the giblets: Place the giblets in a small saucepan and cover with about 1½ cups (350 ml) of water, then cover the pan with a lid and bring to a boil. Reduce the heat to low and simmer for 30 minutes. Strain the giblet pieces, reserving the flavorful cooking liquid. Discard the giblets. 3. About 10 minutes before the bird is done, steam the asparagus. 4. When the chicken is done, remove it from the oven and transfer the bird to a serving platter. Remove the stuffing and surround the chicken with the steamed asparagus. 5. Place the roasting pan on the stovetop over medium heat. Add ½ cup (120 ml) of the giblet cooking liquid and the melted duck fat to the pan and whisk to combine. Add the tapioca starch and continue to whisk until the gravy has thickened. 6. Drizzle the gravy over the bird or serve on the side.

Per Serving:

Calories: 580 | fat: 41g | protein: 50g | carbs: 4g | net carbs: 2g | fiber: 2g

BLT Chicken Salad

Prep time: 15 minutes | Cook time: 17 minutes | Serves 4

4 slices bacon	1 cup water
2 (6-ounce / 170-g) chicken breasts	2 cups chopped romaine lettuce
	Sauce:
1 teaspoon salt	⅓ cup mayonnaise
½ teaspoon garlic powder	1 ounce (28 g) chopped pecans
¼ teaspoon dried parsley	½ cup diced Roma tomatoes
¼ teaspoon pepper	½ avocado, diced
¼ teaspoon dried thyme	1 tablespoon lemon juice

1. Press the Sauté button to heat your Instant Pot. 2. Add the bacon and cook for about 7 minutes, flipping occasionally, until crisp. Remove and place on a paper towel to drain. When cool enough to handle, crumble the bacon and set aside. 3. Sprinkle the chicken with salt, garlic powder, parsley, pepper, and thyme. 4. Pour the water into the Instant Pot. Use a wooden spoon to ensure nothing is stuck to the bottom of the pot. Add the trivet to the pot and place the chicken on top of the trivet. 5. Secure the lid. Select the Manual mode and set the cooking time for 10 minutes at High Pressure. 6. Meanwhile, whisk together all the ingredients for the sauce in a large salad bowl. 7. Once cooking is complete, do a quick pressure release. Carefully open the lid. 8. Remove the chicken and let sit for 10 minutes. Cut the chicken into cubes and transfer to the salad bowl, along with the cooked bacon. Gently stir until the chicken is thoroughly coated. Mix in the lettuce right before serving.

Per Serving:

Calories: 431 | fat: 33g | protein: 24g | carbs: 5g | net carbs: 2g | fiber: 3g

Spicy Creamy Chicken Soup

Prep time: 10 minutes | Cook time: 30 minutes | Serves 15

2 (32-ounce / 907-g) cartons chicken broth or bone broth	tomatoes and green chilies, undrained
1 (8-ounce / 227-g) brick cream cheese, cubed	½ cup ranch dressing
	½ cup heavy cream
4 (12½-ounce / 354-g) cans chicken or 1¾ pounds (794 g) chopped cooked boneless skinless chicken breasts or rotisserie chicken	1 teaspoon garlic powder
	1 teaspoon sea salt
	1 teaspoon freshly ground black pepper
	15 ounces (425 g) grated
2 (10-ounce / 283-g) cans diced	Cheddar cheese

1. In a stockpot over medium heat, combine the broth, cream cheese, chicken, tomatoes and green chilies, ranch dressing, heavy cream, garlic powder, salt, and pepper. 2. Simmer for 30 minutes, stirring occasionally. 3. Portion into individual bowls and sprinkle each with ¼ cup of Cheddar cheese. Enjoy!

Per Serving (8-ounce):

Calories: 383 | fat: 27g | protein: 27g | carbs: 7g | net carbs: 7g | fiber: 0g

One Pot Chicken with Mushrooms

Prep time: 10 minutes | Cook time: 20 minutes | Serves 6

2 cups sliced mushrooms	1 teaspoon Dijon mustard
½ teaspoon onion powder	1 tablespoon tarragon, chopped
½ teaspoon garlic powder	2 pounds chicken thighs
¼ cup butter	Salt and black pepper, to taste

1. Season the thighs with salt, pepper, garlic, and onion powder. Melt the butter in a skillet, and cook the chicken until browned; set aside. Add mushrooms to the same fat and cook for about 5 minutes. 2. Stir in Dijon mustard and ½ cup of water. Return the chicken to the skillet. Season to taste with salt and pepper, reduce the heat and cover, and let simmer for 15 minutes. Stir in tarragon. Serve warm.

Per Serving:

Calories: 404 | fat: 32g | protein: 27g | carbs: 2g | net carbs: 1g | fiber: 1g

Baked Spaghetti Squash Carbonara with Chicken

Prep time: 15 minutes | Cook time: 40 minutes | Serves 6

1 small spaghetti squash	4 garlic cloves, minced
½ cup extra-virgin olive oil, divided	3 large egg yolks
	½ cup heavy cream
6 ounces (170 g) thick-cut bacon (preferably nitrate-free), cut into ½-inch-thick strips	1 cup freshly grated Parmesan cheese, divided
1 pound (454 g) boneless, skinless chicken thighs, cut into ½-inch cubes	¼ teaspoon freshly ground black pepper
	¼ cup fresh Italian parsley, chopped

1. Preheat the oven to 400ºF (205ºC). With a very sharp knife, cut the spaghetti squash in half lengthwise. Scoop out all the seeds, and coat the cut sides of the squash with 1 tablespoon of oil per side. 2. Place squash halves cut-side down in a 9-by-13-inch glass baking dish and roast until just barely tender, 20 to 25 minutes. Remove from the oven and flip the halves to cut-side up and allow to cool for 10 minutes. 3. Meanwhile, prepare the filling. Cook the bacon in a large skillet over medium heat and fry until crispy and fat has been rendered, 4 to 5 minutes. 4. Using a slotted spoon, transfer the cooked bacon to a large bowl and cover to keep warm, reserving the rendered fat. 5. Add the remaining 2 tablespoons of olive oil to the fat in the skillet and heat over medium heat. Sauté the cubed chicken until golden and cooked through, stirring frequently, 5 to 6 minutes. Add the minced garlic and sauté for another 30 seconds. 6. Transfer the cooked chicken, garlic, and all the cooking fat to the bowl with the cooked bacon, and cover. 7. In a small bowl, beat together the egg yolks, heavy cream, ¼ cup of Parmesan, and pepper. Set aside. 8. When the cooked squash is just cool enough to handle, but still very warm (you can use potholders to handle the squash), use a fork to gently scrape the cooked flesh in rows to form long pasta-like strings and place in a large bowl. Reserve the baking dish and keep the oven on. Add the remaining ¼ cup of olive oil to the squash and toss to coat well. 9. Tossing with tongs, slowly pour the egg-and-cream mixture onto the warm squash, tossing until the eggs thicken and the cheese melts. Add the cooked bacon, chicken, and reserved fats, and toss to coat well. 10. Transfer the squash mixture and sauce to the glass baking dish, top with the remaining ¾ cup of Parmesan cheese, and cover with aluminum foil. Bake for 10 minutes. Remove the foil and bake for an additional 5 minutes, or until bubbly and cheese is golden and melted. Serve warm, garnished with chopped parsley.

Per Serving:

Calories: 565 | fat: 47g | protein: 26g | carbs: 10g | net carbs: 9g | fiber: 1g

Buffalo Chicken Cheese Sticks

Prep time: 5 minutes | Cook time: 8 minutes | Serves 2

1 cup shredded cooked chicken	cheese
¼ cup buffalo sauce	1 large egg
1 cup shredded Mozzarella	¼ cup crumbled feta

1. In a large bowl, mix all ingredients except the feta. Cut a piece of parchment to fit your air fryer basket and press the mixture into a ½-inch-thick circle. 2. Sprinkle the mixture with feta and place into the air fryer basket. 3. Adjust the temperature to 400ºF (204ºC) and air fry for 8 minutes. 4. After 5 minutes, flip over the cheese mixture. 5. Allow to cool 5 minutes before cutting into sticks. Serve warm.

Per Serving:

Calories: 413 | fat: 25g | protein: 43g | carbs: 3g | fiber: 0g | sodium: 453mg

Chipotle Dry-Rub Wings

Prep time: 10 minutes | Cook time: 45 minutes | Serves 4

CHIPOTLE RUB:	1 teaspoon garlic powder
1 tablespoon ground chipotle pepper	1 teaspoon onion powder
	1 teaspoon pink Himalayan salt
1 teaspoon paprika	2 pounds chicken wings
1 teaspoon ground cumin	1 teaspoon baking powder
1 teaspoon ground mustard	

1. Preheat the oven to 250°F and place a wire baking rack inside a rimmed baking sheet. 2. Put the seasonings for the rub in a small bowl and stir with a fork. Divide the spice rub into 2 equal portions. 3. Cut the wings in half, if whole (see Tip), and place in a large zip-top plastic bag. Add the baking powder and half of the spice rub to the bag and shake thoroughly to coat the wings. 4. Lay the wings on the baking rack in a single layer. Bake for 25 minutes. 5. Turn the heat up to 450°F and bake the wings for an additional 20 minutes, until golden brown and crispy. 6. Once the wings are done, place them in a large plastic container with the remaining half of the spice rub and shake to coat. Serve immediately.

Per Serving:

Calories: 507 | fat: 36g | protein: 42g | carbs: 3g | net carbs: 3g | fiber: 0g

Chicken Alfredo

Prep time: 5 minutes | Cook time: 20 minutes | Serves 2

2 teaspoons extra-virgin olive oil, divided

8 ounces (227 g) boneless, skinless chicken thighs, cubed

2 tablespoons butter

½ teaspoon minced garlic

½ cup heavy (whipping) cream

⅔ cup grated Parmesan cheese

¼ cup shredded low-moisture

mozzarella cheese

Pinch of red pepper flakes

Pink Himalayan sea salt

Freshly ground black pepper

1 (7-ounce / 198-g) package shirataki noodles, drained, or 7 ounces / 198 g zoodles (spiralized zucchini)

1. In a small sauté pan or skillet, heat 1 teaspoon of olive oil over medium heat and cook the chicken for 10 to 12 minutes, until cooked through. 2. In a medium saucepan, melt the butter over medium heat. Add the garlic and cook for 1 to 2 minutes, until slightly browned. Add the cream and bring to a simmer. 3. Slowly add the Parmesan and mozzarella while stirring. The cheese should melt into the sauce. 4. Reduce the heat, add the chicken, and heat through, without allowing the sauce to boil. Season with the salt and pepper. 5. In the same skillet as you cooked the chicken, add the remaining 1 teaspoon of olive oil and drop in the shirataki noodles. Cook the noodles over medium heat for 2 to 3 minutes, until heated through. 6. Spoon the noodles onto 2 serving plates and top with the sauce.

Per Serving:

Calories: 810 | fat: 70g | protein: 36g | carbs: 11g | net carbs: 9g | fiber: 2g

Turkey with Mushroom Gravy

Prep time: 10 minutes | Cook time: 45 minutes | Serves 4

1 (2-pound / 907-g) piece of turkey breast

½ teaspoon pink Himalayan sea salt, plus more for seasoning

¼ teaspoon freshly ground black pepper, plus more for

seasoning

4 tablespoons (½ stick) butter

2 cups sliced fresh mushrooms

½ medium onion, chopped

1 cup chicken broth

¼ cup sour cream

1. Preheat the oven to 450°F (235°C). 2. Slice the turkey breast into 4 cutlets that are roughly 2 inches thick. 3. Place the cutlets in an 8-inch square baking dish and season lightly with a little salt and pepper. Bake for 30 minutes. 4. In a medium saucepan, melt the butter over medium heat. Add the mushrooms and onion and cook for 3 to 5 minutes, until the onion is almost translucent. 5. Add the broth, sour cream, ½ teaspoon of salt, and ¼ teaspoon of pepper to the pan. Stir to form a sauce, then simmer over low heat for about 5 minutes, until it reaches your desired thickness. Keep warm. 6. When the turkey is almost finished baking, pour the gravy over it and bake for an additional 5 to 10 minutes, until the gravy is bubbling. Serve.

Per Serving:

Calories: 499 | fat: 30g | protein: 51g | carbs: 3g | net carbs: 2g | fiber: 1g

Chicken and Scallions Stuffed Peppers

Prep time: 5 minutes | Cook time: 20 minutes | Serves 5

1 tablespoon butter, at room temperature

½ cup scallions, chopped

1 pound (454 g) ground chicken

½ teaspoon sea salt

½ teaspoon chili powder

⅓ teaspoon paprika

⅓ teaspoon ground cumin

¼ teaspoon shallot powder

6 ounces (170 g) goat cheese, crumbled

1½ cups water

5 bell peppers, tops, membrane, and seeds removed

½ cup sour cream

1. Set your Instant Pot to Sauté and melt the butter. 2. Add the scallions and chicken and sauté for 2 to 3 minutes. 3. Stir in the sea salt, chili powder, paprika, cumin, and shallot powder. Add the crumbled goat cheese, stir, and reserve the mixture in a bowl. 4. Clean your Instant Pot. Pour the water into the Instant Pot and insert the trivet. 5. Stuff the bell peppers with enough of the chicken mixture, and don't pack the peppers too tightly. Put the peppers on the trivet. 6. Lock the lid. Select the Poultry mode and set the cooking time for 15 minutes at High Pressure. 7. When the timer beeps, perform a natural pressure release for 10 minutes, then release any remaining pressure. Carefully remove the lid. 8. Remove from the Instant Pot and serve with the sour cream.

Per Serving:

Calories: 338 | fat: 20g | protein: 30g | carbs: 9g | net carbs: 7g | fiber: 1g

"K.F.C." Keto Fried Chicken

Prep time: 15 minutes | Cook time: 10 minutes | Serves 4

1 cup vegetable oil, for frying

2 large eggs

2 tablespoons heavy whipping cream

⅔ cup blanched almond flour

⅔ cup grated Parmesan cheese

¼ teaspoon salt

½ teaspoon black pepper

½ teaspoon paprika

½ teaspoon ground cayenne

1 pound (approximately 4) boneless, skinless chicken thighs

1 In a medium pot over medium heat add vegetable oil. Make sure it is about 1" deep. Heat oil to 350°F, frequently monitoring to maintain the temperature by adjusting heat during frying. 2 In a medium bowl, add eggs and heavy whipping cream. Beat until well mixed. 3 In a separate medium bowl, add almond flour, Parmesan cheese, salt, pepper, paprika, and cayenne and mix. 4 Cut each thigh into two even pieces. If wet, pat dry. 5 Coat each piece first in the dry breading, then in the egg wash, and then the breading again. 6 Shake off any excess breading and lower the chicken into the hot oil. Fry until deep brown and cooked through, about 3–5 minutes on each side, and then drain on paper towels. 7 Repeat until all chicken is cooked. Serve right away while hot and crispy.

Per Serving:

Calories: 470 | fat: 34g | protein: 31g | carbs: 5g | fiber: 2g | sodium: 507mg

Oregano & Chili Flattened Chicken

Prep time: 10 minutes | Cook time: 30 minutes | Serves 6

6 chicken breasts	2/3 cup olive oil
4 cloves garlic, minced	¼ cup erythritol
½ cup oregano leaves, chopped	Salt and black pepper to taste
½ cup lemon juice	3 small chilies, minced

1. Preheat a grill to 350ºF. 2. In a bowl, mix the garlic, oregano, lemon juice, olive oil, chilies and erythritol. Set aside. 3. While the spices incorporate in flavor, cover the chicken with plastic wraps, and use the rolling pin to pound to ½ -inch thickness. Remove the wrap, and brush the mixture on the chicken on both sides. 4. Place on the grill, cover the lid and cook for 15 minutes. Baste the chicken with more of the spice mixture, and continue cooking for 15 more minutes.

Per Serving:
Calories: 269 | fat: 17g | protein: 26g | carbs: 3g | net carbs: 3g | fiber: 0g

Keto Greek Avgolemono

Prep time: 10 minutes | Cook time: 30 minutes | Serves 4

4 bone-in, skin-on chicken thighs	4 tablespoons extra-virgin olive oil or MCT oil, for drizzling (optional)
¼ cup diced onions	Cracklings:
1 sprig fresh thyme	Chicken skin (from above)
4 cups chicken bone broth, homemade or store-bought, plus more if needed	½ teaspoon fine sea salt
Fine sea salt and freshly ground black pepper, to taste	½ teaspoon freshly ground black pepper
2 large eggs	1½ teaspoons Paleo fat, such as lard, tallow, or avocado oil
2 tablespoons lemon juice	

1. Remove the skin from the chicken thighs and set aside (you will use it to make cracklings). Place the skinless chicken, diced onions, and thyme in a large pot and fill with broth so that the broth covers the thighs by 1 inch. Add a couple pinches each of salt and pepper. Bring to a boil and cook for 20 minutes, or until the chicken is tender and easily falls off the bone. 2. While the chicken is cooking, make the cracklings: Cut the chicken skin into ¼-inch pieces and season with the ½ teaspoon each of salt and pepper. Heat the Paleo fat in a skillet over medium-high heat, then add the chicken skin and fry until golden brown and crispy, about 8 minutes. Set the cracklings aside on a paper towel to drain. 3. When the chicken thighs are done, place them in individual serving bowls and set aside. 4. In a medium bowl, whisk the eggs and lemon juice. While whisking, very slowly pour in ½ cup of the hot broth (if you add the hot broth too quickly, the eggs will curdle). Slowly whisk another cup of hot soup into the egg mixture. 5. Pour the hot egg mixture into the pot while stirring to create a creamy soup without the cream. Reduce the heat and simmer for 10 minutes, stirring constantly. The soup will thicken slightly as it cooks. 6. Pour one-quarter (about 1 cup) of the creamy soup over each chicken thigh. Top with the cracklings. Drizzle each bowl with

1 tablespoon of olive oil, if desired. 7. This dish is best served fresh to avoid curdled eggs from reheating, but leftovers can be stored in an airtight container in the fridge for up to 2 days. Reheat in a saucepan over medium-low heat until warmed, stirring constantly to keep the eggs from curdling.

Per Serving:
Calories: 275 | fat: 20g | protein: 22g | carbs: 2g | net carbs: 1g | fiber: 1g

Fluffy Chicken

Prep time: 5 minutes | Cook time: 0 minutes | Serves 8

½ cup chicken broth	8 ounces full-fat cream cheese, softened
1 (1-ounce) package ranch powder seasoning mix	8 slices no-sugar-added bacon, cooked and crumbled
2 pounds boneless, skinless chicken breasts	½ cup shredded Cheddar cheese

1 Add chicken broth to slow cooker and stir in ranch powder seasoning packet. 2 Add chicken and cover. Cook 2 hours 45 minutes on high or 5 hours 15 minutes on low. 3 Remove lid. Drain excess broth, leaving around ½ cup for moisture depending on preference. 4 Shred chicken. 5 In a small microwave-safe bowl, microwave cream cheese 20–30 seconds. Combine with crumbled bacon and Cheddar cheese. 6 Add cream cheese mixture to shredded chicken. Cover and heat 10 minutes on high temperature until cheeses melt. Serve warm.

Per Serving:
Calories: 325 | fat: 16g | protein: 33g | carbs: 3g | net carbs: 2g | fiber: 0g

Bacon Wrapped Chicken with Grilled Asparagus

Prep time: 5 minutes | Cook time: 40 minutes | Serves 4

6 chicken breasts	1 pound (454 g) asparagus spears
Pink salt and black pepper to taste	3 tablespoons olive oil
8 bacon slices	2 tablespoons fresh lemon juice
3 tablespoons olive oil	Manchego cheese for topping

1. Preheat the oven to 400ºF. 2. Season chicken breasts with salt and black pepper, and wrap 2 bacon slices around each chicken breast. Arrange on a baking sheet that is lined with parchment paper, drizzle with oil and bake for 25-30 minutes until bacon is brown and crispy. 3. Preheat your grill to high heat. 4. Brush the asparagus spears with olive oil and season with salt. Grill for 8-10 minutes, frequently turning until slightly charred. Remove to a plate and drizzle with lemon juice. Grate over Manchego cheese so that it melts a little on contact with the hot asparagus and forms a cheesy dressing.

Per Serving:
Calories: 464 | fat: 36g | protein: 32g | carbs: 3g | net carbs: 3g | fiber: 0g

Chicken and Grape Tomatoes

Prep time: 15 minutes | Cook time: 8 hours | Serves 2

1 pint grape tomatoes	each
4 garlic cloves, smashed	1 teaspoon fresh thyme
Zest of 1 lemon	½ teaspoon fresh rosemary
1 teaspoon extra-virgin olive oil	⅛ teaspoon sea salt
2 bone-in, skinless chicken thighs, about 8 ounces (227 g)	Freshly ground black pepper

1. Put the tomatoes, garlic, lemon zest, and olive oil in the slow cooker. Gently stir to mix. 2. Place the chicken thighs over the tomato mixture and season them with the thyme, rosemary, salt, and a few grinds of black pepper. 3. Cover and cook on low for 8 hours.

Per Serving:

Calories: 284 | fat: 10g | protein: 40g | carbs: 9g | net carbs: 7g | sugars: 5g | fiber: 2g | sodium: 366mg | cholesterol: 182mg

Roasted Red Pepper and Mozzarella Stuffed Chicken Breasts

Prep time: 15 minutes | Cook time: 6 to 8 hours | Serves 2

1 teaspoon extra-virgin olive oil	into thin strips
2 boneless, skinless chicken breasts	2 ounces (57 g) sliced mozzarella cheese
⅛ teaspoon sea salt	¼ cup roughly chopped fresh basil
Freshly ground black pepper	
2 roasted red bell peppers, cut	

1. Grease the inside of the slow cooker with the olive oil. 2. Slice the chicken breasts through the center horizontally until nearly sliced in half. Open as if opening a book. Season all sides of the chicken with the salt and pepper. 3. Place a layer of the roasted peppers on one inside half of each chicken breast. Top the peppers with the mozzarella slices. Then sprinkle the cheese with the fresh basil. Fold the other half of the chicken over the filling. 4. Carefully place the stuffed chicken breasts into the slow cooker, making sure the filling does not escape. Cover and cook on low for 6 to 8 hours, or until the chicken is cooked through.

Per Serving:

Calories: 463 | fat: 15g | protein: 70g | carbs: 8g | net carbs: 5g | sugars: 5g | fiber: 3g | sodium: 287mg | cholesterol: 214mg

Turkey Meatloaf Florentine Muffins

Prep time: 10 minutes | Cook time: 25 minutes | Serves 6

½ pound (227 g) frozen spinach, thawed	4 cloves garlic, minced
2 pounds (907 g) ground turkey	2 teaspoons sea salt
½ cup (2 ounces / 57 g) blanched almond flour	½ teaspoon black pepper
	2¼ cups (9 ounces / 255 g) shredded Mozzarella cheese, divided into 1½ cups (6 ounces
2 large eggs	

/ 170 g) and ¾ cup (3 ounces / 85 g) — ⅓ cup no-sugar-added marinara sauce

1. Preheat the oven to 375ºF (190ºC). Lightly grease 12 cups of a muffin tin and place on top of a sheet pan for easier cleanup. 2. Drain the spinach and squeeze it tightly in a kitchen towel to remove as much water as possible. 3. In a large bowl, mix together the spinach, turkey, almond flour, eggs, garlic, sea salt, and black pepper. Mix until just combined, but do not overwork the meat. 4. Fill each muffin cup with 2 tablespoons of the turkey mixture. Create a well with the back of a measuring spoon or your hands. Pack each well with 2 tablespoons Mozzarella (1½ cups or 6 ounces / 170 g total). Top with 2 more tablespoons turkey mixture, lightly pressing down along the sides to seal the filling inside. 5. Spread 1 teaspoon marinara sauce over each meatloaf muffin. Sprinkle each with another 1 tablespoon Mozzarella (¾ cup or 3 ounces / 85 g total). 6. Bake for 20 to 25 minutes, until the internal temperature reaches at least 160ºF (71ºC). Let rest for 5 minutes before serving (temperature will rise another 5 degrees while resting).

Per Serving:

Calories: 380 | fat: 16g | protein: 52g | carbs: 6g | net carbs: 4g | fiber: 2g

Thanksgiving Turkey

Prep time: 5 minutes | Cook time: 60 minutes | Serves 8

1 turkey breast (7 pounds / 3.2 kg), giblets removed	½ onion, quartered
4 tablespoons butter, softened	1 rib celery, cut into 3 or 4 pieces
2 teaspoons ground sage	1 cup chicken broth
2 teaspoons garlic powder	2 or 3 bay leaves
2 teaspoons salt	1 teaspoon xanthan gum
2 teaspoons black pepper	

1. Pat the turkey dry with a paper towel. 2. In a small bowl, combine the butter with the sage, garlic powder, salt, and pepper. Rub the butter mixture all over the top of the bird. Place the onion and celery inside the cavity. 3. Place the trivet in the pot. Add the broth and bay leaves to the pot. 4. Place the turkey on the trivet. If you need to remove the trivet to make the turkey fit, you can. The turkey will be near the top of the pot, which is fine. 5. Close the lid and seal the vent. Cook on High Pressure for 35 minutes. It is normal if it takes your pot a longer time to come to pressure. 6. Let the steam naturally release for 20 minutes before Manually releasing. Press Cancel. 7. Heat the broiler. 8. Carefully remove the turkey to a sheet pan. Place under the broiler for 5 to 10 minutes to crisp up the skin. 9. While the skin is crisping, use the juices to make a gravy. Pour the juices through a mesh sieve, reserving 2 cups of broth. Return the reserved broth to the pot. Turn the pot to Sauté mode. When the broth starts to boil, add the xanthan gum and whisk until the desired consistency is reached. Add more xanthan gum if you like a thicker gravy. 10. Remove the turkey from the broiler and place on a platter. Carve as desired and serve with the gravy.

Per Serving:

Calories: 380 | fat: 18g | protein: 47g | carbs: 3g | net carbs: 1g | fiber: 2g

Indian Chicken Breast

Prep time: 5 minutes | Cook time: 4 minutes | Serves 2

¼ teaspoon cumin seeds	½ cup coconut milk
½ teaspoon turmeric	14 ounces (397 g) chicken
1 teaspoon ground paprika	breast, skinless, boneless
¾ teaspoon chili paste	1 tablespoon coconut oil
½ teaspoon ground coriander	

1. Blend together the cumin seeds, turmeric, ground paprika, chili paste, coriander, coconut milk, and coconut oil. 2. When the mixture is smooth, pour it in the instant pot bowl. 3. Chop the chicken breast roughly and transfer it in the spice mixture. Stir gently with the help of the spatula. 4. Lock the lid and seal it. 5. Set the Manual mode for 4 minutes (High Pressure). 6. After this, make quick-release pressure. Enjoy!

Per Serving:

Calories: 435 | fat: 17g | protein: 44g | carbs: 5g | net carbs: 3g | fiber: 2g

Chicken Thighs with Feta

Prep time: 7 minutes | Cook time: 15 minutes | Serves 2

4 lemon slices	4 ounces (113 g) feta, crumbled
2 chicken thighs	1 teaspoon butter
1 tablespoon Greek seasoning	½ cup water

1. Rub the chicken thighs with Greek seasoning. 2. Then spread the chicken with butter. 3. Pour water in the instant pot and place the trivet. 4. Place the chicken on the foil and top with the lemon slices. Top it with feta. 5. Wrap the chicken in the foil and transfer on the trivet. 6. Cook on the Sauté mode for 10 minutes. Then make a quick pressure release for 5 minutes. 7. Discard the foil from the chicken thighs and serve!

Per Serving:

Calories: 341 | fat: 24g | protein: 27g | carbs: 6g | net carbs: 6g | fiber: 0g

Thanksgiving Turkey Breast

Prep time: 5 minutes | Cook time: 30 minutes | Serves 4

1½ teaspoons fine sea salt	1 teaspoon chopped fresh thyme
1 teaspoon ground black pepper	leaves
1 teaspoon chopped fresh rosemary leaves	1 (2-pound / 907-g) turkey breast
1 teaspoon chopped fresh sage	3 tablespoons ghee or unsalted
1 teaspoon chopped fresh tarragon	butter, melted
	3 tablespoons Dijon mustard

1. Spray the air fryer with avocado oil. Preheat the air fryer to 390ºF (199ºC). 2. In a small bowl, stir together the salt, pepper, and herbs until well combined. Season the turkey breast generously on all sides with the seasoning. 3. In another small bowl, stir together the ghee and Dijon. Brush the ghee mixture on all sides of the turkey breast. 4. Place the turkey breast in the air fryer basket and air fry for 30 minutes, or until the internal temperature reaches 165ºF (74ºC). Transfer the breast to a cutting board and allow it to rest for 10 minutes before cutting it into ½-inch-thick slices. 5. Store leftovers in an airtight container in the refrigerator for up to 4 days or in the freezer for up to a month. Reheat in a preheated 350ºF (177ºC) air fryer for 4 minutes, or until warmed through.

Per Serving:

calorie: 418 | fat: 22g | protein: 51g | carbs: 1g | sugars: 0g | fiber: 1g | sodium: 603mg

Kung Pao Chicken

Prep time: 5 minutes | Cook time: 17 minutes | Serves 5

2 tablespoons coconut oil	½ teaspoon chili powder
1 pound (454 g) boneless,	½ teaspoon finely grated ginger
skinless chicken breasts, cubed	½ teaspoon kosher salt
1 cup cashews, chopped	½ teaspoon freshly ground
6 tablespoons hot sauce	black pepper

1. Set the Instant Pot to Sauté and melt the coconut oil. 2. Add the remaining ingredients to the Instant Pot and mix well. 3. Secure the lid. Select the Manual mode and set the cooking time for 17 minutes at High Pressure. 4. Once cooking is complete, do a quick pressure release. Carefully open the lid. 5. Serve warm.

Per Serving:

Calories: 381 | fat: 25g | protein: 30g | carbs: 10g | net carbs: 8g | fiber: 1g

Simply Terrific Turkey Meatballs

Prep time: 10 minutes | Cook time: 7 to 10 minutes | Serves 4

1 red bell pepper, seeded and coarsely chopped	ground turkey
2 cloves garlic, coarsely chopped	1 egg, lightly beaten
¼ cup chopped fresh parsley	½ cup grated Parmesan cheese
1½ pounds (680 g) 85% lean	1 teaspoon salt
	½ teaspoon freshly ground black pepper

1. Preheat the air fryer to 400ºF (204ºC). 2. In a food processor fitted with a metal blade, combine the bell pepper, garlic, and parsley. Pulse until finely chopped. Transfer the vegetables to a large mixing bowl. 3. Add the turkey, egg, Parmesan, salt, and black pepper. Mix gently until thoroughly combined. Shape the mixture into 1¼-inch meatballs. 4. Working in batches if necessary, arrange the meatballs in a single layer in the air fryer basket; coat lightly with olive oil spray. Pausing halfway through the cooking time to shake the basket, air fry for 7 to 10 minutes, until lightly browned and a thermometer inserted into the center of a meatball registers 165ºF (74ºC).

Per Serving:

Calories: 388 | fat: 25g | protein: 34g | carbs: 5g | fiber: 1g | sodium: 527mg

Tex-Mex Chicken Roll-Ups

Prep time: 10 minutes | Cook time: 14 to 17 minutes | Serves 8

2 pounds (907 g) boneless, skinless chicken breasts or thighs	black pepper, to taste
1 teaspoon chili powder	6 ounces (170 g) Monterey Jack cheese, shredded
½ teaspoon smoked paprika	4 ounces (113 g) canned diced green chiles
½ teaspoon ground cumin	Avocado oil spray
Sea salt and freshly ground	

1. Place the chicken in a large zip-top bag or between two pieces of plastic wrap. Using a meat mallet or heavy skillet, pound the chicken until it is about ¼ inch thick. 2. In a small bowl, combine the chili powder, smoked paprika, cumin, and salt and pepper to taste. Sprinkle both sides of the chicken with the seasonings. 3. Sprinkle the chicken with the Monterey Jack cheese, then the diced green chiles. 4. Roll up each piece of chicken from the long side, tucking in the ends as you go. Secure the roll-up with a toothpick. 5. Set the air fryer to 350ºF (177ºC). Spray the outside of the chicken with avocado oil. Place the chicken in a single layer in the basket, working in batches if necessary, and roast for 7 minutes. Flip and cook for another 7 to 10 minutes, until an instant-read thermometer reads 160ºF (71ºC). 6. Remove the chicken from the air fryer and allow it to rest for about 5 minutes before serving.

Per Serving:

Calories: 220 | fat: 10g | protein: 31g | carbs: 1g | fiber: 0g | sodium: 355mg

Chettinad Chicken

Prep time: 15 minutes | Cook time: 4 to 6 hours | Serves 6

1 tablespoon white poppy seeds	20 curry leaves
1 teaspoon coriander seeds	3 onions, finely sliced
2 teaspoons cumin seeds	2 star anise
1 teaspoon fennel seeds	4 tomatoes
4 to 5 dried red chiles	1 teaspoon turmeric
2-inch piece cinnamon stick	Sea salt
6 green cardamom pods	1 teaspoon chili powder
4 cloves	12 chicken thighs on the bone, skinned and trimmed
1½ cups grated coconut	
4 garlic cloves	Juice of 2 or 3 limes
1 tablespoon freshly grated ginger	Handful fresh coriander leaves, chopped
2 tablespoons coconut oil	

1. In a frying pan, toast the poppy seeds, coriander seeds, cumin seeds, fennel seeds, dried red chiles, cinnamon, green cardamom pods, and cloves until fragrant, about 1 minute. Remove from the pan and set aside to cool. Once cooled, grind to a fine powder in a spice grinder. 2. In the same pan, toast the grated coconut for 3 to 4 minutes until it just starts to turn golden. Remove from the pan and spread on a plate to cool. Once cooled, grind and mix with the ground spices. 3. Crush the garlic and ginger in a mortar and pestle and set aside. 4. Either heat the slow cooker to sauté or use a pan on the stove. Heat the coconut oil and add the curry leaves, when they stop spluttering, add the sliced onions and fry them until they are light brown. Stir in the crushed garlic and ginger, and stir for a minute or two. 5. Add to the slow cooker along with the ground spices and anise. Chop and add the tomatoes, the turmeric, and the salt, and stir in the chili powder. 6. Place the chicken pieces in the cooker, cover and cook on low for 6 hours, or on high for 4 hours, until tender and cooked through. 7. Check the seasoning and adjust if needed, squeeze in the lime juice, and serve topped with fresh coriander leaves.

Per Serving:

Calories: 628 | fat: 28g | protein: 79g | carbs: 13g | net carbs: 9g | sugars: 6g | fiber: 4g | sodium: 393mg | cholesterol: 363mg

Broccoli Chicken Divan

Prep time: 15 minutes | Cook time: 10 minutes | Serves 4

1 cup chopped broccoli	¼ cup chicken broth
2 tablespoons cream cheese	½ cup grated Cheddar cheese
½ cup heavy cream	6 ounces (170 g) chicken fillet, cooked and chopped
1 tablespoon curry powder	

1. Mix up broccoli and curry powder and put the mixture in the instant pot. 2. Add heavy cream and cream cheese. 3. Then add chicken and mix up the ingredients. 4. Then add chicken broth and heavy cream. 5. Top the mixture with Cheddar cheese. Close and seal the lid. 6. Cook the meal on Manual mode (High Pressure) for 10 minutes. Allow the natural pressure release for 5 minutes, open the lid and cool the meal for 10 minutes.

Per Serving:

Calories: 222 | fat: 15g | protein: 18g | carbs: 3g | net carbs: 2g | fiber: 1g

Greek Chicken Stir-Fry

Prep time: 15 minutes | Cook time: 15 minutes | Serves 2

1 (6-ounce / 170-g) chicken breast, cut into 1-inch cubes	and sliced
½ medium zucchini, chopped	1 tablespoon coconut oil
½ medium red bell pepper, seeded and chopped	1 teaspoon dried oregano
¼ medium red onion, peeled	½ teaspoon garlic powder
	¼ teaspoon dried thyme

1. Place all ingredients into a large mixing bowl and toss until the coconut oil coats the meat and vegetables. Pour the contents of the bowl into the air fryer basket. 2. Adjust the temperature to 375ºF (191ºC) and air fry for 15 minutes. 3. Shake the basket halfway through the cooking time to redistribute the food. Serve immediately.

Per Serving:

Calories: 183 | fat: 9g | protein: 20g | carbs: 4g | fiber: 1g | sodium: 44mg

Turmeric Chicken Nuggets

Prep time: 10 minutes | Cook time: 9 minutes | Serves 5

8 ounces (227 g) chicken fillet	½ cup almond flour
1 teaspoon ground turmeric	2 eggs, beaten
½ teaspoon ground coriander	½ cup butter

1. Chop the chicken fillet roughly into the medium size pieces. 2. In the mixing bowl, mix up ground turmeric, ground coriander, and almond flour. 3. Then dip the chicken pieces in the beaten egg and coat in the almond flour mixture. 4. Toss the butter in the instant pot and melt it on Sauté mode for 4 minutes. 5. Then put the coated chicken in the hot butter and cook for 5 minutes or until the nuggets are golden brown.

Per Serving:

Calories: 343 | fat: 29g | protein: 18g | carbs: 3g | net carbs: 2g | fiber: 1g

Slow-Cooked Mexican Turkey Soup

Prep time: 10 minutes | Cook time: 4 hours | Serves 4

1½ pounds turkey breasts, skinless, boneless, cubed	¼ teaspoon cayenne red pepper
4 cups chicken stock	4 ounces canned diced green chilies
1 chopped onion	1 teaspoon fresh cilantro, chopped
1 cup canned chunky salsa	
8 ounces cheddar cheese	

1. In a slow cooker, combine the turkey with salsa, onion, green chilies, cayenne pepper, chicken stock, and cheese, and cook for 4 hours on High while covered. Open the slow cooker, sprinkle with fresh cilantro and ladle in bowls to serve.

Per Serving:

Calories: 443 | fat: 31g | protein: 34g | carbs: 7g | net carbs: 5g | fiber: 2g

Chicken Cauliflower Bake

Prep time: 10 minutes | Cook time: 45 minutes | Serves 6

3 cups cubed leftover chicken	1 cup pork rinds, crushed
3 cups spinach	½ cup unsweetened almond milk
2 cauliflower heads, cut into florets	3 tablespoons olive oil
3 cups water	3 cloves garlic, minced
3 eggs, lightly beaten	Salt and black pepper to taste
2 cups grated sharp cheddar cheese	Cooking spray

1. Preheat the oven to 350ºF and grease a baking dish with cooking spray. Set aside. 2. Pour the cauli florets and water in a pot; bring to boil over medium heat. Cover and steam the cauli florets for 8 minutes. Drain them through a colander and set aside. 3. Also, combine the cheddar cheese and pork rinds in a large bowl and mix in the chicken. Set aside. 4. Heat the olive oil in a skillet and cook the garlic and spinach until the spinach has wilted, about 5 minutes. Season with salt and black pepper, and add the spinach mixture and cauli florets to the chicken bowl. 5. Top with the eggs and almond milk, mix and transfer everything to the baking dish. Layer the top of the ingredients and place the dish in the oven to bake for 30 minutes. 6. By this time the edges and top must have browned nicely, then remove the chicken from the oven, let rest for 5 minutes, and serve. Garnish with steamed and seasoned green beans.

Per Serving:

Calories: 395 | fat: 31g | protein: 24g | carbs: 5g | net carbs: 3g | fiber: 2g

Bacon-Wrapped Chicken Tenders

Prep time: 15 minutes | Cook time: 15 minutes | Serves 2

4 ounces (113 g) chicken fillet	¼ teaspoon salt
2 bacon slices	1 teaspoon olive oil
½ teaspoon ground paprika	1 cup water, for cooking

1. Cut the chicken fillet on 2 tenders and sprinkle them with salt, ground paprika, and olive oil. 2. Wrap the chicken tenders in the bacon and transfer in the steamer rack, 3. Pour water and insert the steamer rack with the chicken tenders in the instant pot. 4. Close and seal the lid and cook the meal on Manual mode (High Pressure) for 15 minutes. 5. When the time is finished, allow the natural pressure release for 10 minutes.

Per Serving:

Calories: 232 | fat: 14g | protein: 23g | carbs: 1g | net carbs: 1g | fiber: 0g

Indoor BBQ Chicken

Prep time: 10 minutes | Cook time: 45 minutes | Serves 4

1 tablespoon sriracha sauce	1 tablespoon paprika
2 teaspoons chili powder	1 (1-gram) packet 0g net carb sweetener
2 teaspoons garlic powder	
2 teaspoons onion powder	½ teaspoon xanthan gum
1 teaspoon salt	1 cup crushed tomatoes
1 teaspoon black pepper	4 medium chicken thighs with skin
1 tablespoon apple cider vinegar	

1 Preheat oven to 375°F. Line a baking sheet with parchment paper or greased foil. 2 In a small saucepan over medium-high heat, make the barbecue sauce by mixing all the ingredients except the chicken and bring to boil. Let simmer 5 minutes, stirring regularly. 3 Using a basting brush, apply about half the barbecue sauce to both sides of thighs. Place chicken on baking sheet. 4 Cook 20 minutes. Flip chicken and reapply remaining sauce. Cook another 20 minutes until chicken is thoroughly cooked. 5 Serve warm or cold.

Per Serving:

Calories: 262 | fat: 19g | protein: 34g | carbs: 10g | net carbs: 7g | fiber: 3g

Cheese Stuffed Chicken

Prep time: 15 minutes | Cook time: 20 minutes | Serves 4

12 ounces (340 g) chicken fillet
4 ounces (113 g) provolone cheese, sliced
1 tablespoon cream cheese
½ teaspoon dried cilantro
½ teaspoon smoked paprika
1 cup water, for cooking

1. Beat the chicken fillet well and rub it with dried cilantro and smoked paprika. 2. Then spread it with cream cheese and top with Provolone cheese. 3. Roll the chicken fillet into the roll and wrap in the foil. 4. Pour water and insert the rack in the instant pot. 5. Place the chicken roll on the rack. Close and seal the lid. 6. Cook it on Manual mode (High Pressure) for 20 minutes. 7. Make a quick pressure release and slice the chicken roll into the servings.

Per Serving:

Calories: 271 | fat: 15g | protein: 32g | carbs: 1g | net carbs: 1g | fiber: 0g

Parmesan Baked Chicken

Prep time: 5 minutes | Cook time: 20 minutes | Serves 2

2 tablespoons ghee
2 boneless skinless chicken breasts
Pink Himalayan salt
Freshly ground black pepper
½ cup mayonnaise
¼ cup grated Parmesan cheese
1 tablespoon dried Italian seasoning
¼ cup crushed pork rinds

1. Preheat the oven to 425°F. Choose a baking dish that is large enough to hold both chicken breasts and coat it with the ghee. 2. Pat dry the chicken breasts with a paper towel, season with pink Himalayan salt and pepper, and place in the prepared baking dish. 3. In a small bowl, mix to combine the mayonnaise, Parmesan cheese, and Italian seasoning. 4. Slather the mayonnaise mixture evenly over the chicken breasts, and sprinkle the crushed pork rinds on top of the mayonnaise mixture. 5. Bake until the topping is browned, about 20 minutes, and serve.

Per Serving:

Calories: 850 | fat: 67g | protein: 60g | carbs: 2g | net carbs: 2g | fiber: 0g

Buttered Chicken

Prep time: 15 minutes | Cook time: 15 minutes | Serves 4

1 (14½-ounce / 411-g) can diced tomatoes, undrained
5 or 6 garlic cloves, minced
1 tablespoon minced fresh ginger
1 teaspoon ground turmeric
1 teaspoon cayenne
1 teaspoon smoked paprika
2 teaspoons garam masala,
divided
1 teaspoon ground cumin
1 teaspoon salt
1 pound (454 g) boneless, skinless chicken breasts or thighs
½ cup unsalted butter, cut into cubes, or ½ cup coconut oil
½ cup heavy (whipping) cream
or full-fat coconut milk
¼ to ½ cup chopped fresh cilantro
4 cups cauliflower rice or cucumber noodles

1. Put the tomatoes, garlic, ginger, turmeric, cayenne, paprika, 1 teaspoon of garam masala, cumin, and salt in the inner cooking pot of the Instant Pot. Mix thoroughly, then place the chicken pieces on top of the sauce. 2. Lock the lid into place. Select Manual and adjust the pressure to High. Cook for 10 minutes. When the cooking is complete, let the pressure release naturally. Unlock the lid. Carefully remove the chicken and set aside. 3. Using an immersion blender in the pot, blend together all the ingredients into a smooth sauce. (Or use a stand blender, but be careful with the hot sauce and be sure to leave the inside lid open to vent.) After blending, let the sauce cool before adding the remaining ingredients or it will be thinner than is ideal. 4. Add the butter cubes, cream, remaining 1 teaspoon of garam masala, and cilantro. Stir until well incorporated. The sauce should be thick enough to coat the back of a spoon when you're done. 5. Remove half the sauce and freeze it for later or refrigerate for up to 2 to 3 days. 6. Cut the chicken into bite-size pieces. Add it back to the sauce. 7. Preheat the Instant Pot by selecting Sauté and adjust to Less for low heat. Let the chicken heat through. Break it up into smaller pieces if you like, but don't shred it. 8. Serve over cauliflower rice or raw cucumber noodles.

Per Serving:

Calories: 512 | fat: 36g | protein: 31g | carbs: 16g | net carbs: 10g | fiber: 6g

Poulet en Papillote

Prep time: 10 minutes | Cook time: 45 minutes | Serves 4

4 chicken breasts, skinless, scored
4 tablespoons white wine
2 tablespoons olive oil + extra for drizzling
4 tablespoons butter
3 cups mixed mushrooms, teared up
1 medium celeriac, peeled, chopped
2 cups water
3 cloves garlic, minced
4 sprigs thyme, chopped
3 lemons, juiced
Salt and black pepper to taste
2 tablespoons Dijon mustard

1. Preheat the oven to 450ºF. 2. Arrange the celeriac on a baking sheet, drizzle it with a little oil, and bake for 20 minutes; set aside. 3. In a bowl, evenly mix the chicken, roasted celeriac, mushrooms, garlic, thyme, lemon juice, salt, black pepper, and mustard. Make 4 large cuts of foil, fold them in half, and then fold them in half again. Tightly fold the two open edges together to create a bag. 4. Now, share the chicken mixture into each bag, top with the white wine, olive oil, and a tablespoon of butter. Seal the last open end securely making sure not to pierce the bag. Put the bag on a baking tray and bake the chicken in the middle of the oven for 25 minutes.

Per Serving:

Calories: 333 | fat: 21g | protein: 29g | carbs: 7g | net carbs: 3g | fiber: 4g

Chapter 5 Beef, Pork, and Lamb

Cardamom Beef Stew Meat with Broccoli

Prep time: 10 minutes | Cook time: 50 minutes | Serves 2

9 ounces (255 g) beef stew meat, chopped

1 teaspoon ground cardamom

½ teaspoon salt

1 cup chopped broccoli

1 cup water

1. Preheat the instant pot on the Sauté mode. 2. When the title "Hot" is displayed, add chopped beef stew meat and cook it for 4 minutes (for 2 minutes from each side). 3. Then add the ground cardamom, salt, and broccoli. 4. Add water and close the instant pot lid. 5. Sauté the stew for 45 minutes to get the tender taste. 6. Enjoy!

Per Serving:

Calories: 256 | fat: 8g | protein: 40g | carbs: 4g | net carbs: 2g | fiber: 2g

Pork Burgers with Sriracha Mayo

Prep time: 10 minutes | Cook time: 10 minutes | Serves 2

12 ounces ground pork

2 scallions, white and green parts, thinly sliced

1 tablespoon toasted sesame oil

Pink Himalayan salt

Freshly ground black pepper

1 tablespoon ghee

1 tablespoon Sriracha sauce

2 tablespoons mayonnaise

1. In a large bowl, mix to combine the ground pork with the scallions and sesame oil, and season with pink Himalayan salt and pepper. Form the pork mixture into 2 patties. Create an imprint with your thumb in the middle of each burger so the pork will heat evenly. 2. In a large skillet over medium-high heat, heat the ghee. When the ghee has melted and is very hot, add the burger patties and cook for 4 minutes on each side. 3. Meanwhile, in a small bowl, mix the Sriracha sauce and mayonnaise. 4. Transfer the burgers to a plate and let rest for at least 5 minutes. 5. Top the burgers with the Sriracha mayonnaise and serve.

Per Serving:

Calories: 575 | fat: 49g | protein: 31g | carbs: 2g | net carbs: 1g | fiber: 1g

Keto Chili

Prep time: 20 minutes | Cook time: 5 - 8 hours | Serves 6

1 pound ground beef

1 pound bulk sausage, mild or hot

1 green bell pepper, diced

½ medium yellow onion, chopped

3 to 4 cloves garlic, minced, or 1 tablespoon garlic powder

1 (14½-ounce) can diced tomatoes (with juices)

1 (6-ounce) can tomato paste

1 tablespoon chili powder

1½ teaspoons ground cumin

⅓ cup water

Topping Suggestions

Shredded cheddar cheese

Sliced green onions

Sour cream

Sliced jalapeños

1 In a large pot, brown the ground beef and sausage, using a wooden spoon to break up the clumps. Drain the meat, reserving half of the drippings. 2 Transfer the drained meat to a slow cooker. Add the reserved drippings, bell pepper, onion, garlic, tomatoes with juices, tomato paste, chili powder, cumin, and water and mix well. 3 Place the lid on the slow cooker and cook on low for 6 to 8 hours or on high for 5 hours, until the veggies are soft. 4 Serve topped with shredded cheese, green onions, sour cream, and/or sliced jalapeños, if desired.

Per Serving:

Calories: 387 | fat: 25g | protein: 34g | carbs: 11g | net carbs: 8g | fiber: 3g

Stuffed Cabbage Rolls

Prep time: 10 minutes | Cook time: 1 hour 30 minutes | Serves 8

1 large head cabbage, separated into 16 leaves

1 pound (454 g) ground beef

1 pound (454 g) sausage

1 small onion, chopped

2 garlic cloves, minced

Salt, to taste

Freshly ground black pepper, to taste

1 cup chicken broth

½ cup canned no-sugar-added tomato sauce, warmed

Grated Parmesan cheese, for topping

1. Bring a large saucepan of water to a boil over high heat. Add the cabbage leaves and boil for 2 to 3 minutes or until soft. Remove from the water and set aside to drain. Discard the water. 2. In a large bowl, mix together the beef, sausage, onion, and garlic. Season well with salt and pepper. Spoon the meat mixture into each leaf and fold the sides over, rolling each leaf up to hold the meat mixture. Secure with a toothpick and transfer to the pan. 3. Add the chicken broth. Cover the pan and simmer over low heat for about 1 hour, 30 minutes or until the meat is cooked through. Remove the rolls from the broth and top with the warmed tomato sauce and a sprinkle of Parmesan. Refrigerate leftovers in an airtight container for up to 3 days.

Per Serving (2 rolls):

Calories: 331 | fat: 23g | protein: 22g | carbs: 11g | net carbs: 7g | fiber: 4g

Cheeseburger "Mac" Helper

Prep time: 5 minutes | Cook time: 20 or 40 minutes | serves 4

1 pound ground beef	½ teaspoon ground black
½ cup chopped onions, or	pepper
2 tablespoons dried minced	1 (8-ounce) can tomato sauce
onions	1 (12-ounce) bag frozen
2 teaspoons paprika	cauliflower florets
1 teaspoon chili powder	2 cups shredded cheddar cheese
1 teaspoon garlic powder	Fresh flat-leaf parsley, for
1 teaspoon dried parsley	garnish (optional)
½ teaspoon salt	

1. In a large skillet over medium heat, cook the ground beef with the onions, crumbling the meat with a large spoon as it cooks, until the meat is browned and the onions are translucent, about 10 minutes. Drain the fat, if necessary. 2. Stir in the paprika, chili powder, garlic powder, parsley, salt, pepper, and tomato sauce and simmer for 5 minutes. 3. Stir in the cauliflower, cover, and continue cooking, stirring occasionally, until the cauliflower is tender. 4. Stir in the cheese and serve immediately, or reduce the heat to low and simmer for an additional 20 minutes for more depth of flavor, then stir in the cheese. Garnish with parsley, if desired. Leftovers can be stored in an airtight container in the refrigerator for up to 5 days.

Per Serving:
Calories: 381 | fat: 28g | protein: 24g | carbs: 9g | net carbs: 6g | fiber: 3g

Beef and Sausage Medley

Prep time: 10 minutes | Cook time: 27 minutes | Serves 8

1 teaspoon butter	1½ cups roasted vegetable broth
2 beef sausages, casing	2 cloves garlic, minced
removed and sliced	1 teaspoon Old Bay seasoning
2 pounds (907 g) beef steak,	2 bay leaves
cubed	1 sprig thyme
1 yellow onion, sliced	1 sprig rosemary
2 fresh ripe tomatoes, puréed	½ teaspoon paprika
1 jalapeño pepper, chopped	Sea salt and ground black
1 red bell pepper, chopped	pepper, to taste

1. Press the Sauté button to heat up the Instant Pot. Melt the butter and cook the sausage and steak for 4 minutes, stirring periodically. Set aside. 2. Add the onion and sauté for 3 minutes or until softened and translucent. Add the remaining ingredients, including reserved beef and sausage. 3. Secure the lid. Choose Manual mode and set time for 20 minutes on High Pressure. 4. Once cooking is complete, use a quick pressure release.Carefully remove the lid. 5. Serve immediately.

Per Serving:
Calories: 319 | fat: 14g | protein: 43g | carbs: 6g | net carbs: 2g | fiber: 4g

Pork Steaks with Pico de Gallo

Prep time: 15 minutes | Cook time: 12 minutes | Serves 6

1 tablespoon butter	black pepper, or more to taste
2 pounds (907 g) pork steaks	Pico de Gallo:
1 bell pepper, deseeded and	1 tomato, chopped
sliced	1 chili pepper, seeded and
½ cup shallots, chopped	minced
2 garlic cloves, minced	½ cup red onion, chopped
¼ cup dry red wine	2 garlic cloves, minced
1 cup chicken bone broth	1 tablespoon fresh cilantro,
¼ cup water	finely chopped
Salt, to taste	Sea salt, to taste
¼ teaspoon freshly ground	

1. Press the Sauté button to heat up the Instant Pot. Melt the butter and sear the pork steaks about 4 minutes or until browned on both sides. 2. Add bell pepper, shallot, garlic, wine, chicken bone broth, water, salt, and black pepper to the Instant Pot. 3. Secure the lid. Choose the Manual mode and set cooking time for 8 minutes at High pressure. 4. Meanwhile, combine the ingredients for the Pico de Gallo in a small bowl. Refrigerate until ready to serve. 5. Once cooking is complete, use a quick pressure release. Carefully remove the lid. 6. Serve warm pork steaks with the chilled Pico de Gallo on the side.

Per Serving:
Calories: 448 | fat: 29g | protein: 39g | carbs: 4g | net carbs: 2g | fiber: 2g

Beef Zucchini Boats

Prep time: 10 minutes | Cook time: 33 minutes | Serves 4

2 garlic cloves, minced	¼ cup fresh cilantro, chopped
1 teaspoon cumin	½ cup Monterey Jack cheese,
1 tablespoon olive oil	shredded
1 pound ground beef	1½ cups enchilada sauce
½ cup onions, chopped	1 avocado, chopped, for serving
1 teaspoon smoked paprika	Green onions, chopped, for
Salt and black pepper, to taste	serving
4 zucchinis	Tomatoes, chopped, for serving

1. Set a pan over high heat and warm the oil. Add the onions, and cook for 2 minutes. Stir in the beef, and brown for 4-5 minutes. Stir in the paprika, pepper, garlic, cumin, and salt; cook for 2 minutes. 2. Slice the zucchini in half lengthwise and scoop out the seeds. Set the zucchini in a greased baking pan, stuff each with the beef, scatter enchilada sauce on top, and spread with the Monterey cheese. 3. Bake in the oven at 350ºF for 20 minutes while covered. Uncover, spread with cilantro, and bake for 5 minutes. Top with tomatoes, green onions and avocado, place on serving plates and enjoy.

Per Serving:
Calories: 422 | fat: 33g | protein: 39g | carbs: 15g | net carbs: 8g | fiber: 7g

Cuban Pork Shoulder

Prep time: 20 minutes | Cook time: 35 minutes | Serves 3

9 ounces (255 g) pork shoulder, boneless, chopped	½ teaspoon ground black pepper
1 tablespoon avocado oil	¼ cup apple cider vinegar
1 teaspoon ground cumin	1 cup water

1. In the mixing bowl, mix up avocado oil, ground cumin, ground black pepper, and apple cider vinegar. 2. Mix up pork shoulder and spice mixture together and transfer on the foil. Wrap the meat mixture. 3. Pour water and insert the steamer rack in the instant pot. 4. Put the wrapped pork shoulder on the rack. Close and seal the lid. 5. Cook the Cuban pork for 35 minutes. 6. Then allow the natural pressure release for 10 minutes.

Per Serving:

Calories: 262 | fat: 19g | protein: 20g | carbs: 1g | net carbs: 1g | fiber: 0g

Southern Pulled Pork "Spaghetti"

Prep time: 5 minutes | Cook time: 0 minutes | Serves 6

PORK "SPAGHETTI":	1 red bell pepper, diced
2 pounds (910 g) boneless pork shoulder	1 small white onion, diced
	8 cremini mushrooms, diced
1 cup (240 ml) chicken bone broth	1 pound (455 g) ground pork
1 teaspoon finely ground sea salt	¾ cup (120 g) sugar-free barbecue sauce
BARBECUE PORK SAUCE:	½ cup (120 ml) reserved pork shoulder cooking liquid (from above)
2 tablespoons avocado oil	

1. Make the "spaghetti": Place all the ingredients for the spaghetti in a pressure cooker or slow cooker. 2. If using a pressure cooker, seal the lid and cook on high pressure for 45 minutes. Allow the pressure to release naturally before removing the lid. Remove ½ cup (120 ml) of the cooking liquid and set aside for the sauce. Drain the meat almost completely, leaving ¼ cup (60 ml) of the cooking liquid in the cooker. If using a slow cooker, cook on high for 4 hours or low for 6 hours. When the meat is done, remove ½ cup (120 ml) of the cooking liquid and set aside for the sauce. Drain the meat almost completely, leaving ⅓ cup (80 ml) of the cooking liquid in the cooker. 3. Meanwhile, make the sauce: Heat the oil in a large frying pan over medium heat. Add the bell pepper, onion, and mushrooms and sauté for 5 minutes, until softened. Add the ground pork and cook until no longer pink, 5 to 7 minutes, stirring to break up the meat as it cooks. Add the barbecue sauce and the reserved cooking liquid. Stir to combine, then cover and cook for another 3 minutes, just to heat through. 4. Shred the meat with two forks. Divide the shredded pork among 6 dinner plates, top with the barbecue pork sauce, and dig in!

Per Serving:

Calories: 683 | fat: 46g | protein: 58g | carbs: 7g | net carbs: 5g | fiber: 2g

Pork Casserole

Prep time: 15 minutes | Cook time: 30 minutes | Serves 4

1 pound (454 g) ground pork	1 (15 -ounce / 425-g) can diced tomatoes
1 large yellow squash, thinly sliced	½ cup pork rinds, crushed
Salt and black pepper to taste	¼ cup chopped parsley
1 clove garlic, minced	1 cup cottage cheese
4 green onions, chopped	1 cup Mexican cheese blend
1 cup chopped cremini mushrooms	3 tablespoons olive oil
	⅓ cup water

1. Preheat the oven to 370°F. 2. Heat the olive oil in a skillet over medium heat, add the pork, season it with salt and black pepper, and cook for 3 minutes or until no longer pink. Stir occasionally while breaking any lumps apart. 3. Add the garlic, half of the green onions, mushrooms, and 2 tablespoons of pork rinds. Cook for 3 minutes. Stir in the tomatoes, half of the parsley, and water. Cook further for 3 minutes, and then turn the heat off. 4. Mix the remaining parsley, cottage cheese, and Mexican cheese blend. Set aside. Sprinkle the bottom of a baking dish with 3 tablespoons of pork rinds; top with half of the squash and a season of salt, 2/3 of the pork mixture, and the cheese mixture. Repeat the layering process a second time to exhaust the ingredients. 5. Cover the baking dish with foil and bake for 20 minutes. After, remove the foil and brown the top of the casserole with the broiler side of the oven for 2 minutes. Remove the dish when ready and serve warm.

Per Serving:

Calories: 717 | fat: 58g | protein: 36g | carbs: 14g | net carbs: 9g | fiber: 5g

Cajun Bacon Pork Loin Fillet

Prep time: 30 minutes | Cook time: 20 minutes | Serves 6

1½ pounds (680 g) pork loin fillet or pork tenderloin	Salt, to taste
	6 slices bacon
3 tablespoons olive oil	Olive oil spray
2 tablespoons Cajun spice mix	

1. Cut the pork in half so that it will fit in the air fryer basket. 2. Place both pieces of meat in a resealable plastic bag. Add the oil, Cajun seasoning, and salt to taste, if using. Seal the bag and massage to coat all of the meat with the oil and seasonings. Marinate in the refrigerator for at least 1 hour or up to 24 hours. 3. Remove the pork from the bag and wrap 3 bacon slices around each piece. Spray the air fryer basket with olive oil spray. Place the meat in the air fryer. Set the air fryer to 350°F (177°C) for 15 minutes. Increase the temperature to 400°F (204°C) for 5 minutes. Use a meat thermometer to ensure the meat has reached an internal temperature of 145°F (63°C). 4. Let the meat rest for 10 minutes. Slice into 6 medallions and serve.

Per Serving:

Calories: 289 | fat: 19g | protein: 27g | carbs: 0g | net carbs: 0g | fiber: 0g

Pepperoni Low-Carb Tortilla Pizza

Prep time: 5 minutes | Cook time: 5 minutes | Serves 2

2 tablespoons olive oil	1 cup shredded mozzarella
2 large low-carb tortillas (I use	cheese
Mission brand)	2 teaspoons dried Italian
4 tablespoons low-sugar tomato	seasoning
sauce (I use Rao's)	½ cup pepperoni

1. In a medium skillet over medium-high heat, heat the olive oil. Add the tortilla. 2. Spoon the tomato sauce onto the tortilla, spreading it out. Sprinkle on the cheese, Italian seasoning, and pepperoni. Work quickly so the tortilla doesn't burn. 3. Cook until the tortilla is crispy on the bottom, about 3 minutes. Transfer to a cutting board, and cut into slices. Put the slices on a serving plate and serve hot.

Per Serving:

Calories: 547 | fat: 44g | protein: 27g | carbs: 17g | net carbs: 8g | fiber: 9g

Moroccan Lamb Stew

Prep time: 5 minutes | Cook time: 50 minutes | Serves 3

½ cup coconut milk	13 ounces (369 g) lamb
1 teaspoon butter	shoulder, chopped
½ teaspoon dried rosemary	1 teaspoon ground anise
¼ teaspoon salt	¾ cup water
½ teaspoon ground coriander	

1. Slice the mushrooms and place them in the instant pot bowl. 2. Add all remaining ingredients. Close and seal the lid. 3. Set Manual mode for 45 minutes. 4. When the time is over, make natural pressure release for 10 minutes.

Per Serving:

Calories: 332 | fat: 20g | protein: 35g | carbs: 3g | net carbs: 2g | fiber: 1g

Chicken Fried Steak with Cream Gravy

Prep time: 5 minutes | Cook time: 10 minutes | Serves 4

4 small thin cube steaks (about	Cream Gravy:
1 pound / 454 g)	½ cup heavy cream
½ teaspoon salt	2 ounces (57 g) cream cheese
½ teaspoon freshly ground	¼ cup bacon grease
black pepper	2 to 3 tablespoons water
¼ teaspoon garlic powder	2 to 3 dashes Worcestershire
1 egg, lightly beaten	sauce
1 cup crushed pork rinds (about	Salt and freshly ground black
3 ounces / 85 g)	pepper, to taste

1. Preheat the air fryer to 400°F (204°C). 2. Working one at a time, place the steak between two sheets of parchment paper and use a meat mallet to pound to an even thickness. 3. In a small bowl, combine the salt, pepper, and garlic power. Season both sides of each steak with the mixture. 4. Place the egg in a small shallow dish and the pork rinds in another small shallow dish. Dip each steak first in the egg wash, followed by the pork rinds, pressing lightly to form an even coating. Working in batches if necessary, arrange the steaks in a single layer in the air fryer basket. Air fry for 10 minutes until crispy and cooked through. 5. To make the cream gravy: In a heavy-bottomed pot, warm the cream, cream cheese, and bacon grease over medium heat, whisking until smooth. Lower the heat if the mixture begins to boil. Continue whisking as you slowly add the water, 1 tablespoon at a time, until the sauce reaches the desired consistency. Season with the Worcestershire sauce and salt and pepper to taste. Serve over the chicken fried steaks.

Per Serving:

Calories: 527 | fat: 46g | protein: 28g | carbs: 1g | net carbs: 1g | fiber: 0g

Herby Beef & Veggie Stew

Prep time: 15 minutes | Cook time: 26 minutes | Serves 4

1 pound (454 g) ground beef	1 tablespoon dried oregano
2 tablespoons olive oil	1 tablespoon dried basil
1 onion, chopped	1 tablespoon dried marjoram
2 garlic cloves, minced	Salt and black pepper, to taste
14 ounces (397 g) canned diced	2 carrots, sliced
tomatoes	2 celery stalks, chopped
1 tablespoon dried rosemary	1 cup vegetable broth
1 tablespoon dried sage	

1. Set a pan over medium heat, add in the olive oil, onion, celery, and garlic, and sauté for 5 minutes. Place in the beef, and cook for 6 minutes. Stir in the tomatoes, carrots, broth, black pepper, oregano, marjoram, basil, rosemary, salt, and sage, and simmer for 15 minutes. Serve and enjoy!

Per Serving:

Calories: 250 | fat: 13g | protein: 26g | carbs: 9g | net carbs: 6g | fiber: 3g

Almond Butter Beef Stew

Prep time: 10 minutes | Cook time: 60 minutes | Serves 3

10 ounces (283 g) beef chuck	½ teaspoon salt
roast, chopped	1 teaspoon dried basil
½ cup almond butter	1 cup water
½ teaspoon cayenne pepper	

1. Place the almond butter in the instant pot and start to preheat it on the Sauté mode. 2. Meanwhile, mix up together the cayenne pepper, salt, and dried basil. 3. Sprinkle the beef with the spices and transfer the meat in the melted almond butter. 4. Close the instant pot lid and lock it. 5. Set the Manual mode and put a timer on 60 minutes (Low Pressure).

Per Serving:

Calories: 360 | fat: 28g | protein: 25g | carbs: 1g | net carbs: 1g | fiber: 0g

Steaks with Walnut-Blue Cheese Butter

Prep time: 30 minutes | Cook time: 10 minutes | Serves 6

½ cup unsalted butter, at room temperature	1 teaspoon minced garlic
½ cup crumbled blue cheese	¼ teaspoon cayenne pepper
2 tablespoons finely chopped walnuts	Sea salt and freshly ground black pepper, to taste
1 tablespoon minced fresh rosemary	1½ pounds (680 g) New York strip steaks, at room temperature

1. In a medium bowl, combine the butter, blue cheese, walnuts, rosemary, garlic, and cayenne pepper and salt and black pepper to taste. Use clean hands to ensure that everything is well combined. Place the mixture on a sheet of parchment paper and form it into a log. Wrap it tightly in plastic wrap. Refrigerate for at least 2 hours or freeze for 30 minutes. 2. Season the steaks generously with salt and pepper. 3. Place the air fryer basket or grill pan in the air fryer. Set the air fryer to 400ºF (204ºC) and let it preheat for 5 minutes. 4. Place the steaks in the basket in a single layer and air fry for 5 minutes. Flip the steaks, and cook for 5 minutes more, until an instant-read thermometer reads 120ºF (49ºC) for medium-rare (or as desired). 5. Transfer the steaks to a plate. Cut the butter into pieces and place the desired amount on top of the steaks. Tent a piece of aluminum foil over the steaks and allow to sit for 10 minutes before serving. 6. Store any remaining butter in a sealed container in the refrigerator for up to 2 weeks.

Per Serving:

Calories: 283 | fat: 18g | protein: 30g | carbs: 1g | net carbs: 1g | fiber: 0g

Sausage and Cauliflower Arancini

Prep time: 30 minutes | Cook time: 28 to 32 minutes | Serves 6

Avocado oil spray	4 ounces (113 g) Cheddar cheese, shredded
6 ounces (170 g) Italian sausage, casings removed	1 large egg
¼ cup diced onion	½ cup finely ground blanched almond flour
1 teaspoon minced garlic	¼ cup finely grated Parmesan cheese
1 teaspoon dried thyme	
Sea salt and freshly ground black pepper, to taste	Keto-friendly marinara sauce, for serving
2½ cups cauliflower rice	
3 ounces (85 g) cream cheese	

1. Spray a large skillet with oil and place it over medium-high heat. Once the skillet is hot, put the sausage in the skillet and cook for 7 minutes, breaking up the meat with the back of a spoon. 2. Reduce the heat to medium and add the onion. Cook for 5 minutes, then add the garlic, thyme, and salt and pepper to taste. Cook for 1 minute more. 3. Add the cauliflower rice and cream cheese to the skillet. Cook for 7 minutes, stirring frequently, until the cream cheese melts and the cauliflower is tender. 4. Remove the skillet from the heat and stir in the Cheddar cheese. Using a cookie scoop, form the mixture into 1½-inch balls. Place the balls on a parchment paper-lined baking sheet. Freeze for 30 minutes. 5. Place the egg in a shallow bowl and beat it with a fork. In a separate bowl, stir together the almond flour and Parmesan cheese. 6. Dip the cauliflower balls into the egg, then coat them with the almond flour mixture, gently pressing the mixture to the balls to adhere. 7. Set the air fryer to 400ºF (204ºC). Spray the cauliflower rice balls with oil, and arrange them in a single layer in the air fryer basket, working in batches if necessary. Air fry for 5 minutes. Flip the rice balls and spray them with more oil. Air fry for 3 to 7 minutes longer, until the balls are golden brown. 8. Serve warm with marinara sauce.

Per Serving:

Calories: 312 | fat: 26g | protein: 14g | carbs: 6g | net carbs: 4g | fiber: 2g

Paprika Pork Ribs

Prep time: 10 minutes | Cook time: 30 minutes | Serves 4

1 pound (454 g) pork ribs	3 tablespoons avocado oil
1 tablespoon ground paprika	1 teaspoon salt
1 teaspoon ground turmeric	½ cup beef broth

1. Rub the pork ribs with ground paprika, turmeric, salt, and avocado oil. 2. Then pour the beef broth in the instant pot. 3. Arrange the pork ribs in the instant pot. Close and seal the lid. 4. Cook the pork ribs for 30 minutes on Manual mode (High Pressure). 5. When the time is finished, make a quick pressure release and chop the ribs into servings.

Per Serving:

Calories: 335 | fat: 22g | protein: 31g | carbs: 2g | net carbs: 1g | fiber: 1g

Italian Beef and Pork Rind Meatloaf

Prep time: 6 minutes | Cook time: 25 minutes | Serves 6

1 pound (454 g) ground beef	½ cup water
1 cup crushed pork rinds	½ cup unsweetened tomato purée
1 egg	
¼ cup grated Parmesan cheese	1 tablespoon chopped fresh parsley
¼ cup Italian dressing	
2 teaspoons Italian seasoning	1 clove garlic, minced

1. In large bowl, combine the beef, pork rinds, egg, cheese, dressing, and Italian seasoning. Stir to mix well. 2. Pour the mixture in a baking pan and level with a spatula. 3. Place the trivet in the pot and add the water. Place the pan on top of the trivet. 4. Close the lid. Select Manual mode and set cooking time for 20 minutes on High Pressure. 5. When timer beeps, use a quick pressure release. Open the lid. 6. Meanwhile, whisk together the tomato purée, parsley, and garlic in a small bowl. Heat the broiler. 7. Remove the pan from the pot. Spread the tomato purée mixture on top. 8. Broil for 5 minutes or until sticky. Slice and serve.

Per Serving:

Calories: 358 | fat: 25g | protein: 29g | carbs: 2g | net carbs: 2g | fiber: 0g

Barbacoa Beef Roast

Prep time: 10 minutes | Cook time: 8 hours | Serves 2

1 pound beef chuck roast	1 (6-ounce) can green jalapeño
Pink Himalayan salt	chiles
Freshly ground black pepper	2 tablespoons apple cider
4 chipotle peppers in adobo	vinegar
sauce (I use La Costeña	½ cup beef broth
12-ounce can)	

1. With the crock insert in place, preheat the slow cooker to low. 2. Season the beef chuck roast on both sides with pink Himalayan salt and pepper. Put the roast in the slow cooker. 3. In a food processor (or blender), combine the chipotle peppers and their adobo sauce, jalapeños, and apple cider vinegar, and pulse until smooth. Add the beef broth, and pulse a few more times. Pour the chile mixture over the top of the roast. 4. Cover and cook on low for 8 hours. 5. Transfer the beef to a cutting board, and use two forks to shred the meat. 6. Serve hot.

Per Serving:
Calories: 723 | fat: 46g | protein: 66g | carbs: 7g | net carbs: 2g | fiber: 5g

Bacon Smothered Pork Chops

Prep time: 10 minutes | Cook time: 20 minutes | Serves 6

7 strips bacon, chopped	5 sprigs fresh thyme + extra to
6 pork chops	garnish
Pink salt and black pepper to	¼ cup chicken broth
taste	½ cup heavy cream

1. Cook bacon in a large skillet on medium heat for 5 minutes. Remove with a slotted spoon onto a paper towel-lined plate to soak up excess fat. 2. Season pork chops with salt and black pepper, and brown in the bacon fat for 4 minutes on each side. Remove to the bacon plate. Stir in the thyme, chicken broth, and heavy cream and simmer for 5 minutes. 3. Return the chops and bacon, and cook further for another 2 minutes. Serve chops and a generous ladle of sauce with cauli mash. Garnish with thyme leaves.

Per Serving:
Calories: 435 | fat: 37g | protein: 22g | carbs: 3g | net carbs: 3g | fiber: 0g

Chili-Stuffed Avocados

Prep time: 10 minutes | Cook time: 30 minutes | Serves 8

2 tablespoons tallow or bacon	2 teaspoons paprika
grease	¾ teaspoon finely ground gray
1 pound (455 g) ground beef	sea salt
(20% to 30% fat)	¼ teaspoon ground cinnamon
1 (14½-ounce/408-g/428-ml)	2 tablespoons finely chopped
can whole tomatoes with juices	fresh parsley
1½ tablespoons chili powder	4 large Hass avocados, sliced in
2 small cloves garlic, minced	half, pits removed (leave skin

on), for serving

1. Place the tallow into a large saucepan. Melt on medium heat before adding the ground beef. Cook until beef is no longer pink, 7 to 8 minutes, stirring often to break the meat up into small clumps. 2. Add the tomatoes, chili powder, garlic, paprika, salt, and cinnamon. Cover and bring to a boil on high heat. Once boiling, reduce the heat to medium-low and simmer for 20 to 25 minutes, with the cover slightly askew to let steam out. 3. Once thickened, remove from the heat and stir in the chopped parsley. 4. Place an avocado half on a small serving plate or on a platter if you plan to serve them family style. Scoop ⅓ scant cup (180g) of chili into the hollow of
Per Serving:
Calories: 385 | fat: 31g | protein: 17g | carbs: 10g | net carbs: 3g | fiber: 7g

Herbed Lamb Shank

Prep time: 15 minutes | Cook time: 35 minutes | Serves 2

2 lamb shanks	¼ teaspoon chili powder
1 rosemary spring	¾ teaspoon ground ginger
1 teaspoon coconut flour	½ cup beef broth
¼ teaspoon onion powder	½ teaspoon avocado oil

1. Put all ingredients in the Instant Pot. Stir to mix well. 2. Close the lid. Select Manual mode and set cooking time for 35 minutes on High Pressure. 3. When timer beeps, use a natural pressure release for 15 minutes, then release any remaining pressure. Open the lid. 4. Discard the rosemary sprig and serve warm.

Per Serving:
Calories: 179 | fat: 7g | protein: 25g | carbs: 2g | net carbs: 1g | fiber: 1g

Beef Meatballs

Prep time: 5 minutes | Cook time: 32 minutes | Serves 5

½ cup pork rinds, crushed	¼ cup free-sugar ketchup
1 egg	3 teaspoons Worcestershire
Salt and black pepper, to taste	sauce
1½ pounds ground beef	½ teaspoon dry mustard
10 ounces canned onion soup	¼ cup water
1 tablespoon almond flour	

1. In a bowl, combine ⅓ cup of the onion soup with the beef, pepper, pork rinds, egg, and salt. Heat a pan over medium heat, shape the mixture into 12 meatballs. Brown in the pan for 12 minutes on both sides. 2. In a separate bowl, combine the rest of the soup with the almond flour, dry mustard, ketchup, Worcestershire sauce, and water. Pour this over the beef meatballs, cover the pan, and cook for 20 minutes as you stir occasionally. Split among serving bowls and serve.

Per Serving:
Calories: 417 | fat: 30g | protein: 31g | carbs: 6g | net carbs: 5g | fiber: 1g

Cajun Sausage and Rice

Prep time: 10 minutes | Cook time: 25 minutes | serves 4

2 tablespoons avocado oil

14 ounces fully cooked andouille sausage, sliced

½ cup diced onions

½ cup diced green bell peppers

1 rib celery, diced

1 (12-ounce) bag frozen riced cauliflower

1 cup vegetable broth

1 teaspoon Creole seasoning

1 bay leaf

1. Heat the oil in a large, deep skillet over medium heat. Brown the sausage for 2 to 3 minutes. Add the onions, green peppers, and celery to the skillet and cook until the vegetables are tender and the onions are translucent. 2. Add the cauliflower, broth, Creole seasoning, and bay leaf to the skillet. Continue cooking, stirring occasionally, until the cauliflower is tender. 3. Reduce the heat to low and simmer for 10 more minutes, until the mixture is slightly thickened. Remove the bay leaf before serving.

Per Serving:

Calories: 308 | fat: 25g | protein: 17g | carbs: 7g | net carbs: 4g | fiber: 3g

Hunan Beef-Stuffed Peppers

Prep time: 7 minutes | Cook time: 15 minutes | Serves 4

Marinade:

½ cup beef bone broth, homemade or store-bought

¼ cup coconut aminos or wheat-free tamari

3 tablespoons MCT oil

1 tablespoon minced garlic

1 tablespoon grated fresh ginger

1 tablespoon freshly ground black pepper

1 teaspoon fish sauce (optional, for umami)

4 dried Thai chiles

¼ teaspoon guar gum (optional)

1 pound (454 g) flank steak, sliced very thinly against the grain

2 bell peppers, any color, cored and cut in half lengthwise, for serving

¼ cup coconut oil

½ cup thinly sliced onions

1 red bell pepper, cut into thin strips

1 green bell pepper, cut into thin strips

Fine sea salt, as needed

1. Place the ingredients for the marinade, except for the guar gum, in a shallow bowl. Give them a stir to combine, then add the steak to the marinade and toss to coat well. Cover and refrigerate for at least 2 hours and up to overnight. 2. Remove the beef and reserve the marinade. If you used store-bought beef broth in the marinade, sift the guar gum into the marinade. (It will help thicken the sauce as it cooks.) 3. To blanch the peppers, bring a large pot of water to a boil. Blanch the peppers in the boiling water for 3 minutes. Drain the peppers in a colander and rinse with ice-cold water (this will preserve their bright color). 4. Heat a wok or large skillet over high heat, then put the coconut oil in the wok. When the oil is hot, sear the slices of beef for 10 seconds, then remove from the pan and set aside. 5. Place the onions and bell peppers in the hot oil and stir-fry for 5 minutes. Add the beef and marinade, bring to a boil, and cook until the marinade has thickened, 5 to 7 minutes. Taste and add salt,

if needed. 6. Serve the stir-fry in the blanched bell pepper halves. Store extras in an airtight container in the fridge for up to 5 days or in the freezer for up to a month.

Per Serving:

Calories: 480 | fat: 34g | protein: 27g | carbs: 17g | net carbs: 10g | fiber: 7g

Mustard Lamb Chops

Prep time: 5 minutes | Cook time: 14 minutes | Serves 4

Oil, for spraying

1 tablespoon Dijon mustard

2 teaspoons lemon juice

½ teaspoon dried tarragon

4 (1¼-inch-thick) loin lamb chops

¼ teaspoon salt

¼ teaspoon freshly ground black pepper

1. Preheat the air fryer to 390ºF (199ºC). Line the air fryer basket with parchment and spray lightly with oil. 2. In a small bowl, mix together the mustard, lemon juice, tarragon, salt, and black pepper. 3. Pat dry the lamb chops with a paper towel. Brush the chops on both sides with the mustard mixture. 4. Place the chops in the prepared basket. You may need to work in batches, depending on the size of your air fryer. 5. Cook for 8 minutes, flip, and cook for another 6 minutes, or until the internal temperature reaches 125ºF (52ºC) for rare, 145ºF (63ºC) for medium-rare, or 155ºF (68ºC) for medium.

Per Serving:

Calories: 96 | fat: 4g | protein: 14g | carbs: 0g | fiber: 0g | sodium: 233mg

Spicy Lamb Sirloin Chops

Prep time: 30 minutes | Cook time: 15 minutes | Serves 4

½ yellow onion, coarsely chopped

4 coin-size slices peeled fresh ginger

5 garlic cloves

1 teaspoon garam masala

1 teaspoon ground fennel

1 teaspoon ground cinnamon

1 teaspoon ground turmeric

½ to 1 teaspoon cayenne pepper

½ teaspoon ground cardamom

1 teaspoon kosher salt

1 pound (454 g) lamb sirloin chops

1. In a blender, combine the onion, ginger, garlic, garam masala, fennel, cinnamon, turmeric, cayenne, cardamom, and salt. Pulse until the onion is finely minced and the mixture forms a thick paste, 3 to 4 minutes. 2. Place the lamb chops in a large bowl. Slash the meat and fat with a sharp knife several times to allow the marinade to penetrate better. Add the spice paste to the bowl and toss the lamb to coat. Marinate at room temperature for 30 minutes or cover and refrigerate for up to 24 hours. 3. Place the lamb chops in a single layer in the air fryer basket. Set the air fryer to 325ºF (163ºC) for 15 minutes, turning the chops halfway through the cooking time. Use a meat thermometer to ensure the lamb has reached an internal temperature of 145ºF (63ºC) (medium-rare).

Per Serving:

Calories: 179 | fat: 7g | protein: 24g | carbs: 4g | fiber: 1g | sodium: 657mg

Beef and Cauliflower Burgers

Prep time: 15 minutes | Cook time: 15 minutes | Serves 2

½ cup shredded cauliflower

5 ounces (142 g) ground beef

1 teaspoon garlic salt

¼ teaspoon ground cumin

1 tablespoon scallions, diced

1 egg, beaten

1 tablespoon coconut oil

¼ cup hot water

1. In the mixing bowl, mix up shredded cauliflower, ground beef, garlic salt, ground cumin, and diced scallions. 2. When the meat mixture is homogenous, add egg and stir it well. 3. Make the burgers from the cauliflower and meat mixture. 4. After this, heat up the coconut oil on Sauté mode. 5. Place the burgers in the hot oil in one layer and cook them for 5 minutes from each side. 6. Then add water and close the lid. Cook the meal on Sauté mode for 5 minutes more.

Per Serving:

Calories: 235 | fat: 13g | protein: 25g | carbs: 3g | net carbs: 2g | fiber: 1g

Steak Diane

Prep time: 10 minutes | Cook time: 15 minutes | Serves 4

4 tablespoons Paleo fat, such as lard, coconut oil, or avocado oil, divided

4 (4-ounce / 113-g) beef or venison tenderloins

1¼ teaspoons fine sea salt, plus more for the sauce

½ teaspoon freshly ground black pepper, plus more for the sauce

¼ cup minced shallots or onions

1 teaspoon minced garlic

½ pound (227 g) button mushrooms, sliced ¼ inch thick (small mushrooms can be left whole)

¼ cup beef bone broth, homemade or store-bought

¼ cup full-fat coconut milk

2 teaspoons Dijon mustard

1. Heat a cast-iron skillet over medium-high heat; once hot, place 1 tablespoon of the fat in the pan. While the pan is heating, prepare the tenderloins: Pat the tenderloins dry and season them well with the salt and pepper. 2. When the fat is hot, place the tenderloins in the skillet and sear for 3 minutes, then flip them over and sear for another 3 minutes. Remove from the skillet for rare meat, or continue to cook until done to your liking. Allow to rest for 10 minutes before slicing or serving. 3. While the meat is resting, make the pan sauce: Add the remaining 3 tablespoons of fat to the pan, then add the shallots, garlic, and mushrooms, season with a couple pinches each of salt and pepper, and sauté until the mushrooms are golden brown on both sides, about 6 minutes. (Add the mushrooms to the pan in batches if necessary to avoid overcrowding.) Pour in the broth and, using a whisk, scrape up the brown bits from the bottom of the pan to incorporate them into the sauce. Add the coconut milk and mustard, stir to combine, and heat until simmering. Simmer over low heat until thickened, about 3 minutes. Season to taste with salt and pepper. 4. Serve the steaks with the sauce.

Per Serving:

Calories: 332 | fat: 20g | protein: 36g | carbs: 2g | net carbs: 1g | fiber: 1g

Blue Pork

Prep time: 5 minutes | Cook time: 20 minutes | Serves 2

1 teaspoon coconut oil

2 pork chops

2 ounces (57 g) blue cheese,

crumbled

1 teaspoon lemon juice

¼ cup heavy cream

1. Heat the coconut oil in the Instant Pot on Sauté mode. 2. Put the pork chops in the Instant Pot and cook on Sauté mode for 5 minutes on each side. 3. Add the lemon juice and crumbled cheese. Stir to mix well. 4. Add heavy cream and close the lid. 5. Select Manual mode and set cooking time for 10 minutes on High Pressure. 6. When timer beeps, perform a natural pressure release for 5 minutes, then release any remaining pressure. Open the lid. 7. Serve immediately.

Per Serving:

Calories: 300 | fat: 26g | protein: 15g | carbs: 1g | net carbs: 1g | fiber: 0g

Osso Buco with Gremolata

Prep time: 35 minutes | Cook time: 1 hour 2 minutes | Serves 6

4 bone-in beef shanks

Sea salt, to taste

2 tablespoons avocado oil

1 small turnip, diced

1 medium onion, diced

1 medium stalk celery, diced

4 cloves garlic, smashed

1 tablespoon unsweetened tomato purée

½ cup dry white wine

1 cup chicken broth

1 sprig fresh rosemary

2 sprigs fresh thyme

3 Roma tomatoes, diced

For the Gremolata:

½ cup loosely packed parsley leaves

1 clove garlic, crushed

Grated zest of 2 lemons

1. On a clean work surface, season the shanks all over with salt. 2. Set the Instant Pot to Sauté and add the oil. When the oil shimmers, add 2 shanks and sear for 4 minutes per side. Remove the shanks to a bowl and repeat with the remaining shanks. Set aside. 3. Add the turnip, onion, and celery to the pot and cook for 5 minutes or until softened. 4. Add the garlic and unsweetened tomato purée and cook 1 minute more, stirring frequently. 5. Deglaze the pot with the wine, scraping the bottom with a wooden spoon to loosen any browned bits. Bring to a boil. 6. Add the broth, rosemary, thyme, and shanks, then add the tomatoes on top of the shanks. 7. Secure the lid. Press the Manual button and set cooking time for 40 minutes on High Pressure. 8. Meanwhile, for the gremolata: In a small food processor, combine the parsley, garlic, and lemon zest and pulse until the parsley is finely chopped. Refrigerate until ready to use. 9. When timer beeps, allow the pressure to release naturally for 20 minutes, then release any remaining pressure. Open the lid. 10. To serve, transfer the shanks to large, shallow serving bowl. Ladle the braising sauce over the top and sprinkle with the gremolata.

Per Serving:

Calories: 605 | fat: 30g | protein: 69g | carbs: 8g | net carbs: 6g | fiber: 2g

Garlic Beef Roast

Prep time: 2 minutes | Cook time: 70 minutes | Serves 6

2 pounds (907 g) top round roast	1 teaspoon black pepper
½ cup beef broth	3 whole cloves garlic
2 teaspoons salt	1 bay leaf

1. Add the roast, broth, salt, pepper, garlic, and bay leaf to the pot. 2. Close the lid and seal the vent. Cook on High Pressure for 15 minutes. Let the steam naturally release for 15 minutes before Manually releasing. 3. Remove the beef from the pot and slice or shred it. Store it in an airtight container in the fridge or freezer.

Per Serving:

Calories: 178 | fat: 4g | protein: 32g | carbs: 1g | net carbs: 1g | fiber: 0g

Blackened Steak Nuggets

Prep time: 10 minutes | Cook time: 7 minutes | Serves 2

1 pound (454 g) rib eye steak, cut into 1-inch cubes	¼ teaspoon garlic powder
2 tablespoons salted butter, melted	¼ teaspoon onion powder
½ teaspoon paprika	¼ teaspoon ground black pepper
½ teaspoon salt	⅛ teaspoon cayenne pepper

1. Place steak into a large bowl and pour in butter. Toss to coat. Sprinkle with remaining ingredients. 2. Place bites into ungreased air fryer basket. Adjust the temperature to 400°F (204°C) and air fry for 7 minutes, shaking the basket three times during cooking. Steak will be crispy on the outside and browned when done and internal temperature is at least 150°F (66°C) for medium and 180°F (82°C) for well-done. Serve warm.

Per Serving:

Calories: 661 | fat: 55g | protein: 41g | carbs: 1g | net carbs: 1g | fiber: 0g

Parmesan-Crusted Steak

Prep time: 30 minutes | Cook time: 12 minutes | Serves 6

½ cup (1 stick) unsalted butter, at room temperature	almond flour
1 cup finely grated Parmesan cheese	1½ pounds (680 g) New York strip steak
¼ cup finely ground blanched	Sea salt and freshly ground black pepper, to taste

1. Place the butter, Parmesan cheese, and almond flour in a food processor. Process until smooth. Transfer to a sheet of parchment paper and form into a log. Wrap tightly in plastic wrap. Freeze for 45 minutes or refrigerate for at least 4 hours. 2. While the butter is chilling, season the steak liberally with salt and pepper. Let the steak rest at room temperature for about 45 minutes. 3. Place the grill pan or basket in your air fryer, set it to 400°F (204°C), and let it preheat for 5 minutes. 4. Working in batches, if necessary, place the steak on the grill pan and air fry for 4 minutes. Flip and cook for 3 minutes more, until the steak is brown on both sides. 5. Remove the steak from the air fryer and arrange an equal amount of the Parmesan butter on top of each steak. Return the steak to the air fryer and continue cooking for another 5 minutes, until an instant-read thermometer reads 120°F (49°C) for medium-rare and the crust is golden brown (or to your desired doneness). 6. Transfer the cooked steak to a plate; let rest for 10 minutes before serving.

Per Serving:

Calories: 319 | fat: 20g | protein: 32g | carbs: 3g | net carbs: 2g | fiber: 1g

Italian Sausage Broccoli Sauté

Prep time: 10 minutes | Cook time: 20 minutes | Serves 4

2 tablespoons good-quality olive oil	4 cups small broccoli florets
1 pound Italian sausage meat, hot or mild	1 tablespoon minced garlic
	Freshly ground black pepper, for seasoning

1. Cook the sausage. In a large skillet over medium heat, warm the olive oil. Add the sausage and sauté it until it's cooked through, 8 to 10 minutes. Transfer the sausage to a plate with a slotted spoon and set the plate aside. 2. Sauté the vegetables. Add the broccoli to the skillet and sauté it until it's tender, about 6 minutes. Stir in the garlic and sauté for another 3 minutes. 3. Finish the dish. Return the sausage to the skillet and toss to combine it with the other ingredients. Season the mixture with pepper. 4. Serve. Divide the mixture between four plates and serve it immediately.

Per Serving:

Calories: 486 | fat: 43g | protein: 19g | carbs: 7g | net carbs: 5g | fiber: 2g

Bone-in Pork Chops

Prep time: 5 minutes | Cook time: 10 to 12 minutes | Serves 2

1 pound (454 g) bone-in pork chops	½ teaspoon onion powder
1 tablespoon avocado oil	¼ teaspoon cayenne pepper
1 teaspoon smoked paprika	Sea salt and freshly ground black pepper, to taste

1. Brush the pork chops with the avocado oil. In a small dish, mix together the smoked paprika, onion powder, cayenne pepper, and salt and black pepper to taste. Sprinkle the seasonings over both sides of the pork chops. 2. Set the air fryer to 400°F (204°C). Place the chops in the air fryer basket in a single layer, working in batches if necessary. Air fry for 10 to 12 minutes, until an instant-read thermometer reads 145°F (63°C) at the chops' thickest point. 3. Remove the chops from the air fryer and allow them to rest for 5 minutes before serving.

Per Serving:

Calories: 356 | fat: 16g | protein: 50g | carbs: 1g | fiber: 1g | sodium: 133mg

Cheese Wine Pork Cutlets

Prep time: 30 minutes | Cook time: 15 minutes | Serves 2

1 cup water	½ teaspoon porcini powder
1 cup red wine	Sea salt and ground black
1 tablespoon sea salt	pepper, to taste
2 pork cutlets	1 egg
¼ cup almond meal	¼ cup yogurt
¼ cup flaxseed meal	1 teaspoon brown mustard
½ teaspoon baking powder	⅓ cup Parmesan cheese, grated
1 teaspoon shallot powder	

1. In a large ceramic dish, combine the water, wine and salt. Add the pork cutlets and put for 1 hour in the refrigerator. 2. In a shallow bowl, mix the almond meal, flaxseed meal, baking powder, shallot powder, porcini powder, salt, and ground pepper. In another bowl, whisk the eggs with yogurt and mustard. 3. In a third bowl, place the grated Parmesan cheese. 4. Dip the pork cutlets in the seasoned flour mixture and toss evenly; then, in the egg mixture. Finally, roll them over the grated Parmesan cheese. 5. Spritz the bottom of the air fryer basket with cooking oil. Add the breaded pork cutlets and cook at 395°F (202°C) and for 10 minutes. 6. Flip and cook for 5 minutes more on the other side. Serve warm.

Per Serving:
Calories: 541 | fat: 32g | protein: 53g | carbs: 9g | net carbs: 6g | fiber: 3g

Lamb Stew with Veggies

Prep time: 20 minutes | Cook time: 1 hour 50 minutes | Serves 2

1 garlic clove, minced	½ tablespoon fresh rosemary,
1 parsnip, chopped	chopped
1 onion, chopped	1 leek, chopped
1 tablespoon olive oil	1 tablespoon mint sauce
1 celery stalk, chopped	1 teaspoon stevia
10 ounces lamb fillet, cut into	1 tablespoon tomato puree
pieces	½ head cauliflower, cut into
Salt and black pepper, to taste	florets
1¼ cups vegetable stock	½ head celeriac, chopped
1 carrot, chopped	2 tablespoons butter

1. Set a pot over medium heat and warm the oil, stir in the celery, onion, and garlic, and cook for 5 minutes. Stir in the lamb pieces, and cook for 3 minutes. 2. Add in the stevia, carrot, parsnip, rosemary, mint sauce, stock, leek, tomato puree, boil the mixture, and cook for 1 hour and 30 minutes. 3. Meanwhile, heat a pot with water over medium heat, place in the celeriac, cover, and simmer for 10 minutes. Place in the cauliflower florets, cook for 15 minutes, drain everything, and combine with butter, black pepper, and salt. 4. Mash using a potato masher, and split the mash between 2 plates. Top with vegetable mixture and lamb and enjoy.

Per Serving:
Calories: 479 | fat: 32g | protein: 33g | carbs: 15g | net carbs: 8g | fiber: 7g

Blade Pork with Sauerkraut

Prep time: 15 minutes | Cook time: 37 minutes | Serves 6

2 pounds (907 g) blade pork	1 tablespoon butter
steaks	1½ cups water
Sea salt and ground black	2 cloves garlic, thinly sliced
pepper, to taste	2 pork sausages, casing
½ teaspoon cayenne pepper	removed and sliced
½ teaspoon dried parsley flakes	4 cups sauerkraut

1. Season the blade pork steaks with salt, black pepper, cayenne pepper, and dried parsley. 2. Press the Sauté button to heat up the Instant Pot. Melt the butter and sear blade pork steaks for 5 minutes or until browned on all sides. 3. Clean the Instant Pot. Add water and trivet to the bottom of the Instant Pot. 4. Place the blade pork steaks on the trivet. Make small slits over entire pork with a knife. Insert garlic pieces into each slit. 5. Secure the lid. Choose the Meat/Stew mode and set cooking time for 30 minutes on High pressure. 6. Once cooking is complete, use a natural pressure release for 15 minutes, then release any remaining pressure. Carefully remove the lid. 7. Add the sausage and sauerkraut. Press the Sauté button and cook for 2 minutes more or until heated through. 8. Serve immediately

Per Serving:
Calories: 471 | fat: 27g | protein: 48g | carbs: 8g | net carbs: 2g | fiber: 6g

Pork Fried Cauliflower Rice

Prep time: 10 minutes | Cook time: 20 minutes | Serves 4

1 pound (454 g) ground pork	1 garlic clove, minced
Sea salt and freshly ground	1½ cups riced cauliflower
black pepper, to taste	1 tablespoon sriracha
3 tablespoons toasted sesame	2 tablespoons liquid aminos or
oil	tamari
3 cups thinly sliced cabbage	1 teaspoon rice wine vinegar
1 cup chopped broccoli	1 teaspoon sesame seeds, for
1 red bell pepper, cored and	garnish
chopped	

1. Heat a medium skillet over medium-high heat. Add the pork and sprinkle generously with salt and pepper. Cook, stirring frequently, until browned, about 10 minutes. Remove the meat from the skillet. 2. Reduce the heat to medium and add the sesame oil to the skillet along with the cabbage, broccoli, bell pepper, riced cauliflower, and garlic. Cook for about 5 minutes until slightly softened, then add the sriracha, liquid aminos, and vinegar and mix well. 3. Return the browned pork to the skillet. Simmer together for about 5 minutes more until the cabbage is crisp-tender. Season with salt and pepper, then garnish with the sesame seeds and serve right away.

Per Serving:
Calories: 460 | fat: 36g | protein: 23g | carbs: 11g | net carbs: 5g | fiber: 6g

Baby Back Ribs

Prep time: 5 minutes | Cook time: 25 minutes | Serves 4

2 pounds (907 g) baby back ribs	¼ teaspoon ground cayenne pepper
2 teaspoons chili powder	
1 teaspoon paprika	½ cup low-carb, sugar-free barbecue sauce
½ teaspoon onion powder	
½ teaspoon garlic powder	

1. Rub ribs with all ingredients except barbecue sauce. Place into the air fryer basket. 2. Adjust the temperature to 400ºF (204ºC) and roast for 25 minutes. 3. When done, ribs will be dark and charred with an internal temperature of at least 185ºF (85ºC). Brush ribs with barbecue sauce and serve warm.

Per Serving:

Calories: 571 | fat: 36g | protein: 45g | carbs: 17g | fiber: 1g | sodium: 541mg

Rosemary Pork Belly

Prep time: 10 minutes | Cook time: 75 minutes | Serves 4

10 ounces (283 g) pork belly	¼ teaspoon ground cinnamon
1 teaspoon dried rosemary	1 teaspoon salt
½ teaspoon dried thyme	1 cup water

1. Rub the pork belly with dried rosemary, thyme, ground cinnamon, and salt and transfer in the instant pot bowl. 2. Add water, close and seal the lid. 3. Cook the pork belly on Manual mode (High Pressure) for 75 minutes. 4. Remove the cooked pork belly from the instant pot and slice it into servings.

Per Serving:

Calories: 329 | fat: 19g | protein: 33g | carbs: 0g | net carbs: 0g | fiber: 0g

Easy Smoked Ham Hocks with Smoky Whole-Grain Mustard

Prep time: 5 minutes | Cook time: 10 minutes | Serves 4

Smoky Whole-Grain Mustard:	black pepper
¼ cup prepared yellow mustard	2 tablespoons coconut oil, melted
¼ cup brown mustard seeds	
2 tablespoons Swerve confectioners'-style sweetener or equivalent amount of liquid or powdered sweetener	½ teaspoon liquid smoke
	4 (3-ounce / 85-g) smoked ham hock steaks
¼ cup coconut vinegar or apple cider vinegar	2 cups sauerkraut, warmed, for serving
2 teaspoons chili powder	Cornichons or other pickles of choice, for serving
½ teaspoon freshly ground	

1. To make the mustard: In a small bowl, stir together the prepared mustard, mustard seeds, sweetener, vinegar, chili powder, and pepper. Stir in the melted coconut oil and liquid smoke; mix well to combine. Refrigerate overnight to allow the flavors to blend before using. 2. Preheat the oven to 425ºF (220ºC). Place the smoked ham hocks on a rimmed baking sheet and bake for 10 minutes, or until the skin gets crispy. 3. Place each ham hock on a plate with ½ cup sauerkraut and 2 to 4 tablespoons of the smoky mustard. 4. Store extras in an airtight container in the fridge for up to 3 days. To reheat, place in a skillet over medium heat and sauté for 3 minutes per side, or until warmed to your liking.

Per Serving:

Calories: 195 | fat: 15g | protein: 9g | carbs: 6g | net carbs: 4g | fiber: 2g

Winter Veal and Sauerkraut

Prep time: 10 minutes | Cook time: 1 hour | Serves 4

1 pound veal, cut into cubes	1 onion, chopped
18 ounces sauerkraut, rinsed and drained	2 garlic cloves, minced
	1 tablespoon butter
Salt and black pepper, to taste	½ cup Parmesan cheese, grated
½ cup ham, chopped	½ cup sour cream

1. Heat a pot with the butter over medium heat, add in the onion, and cook for 3 minutes. Stir in garlic, and cook for 1 minute. Place in the veal and ham, and cook until slightly browned. Place in the sauerkraut, and cook until the meat becomes tender, about 30 minutes. Stir in sour cream, pepper, and salt. Top with Parmesan cheese and bake for 20 minutes at 350ºF.

Per Serving:

Calories: 410 | fat: 25g | protein: 32g | carbs: 10g | net carbs: 6g | fiber: 4g

Lemon Butter Pork Chops

Prep time: 5 minutes | Cook time: 25 minutes | Serves 4

½ teaspoon sea salt	5 tablespoons butter, divided
1 teaspoon lemon-pepper seasoning	¼ cup bone broth
	2 tablespoons freshly squeezed lemon juice
1 teaspoon garlic powder	
½ teaspoon dried thyme	1 tablespoon minced garlic
4 (4-ounce / 113-g) boneless pork chops	½ cup heavy (whipping) cream

1. In a small bowl, stir together the salt, lemon-pepper seasoning, garlic powder, and thyme. Rub the spice mixture all over the pork chops. 2. Heat a skillet over medium-high heat and melt 2 tablespoons of butter. Add the pork chops and cook for at least 5 minutes on each side until they are cooked through. Remove the chops from the pan. 3. Reduce the heat to medium-low. Add the bone broth, lemon juice, garlic, and the remaining 3 tablespoons of butter. Add the pork chops and simmer for about 15 minutes, adding the cream 1 tablespoon at a time every few minutes, until the sauce thickens. 4. Remove from the heat and serve.

Per Serving:

Calories: 379 | fat: 29g | protein: 27g | carbs: 2g | net carbs: 2g | fiber: 0g

Beef and Broccoli Roast

Prep time: 10 minutes | Cook time: 4 hours 30 minutes | Serves 2

1 pound beef chuck roast	¼ cup soy sauce (or coconut aminos)
Pink Himalayan salt	
Freshly ground black pepper	1 teaspoon toasted sesame oil
½ cup beef broth, plus more if needed	1 (16-ounce) bag frozen broccoli

1. With the crock insert in place, preheat the slow cooker to low. 2. On a cutting board, season the chuck roast with pink Himalayan salt and pepper, and slice the roast thin. Put the sliced beef in the slow cooker. 3. In a small bowl, mix together the beef broth, soy sauce, and sesame oil. Pour over the beef. 4. Cover and cook on low for 4 hours. 5. Add the frozen broccoli, and cook for 30 minutes more. If you need more liquid, add additional beef broth. 6. Serve hot.

Per Serving:
Calories: 806 | fat: 49g | protein: 74g | carbs: 18g | net carbs: 12g | fiber: 6g

Meatballs in Creamy Almond Sauce

Prep time: 15 minutes | Cook time: 35 minutes | Serves 4 to 6

8 ounces (227 g) ground veal or pork	½ teaspoon ground nutmeg
8 ounces (227 g) ground beef	2 teaspoons chopped fresh flat-leaf Italian parsley, plus ¼ cup, divided
½ cup finely minced onion, divided	
1 large egg, beaten	½ cup extra-virgin olive oil, divided
¼ cup almond flour	¼ cup slivered almonds
1½ teaspoons salt, divided	1 cup dry white wine or chicken broth
1 teaspoon garlic powder	
½ teaspoon freshly ground black pepper	¼ cup unsweetened almond butter

1. In a large bowl, combine the veal, beef, ¼ cup onion, and the egg and mix well with a fork. In a small bowl, whisk together the almond flour, 1 teaspoon salt, garlic powder, pepper, and nutmeg. Add to the meat mixture along with 2 teaspoons chopped parsley and incorporate well. Form the mixture into small meatballs, about 1 inch in diameter, and place on a plate. Let sit for 10 minutes at room temperature. 2. In a large skillet, heat ¼ cup oil over medium-high heat. Add the meatballs to the hot oil and brown on all sides, cooking in batches if necessary, 2 to 3 minutes per side. Remove from skillet and keep warm. 3. In the hot skillet, sauté the remaining ¼ cup minced onion in the remaining ¼ cup olive oil for 5 minutes. Reduce the heat to medium-low and add the slivered almonds. Sauté until the almonds are golden, another 3 to 5 minutes. 4. In a small bowl, whisk together the white wine, almond butter, and remaining ½ teaspoon salt. Add to the skillet and bring to a boil, stirring constantly. Reduce the heat to low, return the meatballs to skillet, and cover. Cook until the meatballs are cooked through, another 8 to 10 minutes. 5. Remove from the heat, stir in the remaining ¼ cup chopped parsley, and serve the meatballs

warm and drizzled with almond sauce.

Per Serving:
Calories: 447 | fat: 36g | protein: 20g | carbs: 7g | fiber: 2g | sodium: 659mg

Braised Short Ribs with Red Wine

Prep time: 10 minutes | Cook time: 1 hour 30 minutes to 2 hours| Serves 4

1½ pounds (680 g) boneless beef short ribs (if using bone-in, use 3½ pounds)	½ teaspoon garlic powder
	¼ cup extra-virgin olive oil
1 teaspoon salt	1 cup dry red wine (such as cabernet sauvignon or merlot)
½ teaspoon freshly ground black pepper	2 to 3 cups beef broth, divided
	4 sprigs rosemary

1. Preheat the oven to 350°F(180°C). 2. Season the short ribs with salt, pepper, and garlic powder. Let sit for 10 minutes. 3. In a Dutch oven or oven-safe deep skillet, heat the olive oil over medium-high heat. 4. When the oil is very hot, add the short ribs and brown until dark in color, 2 to 3 minutes per side. Remove the meat from the oil and keep warm. 5. Add the red wine and 2 cups beef broth to the Dutch oven, whisk together, and bring to a boil. Reduce the heat to low and simmer until the liquid is reduced to about 2 cups, about 10 minutes. 6. Return the short ribs to the liquid, which should come about halfway up the meat, adding up to 1 cup of remaining broth if needed. Cover and braise until the meat is very tender, about 1½ to 2 hours. 7. Remove from the oven and let sit, covered, for 10 minutes before serving. Serve warm, drizzled with cooking liquid.

Per Serving:
Calories: 525 | fat: 37g | protein: 34g | carbs: 5g | fiber: 1g | sodium: 720mg

Eggplant Pork Lasagna

Prep time: 20 minutes | Cook time: 30 minutes | Serves 6

2 eggplants, sliced	1 tablespoon unsweetened tomato purée
1 teaspoon salt	
10 ounces (283 g) ground pork	1 teaspoon butter, softened
1 cup Mozzarella, shredded	1 cup chicken stock

1. Sprinkle the eggplants with salt and let sit for 10 minutes, then pat dry with paper towels. 2. In a mixing bowl, mix the ground pork, butter, and tomato purée. 3. Make a layer of the sliced eggplants in the bottom of the Instant Pot and top with ground pork mixture. 4. Top the ground pork with Mozzarella and repeat with remaining ingredients. 5. Pour in the chicken stock. Close the lid. Select Manual mode and set cooking time for 30 minutes on High Pressure. 6. When timer beeps, use a natural pressure release for 10 minutes, then release the remaining pressure and open the lid. 7. Cool for 10 minutes and serve.

Per Serving:
Calories: 136 | fat: 4g | protein: 16g | carbs: 12g | net carbs: 5g | fiber: 7g

Beef Steak with Cheese Mushroom Sauce

Prep time: 6 minutes | Cook time: 30 minutes | Serves 6

1 tablespoon olive oil	Sauce:
1½ pounds (680 g) beef blade steak	1 tablespoon butter, softened
1 cup stock	2 cups sliced Porcini mushrooms
2 garlic cloves, minced	½ cup thinly sliced onions
Sea salt and ground black pepper, to taste	½ cup sour cream
½ teaspoon cayenne pepper	4 ounces (113 g) goat cheese, crumbled
1 tablespoon coconut aminos	

1. Press the Sauté button to heat up the Instant Pot. Then, heat the olive oil until sizzling. Once hot, cook the blade steak approximately 3 minutes or until delicately browned. 2. Add the stock, garlic, salt, black pepper, cayenne pepper, and coconut aminos. 3. Secure the lid. Choose Manual mode and High Pressure; cook for 20 minutes. Once cooking is complete, use a quick pressure release; carefully remove the lid. 4. Take the meat out of the Instant Pot. Allow it to cool slightly and then, slice it into strips. 5. Press the Sauté button again and add the butter, mushrooms and onions to the Instant Pot. Let it cook for 5 minutes longer or until the mushrooms are fragrant and the onions are softened. 6. Add sour cream and goat cheese; continue to simmer for a couple of minutes more or until everything is thoroughly heated. 7. Return the meat to the Instant Pot and serve. Bon appétit!

Per Serving:

Calories: 311 | fat: 20g | protein: 31g | carbs: 3g | net carbs: 3g | fiber: 0g

Better Than Take-Out Beef with Broccoli

Prep time: 10 minutes | Cook time: 20 minutes | Serves 4

Marinade:	¼ teaspoon red pepper flakes
3 tablespoons coconut aminos (or 2 tablespoons liquid aminos)	Beef and Broccoli:
2 tablespoons coconut oil, melted	1 pound (454 g) beef sirloin or flank, sliced thinly across the grain
2 tablespoons toasted sesame oil	2 cups broccoli florets
2 tablespoons fish sauce	1 tablespoon coconut oil
1 tablespoon coconut vinegar or apple cider vinegar	2 garlic cloves, minced
1 teaspoon onion powder	½ teaspoon sea salt
1 teaspoon garlic powder	¼ teaspoon freshly ground black pepper
½ teaspoon ground ginger	1 tablespoon toasted sesame seeds (optional)

Make the Marinade 1. In a medium bowl, whisk together the coconut aminos, coconut oil, sesame oil, fish sauce, vinegar, onion powder, garlic powder, ginger, and red pepper flakes. Make the Beef and Broccoli 2. In a large plastic bag or medium bowl, pour one-third of the marinade over the beef and let marinate in the refrigerator for a few hours or overnight. Save the rest of the marinade in a small container to use for the sauce. 3. In a large pot, steam the broccoli until just tender. Transfer to a bowl with ice and cold water to stop the cooking. Drain and set aside. 4. In a large skillet or wok, heat the coconut oil over high heat. Remove the beef from the marinade (discard the marinade) and add the beef to the skillet. Let brown for 2 to 3 minutes. Flip the meat and cook for another 2 to 3 minutes. 5. Add the garlic, salt, and pepper and stir to combine. 6. Add the cooked broccoli florets and the reserved marinade. Stir well and let simmer on medium-low heat for 5 to 10 minutes or until the sauce thickens and the meat is cooked through. Top with sesame seeds (if using).

Per Serving:

Calories: 356 | fat: 24g | protein: 29g | carbs: 6g | net carbs: 4g | fiber: 2g

Cottage Pie

Prep time: 20 minutes | Cook time: 30 minutes | Serves 4

Pie:	Topping:
2 tablespoons extra-virgin olive oil	2 (12-ounce / 340-g) packages cauliflower rice, cooked and drained
2 celery stalks, chopped	1 cup shredded low-moisture mozzarella cheese
½ medium onion, chopped	2 tablespoons heavy (whipping) cream
2 garlic cloves, minced	
1 pound (454 g) ground beef (80/20)	2 tablespoons butter
¼ cup chicken broth	½ teaspoon pink Himalayan sea salt
1 tablespoon tomato paste	
1 teaspoon pink Himalayan sea salt	½ teaspoon freshly ground black pepper
1 teaspoon freshly ground black pepper	¼ teaspoon ground white pepper
½ teaspoon ground white pepper	¼ teaspoon garlic powder

1. Preheat the oven to 400°F (205°C). 2. To make the pie: In a large sauté pan or skillet, heat the olive oil over medium heat. Add the celery and onion and cook for 8 to 10 minutes, until the onion is tender. 3. Add the garlic and cook for an additional minute, until fragrant. 4. Add the ground beef, breaking it up with a wooden spoon or spatula. Continue to cook the beef for 7 to 10 minutes, until fully browned. 5. Stir in the broth and tomato paste and stir to coat the meat. Sprinkle in the salt, black pepper, and white pepper. 6. Transfer the meat mixture to a 9-by-13-inch baking dish. 7. To make the topping: In a food processor, combine the cauliflower rice, mozzarella, cream, butter, salt, black pepper, white pepper, and garlic powder. Purée on high speed until the mixture is smooth, scraping down the sides of the bowl as necessary. 8. Spread the cauliflower mash over the top of the meat and smooth the top. 9. Bake for 10 minutes, until the topping is just lightly browned. Let cool for 5 minutes, then serve.

Per Serving:

Calories: 564 | fat: 44g | protein: 30g | carbs: 13g | net carbs: 7g | fiber: 6g

Cardamom Pork Ribs

Prep time: 15 minutes | Cook time: 25 minutes | Serves 3

¼ teaspoon ground cardamom
½ teaspoon minced ginger
4 tablespoons apple cider vinegar
¼ teaspoon sesame seeds

10 ounces (283 g) pork ribs, chopped
¼ teaspoon chili flakes
1 tablespoon avocado oil

1. In the mixing bowl, mix up ground cardamom. Minced ginger, apple cider vinegar, sesame seeds, chili flakes, and avocado oil. 2. Then brush the pork ribs with the cardamom mixture and leave for 10 minutes to marinate. 3. After this, heat up the instant pot on Sauté mode for 2 minutes. 4. Add the marinated pork ribs and all remaining marinade. 5. Cook the pork ribs on Sauté mode for 25 minutes. Flip the ribs on another side every 5 minutes.

Per Serving:

Calories: 271 | fat: 17g | protein: 1g | carbs: 1g | net carbs: 1g | fiber: 0g

Kung Pao Beef

Prep time: 15 minutes | Cook time: 20 minutes | Serves 4

Sauce/Marinade:
¼ cup coconut aminos
1½ tablespoons white wine vinegar
1½ tablespoons sherry wine
1 tablespoon avocado oil
1 teaspoon chili paste
Stir-Fry:
1 pound (454 g) flank steak, thinly sliced against the grain

and cut into bite-size pieces
2 tablespoons avocado oil, divided into 1 tablespoon and 1 tablespoon
2 medium bell peppers (6 ounces / 170 g each), red and green, chopped into bite-size pieces
2 cloves garlic, minced
¼ cup roasted peanuts

1. Make the sauce/marinade: In a small bowl, whisk together the coconut aminos, white wine vinegar, sherry wine, avocado oil, and chili paste. 2. Make the stir-fry: Place the sliced steak into a medium bowl. Pour half of the sauce/marinade (about ¼ cup) over it and stir to coat. Cover and chill for at least 30 minutes, up to 2 hours. 3. About 10 minutes before marinating time is up or when you are ready to cook, in a large wok or sauté pan, heat 1 tablespoon of the oil over medium-high heat. Add the bell peppers and sauté for 7 to 8 minutes, until soft and browned. 4. Add the garlic and sauté for about 1 minute, until fragrant. 5. Remove the peppers and garlic, and cover to keep warm. 6. Add the remaining 1 tablespoon oil to the pan and heat over very high heat. Add the steak, arrange in a single layer, and cook undisturbed for 2 to 4 minutes per side, until browned on each side. If it's not cooked through yet, you can stir-fry for longer. Remove the meat from the pan and cover to keep warm. 7. Add the reserved marinade to the pan. Bring to a vigorous simmer and continue to simmer for a few minutes, until thickened. 8. Add the cooked meat, cooked peppers, and roasted peanuts to the pan and toss in the sauce.

Per Serving:

Calories: 341 | fat: 20g | protein: 27g | carbs: 9g | net carbs: 7g | fiber: 2g

Baked Pork Meatballs in Pasta Sauce

Prep time: 10 minutes | Cook time: 35 minutes | Serves 6

2 pounds (907 g) ground pork
1 tablespoon olive oil
1 cup pork rinds, crushed
3 cloves garlic, minced
½ cup coconut milk
2 eggs, beaten
½ cup grated Parmesan cheese
½ cup grated asiago cheese

Salt and black pepper to taste
¼ cup chopped parsley
2 jars sugar-free marinara sauce
½ teaspoon Italian seasoning
1 cup Italian blend kinds of cheeses
Chopped basil to garnish

1. Preheat the oven to 400ºF, line a cast iron pan with foil and oil it with cooking spray. Set aside. 2. Combine the coconut milk and pork rinds in a bowl. Mix in the ground pork, garlic, Asiago cheese, Parmesan cheese, eggs, salt, and pepper, just until combined. Form balls of the mixture and place them in the prepared pan. Bake in the oven for 20 minutes at a reduced temperature of 370ºF. 3. Transfer the meatballs to a plate. Pour half of the marinara sauce in the baking pan. Place the meatballs back in the pan and pour the remaining marinara sauce all over them. Sprinkle with the Italian blend cheeses, drizzle with the olive oil, and then sprinkle with Italian seasoning. 4. Cover the pan with foil and put it back in the oven to bake for 10 minutes. After, remove the foil, and cook for 5 minutes. Once ready, take out the pan and garnish with basil. Serve on a bed of squash spaghetti.

Per Serving:

Calories: 575 | fat: 43g | protein: 39g | carbs: 8g | net carbs: 5g | fiber: 3g

Beef and Red Cabbage Stew

Prep time: 10 minutes | Cook time: 20 minutes | Serves 4

2 tablespoons butter, at room temperature
1 onion, chopped
2 garlic cloves, minced
1½ pounds (680 g) beef stew meat, cubed
2½ cups beef stock
8 ounces (227 g) sugar-free tomato sauce

2 cups shredded red cabbage
1 tablespoon coconut aminos
2 bay leaves
1 teaspoon dried parsley flakes
½ teaspoon crushed red pepper flakes
Sea salt and ground black pepper, to taste

1. Press the Sauté button to heat up the Instant Pot. Then, melt the butter. Cook the onion and garlic until softened. 2. Add beef stew meat and cook an additional 3 minutes or until browned. Stir the remaining ingredients into the Instant Pot. 3. Secure the lid. Choose Manual mode and High Pressure; cook for 15 minutes. Once cooking is complete, use a quick pressure release; carefully remove the lid. 4. Discard bay leaves and ladle into individual bowls. Enjoy!

Per Serving:

Calories: 320 | fat: 16g | protein: 39g | carbs: 7g | net carbs: 5g | fiber: 2g

Basil and Thyme Pork Loin

Prep time: 10 minutes | Cook time: 17 minutes | Serves 4

1 pound (454 g) pork loin	½ teaspoon salt
1 teaspoon dried basil	2 tablespoons apple cider
1 tablespoon avocado oil	vinegar
1 teaspoon dried thyme	1 cup water, for cooking

1. In the shallow bowl, mix up dried basil, avocado oil, thyme, salt, and apple cider vinegar. 2. Then rub the pork loin with the spice mixture and leave the meat for 10 minutes to marinate. 3. Wrap the meat in foil and put on the steamer rack. 4. Pour water and transfer the steamer rack with meat in the instant pot. 5. Close and seal the lid. Cook the meat on Manual (High Pressure) for 20 minutes. Allow the natural pressure release for 5 minutes. 6. Slice the cooked pork loin.

Per Serving:
Calories: 281 | fat: 16g | protein: 31g | carbs: 0g | net carbs:0 g | fiber: 0g

Garlic Pork Chops with Mint Pesto

Prep time: 10 minutes | Cook time: 2 hours | Serves 4

1 cup parsley	5 tablespoons avocado oil
1 cup mint	Salt, to taste
1½ onions, chopped	4 pork chops
⅓ cup pistachios	5 garlic cloves, minced
1 teaspoon lemon zest	Juice from 1 lemon

1. In a food processor, combine the parsley with avocado oil, mint, pistachios, salt, lemon zest, and 1 onion. Rub the pork with this mixture, place in a bowl, and refrigerate for 1 hour while covered. 2. Remove the chops and set to a baking dish, place in ½ onion, and garlic; sprinkle with lemon juice, and bake for 2 hours in the oven at 250ºF. Split amongst plates and enjoy.

Per Serving:
Calories: 567 | fat: 40g | protein: 37g | carbs: 7g | net carbs: 5g | fiber: 2g

Zucchini Rolls

Prep time: 10 minutes | Cook time: 0 minutes | Serves 4

ROLLS:	DIPPING SAUCE:
1 medium zucchini (about 7 ounces/200 g)	¼ cup (60 ml) extra-virgin olive oil or refined avocado oil
1 cup (120 g) cooked beef strips	2 tablespoons hot sauce
5 medium radishes, sliced thin	2 teaspoons fresh lime juice

1. Place the zucchini on a cutting board and, using a vegetable peeler, peel long strips from the zucchini until it is next to impossible to create a full, long strip. 2. Place a zucchini strip on a cutting board, with a short end facing you. Place a couple of pieces of beef and 3 or 4 radish slices at the short end closest to you. Roll it up, then stab with a toothpick to secure. Repeat with the remaining zucchini strips, placing the completed rolls on a serving plate. 3. In a small serving dish, whisk together the dipping sauce ingredients. Serve the dipping sauce alongside the rolls.

Per Serving:
Calories: 370 | fat: 33g | protein: 14g | carbs: 4g | net carbs: 3g | fiber: 1g

Smothered Bacon and Mushroom Burgers

Prep time: 10 minutes | Cook time: 15 minutes | Serves 4

5 slices bacon, diced	garnish
1 tablespoon plus 1 teaspoon Paleo fat, such as lard, tallow, or coconut oil	Special Sauce:
	¼ cup plus 2 tablespoons mayonnaise, homemade or store-bought
1⅔ pounds (726 g) mushrooms, sliced	¼ cup tomato sauce
⅔ cup thinly sliced onions	2 tablespoons plus 2 teaspoons
2 teaspoons fine sea salt, divided	Swerve confectioners'-style sweetener or equivalent amount
1¼ heaping teaspoons freshly ground black pepper, divided	of liquid or powdered sweetener
1⅓ pounds (590 g) 80% lean ground beef	1½ scant teaspoons coconut vinegar or apple cider vinegar
8 large lettuce leaves, for "buns"	½ rounded teaspoon fine sea salt
Cherry tomatoes, cut in half, for	½ rounded teaspoon freshly ground black pepper

1. Heat a large cast-iron skillet over medium-high heat and sauté the bacon until crispy, about 3 minutes. Add the Paleo fat to the pan, along with the mushrooms and onions, and sauté until the mushrooms are cooked through, about 4 minutes. Season with ¾ teaspoon of the salt and ½ teaspoon of the pepper. Using a slotted spoon, remove the bacon, mushrooms, and onions from the pan and set aside. Leave the fat in the pan. 2. Using your hands, form the meat into four ¾-inch-thick patties. Season the outsides of the patties with the remaining salt and pepper. Fry the burgers in the skillet over medium-high heat on both sides until cooked to your desired doneness. 3. Meanwhile, make the sauce: Place all the ingredients in an 8-ounce (227-g) jar with a lid. Cover and shake vigorously to combine. 4. To serve, place a burger on a lettuce leaf, then top it with one-fourth of the fried bacon, mushroom, and onion mixture, followed by 2 tablespoons of the sauce and another lettuce leaf (for a top "bun"). Repeat with the remaining burgers and toppings, and garnish each plate with cherry tomatoes.

Per Serving:
Calories: 570 | fat: 45g | protein: 25g | carbs: 6g | net carbs: 4g | fiber: 2g

Spinach and Provolone Steak Rolls

Prep time: 10 minutes | Cook time: 12 minutes | Makes 8 rolls

1 (1-pound / 454-g) flank steak, butterflied

8 (1-ounce / 28-g, ¼-inch-thick) deli slices provolone cheese

1 cup fresh spinach leaves

½ teaspoon salt

¼ teaspoon ground black pepper

1. Place steak on a large plate. Place provolone slices to cover steak, leaving 1-inch at the edges. Lay spinach leaves over cheese. Gently roll steak and tie with kitchen twine or secure with toothpicks. Carefully slice into eight pieces. Sprinkle each with salt and pepper. 2. Place rolls into ungreased air fryer basket, cut side up. Adjust the temperature to 400°F (204°C) and air fry for 12 minutes. Steak rolls will be browned and cheese will be melted when done and have an internal temperature of at least 150°F (66°C) for medium steak and 180°F (82°C) for well-done steak. Serve warm.

Per Serving:

Calorie: 155 | fat: 8g | protein: 19g | carbs: 1g | net carbs: 1g | fiber: 0g

Chapter 6 Salads

Basic Chicken Salad in Lettuce Cups

Prep time: 10 minutes | Cook time: 0 minutes | Serves 2

8 ounces (227 g) cooked chicken breast, diced (if using store-bought, make sure it's sugar-free)
½ red bell pepper, diced
¼ cup diced jicama
1 celery stalk, diced
2 tablespoons Primal Kitchen avocado oil mayonnaise
1 teaspoon Dijon mustard
4 slices cooked bacon, chopped

Splash freshly squeezed lemon juice
1 teaspoon fresh dill
Salt and freshly ground black pepper, to taste
4 romaine or butter lettuce leaves
1 tablespoon sliced almonds (optional)
Chopped fresh parsley, for serving (optional)

1. In a mixing bowl, toss together the chicken, bell pepper, jicama, and celery. 2. Add the mayonnaise, mustard, bacon, and lemon juice, then sprinkle in the dill, season with salt and pepper, and stir everything together. 3. Arrange the lettuce leaves on plates and scoop in the chicken salad mixture. 4. Sprinkling almonds and parsley on top before serving is completely optional but gives these cups a little extra flavor and a nutritional boost!

Per Serving:
Calories: 454 | fat: 30g | protein: 36g | carbs: 8g | net carbs: 6g | fiber: 2g

Cheeseburger Salad

Prep time: 10 minutes | Cook time: 10 minutes | Serves 2

1 tablespoon ghee
1 pound ground beef
Pink Himalayan salt
Freshly ground black pepper
½ cup finely chopped dill pickles

2 cups chopped romaine
½ cup shredded Cheddar cheese
2 tablespoons ranch salad dressing (I use Primal Kitchen Ranch)

1. In a medium skillet over medium-high heat, heat the ghee. 2. When the ghee is hot, add the ground beef, breaking it up into smaller pieces with a spoon. Stir, cooking until the beef is browned, about 10 minutes. Season with pink Himalayan salt and pepper. 3. Put the pickles in a large bowl, and add the romaine and cheese. 4. Using a slotted spoon, transfer the browned beef from the skillet to the bowl. 5. Top the salad with the dressing, and toss to thoroughly coat. 6. Divide into two bowls and serve.

Per Serving:
Calories: 662 | fat: 50g | protein: 47g | carbs: 6g | net carbs: 4g | fiber: 2g

Bigass Salad

Prep time: 5 minutes | Cook time: 0 minutes | Serves 1

3 to 4 cups lettuce or mixed greens
1 to 2 cups sliced veggies
¼ cup shredded Cheddar cheese (optional)
1 can (5 ounces / 142 g) tuna

packed in water, drained
¼ cup nuts (walnuts, pecans, almonds)
2 tablespoons sunflower or pumpkin seeds
2 tablespoons olive oil

1. In a large, shallow bowl, layer lettuce, veggies, and cheese in that order. Flake the tuna over the top. 2. When you are ready to eat, sprinkle the nuts and seeds over the top, and drizzle with the olive oil.

Per Serving:
Calories: 843 | fat: 63g | protein: 54g | carbs: 24g | net carbs: 10g | fiber: 14g

Kale Salad with Spicy Lime-Tahini Dressing

Prep time: 15 minutes | Cook time: 0 minutes | Serves 4

DRESSING:
½ cup (120 ml) avocado oil
¼ cup (60 ml) lime juice
¼ cup (60 ml) tahini
2 cloves garlic, minced
1 jalapeño pepper, seeded and finely diced
Handful of fresh cilantro leaves, chopped
½ teaspoon ground cumin
½ teaspoon finely ground sea salt

¼ teaspoon red pepper flakes
SALAD:
6 cups (360 g) destemmed kale leaves, roughly chopped
12 radishes, thinly sliced
1 green bell pepper, sliced
1 medium Hass avocado, peeled, pitted, and cubed (about 4 ounces /110 g of flesh)
¼ cup (30 g) hulled pumpkin seeds

1. Make the dressing: Place the dressing ingredients in a medium-sized bowl and whisk to combine. Set aside. 2. Make the salad: Rinse the kale under hot water for about 30 seconds to soften it and make it easier to digest. Dry the kale well, then place it in a large salad bowl. Add the remaining salad ingredients and toss to combine. 3. Divide the salad evenly among 4 bowls. Drizzle each bowl with ¼ cup (60 ml) of the dressing and serve.

Per Serving:
Calories: 517 | fat: 47g | protein: 11g | carbs: 21g | net carbs: 12g | fiber: 9g

Roasted Vegetable Salad

Prep time: 15 minutes | Cook time: 45 minutes | Serves 4

½ eggplant, diced

1 medium bulb fennel, diced

12 asparagus spears, diced

1 zucchini, diced

12 Brussels sprouts, halved

1 cup cubed fresh pumpkin

1 medium red or white onion, diced

4 tablespoons avocado oil

1 teaspoon minced garlic or garlic powder

1 teaspoon dried oregano or marjoram (or both)

1 teaspoon dried thyme

Salt and freshly ground black pepper, to taste

2 cups mixed greens (or any salad greens of choice)

Freshly grated Parmesan cheese, for serving (optional)

16 ounces (454 g) steak or black cod, for serving (optional)

1. Preheat the oven to 450ºF (235ºC). 2. In a mixing bowl, combine the eggplant, fennel, asparagus, zucchini, Brussels sprouts, pumpkin, and onion. Pour in the avocado oil, add the garlic, oregano or marjoram, and thyme, and season with salt and pepper. Mix together until the vegetables are well coated. 3. Spread the vegetables in an even layer on a baking sheet and roast for 35 to 45 minutes, checking occasionally and stirring every 15 to 20 minutes. (Your oven may be very powerful, so feel free to take the veggies out sooner than 35 minutes if they are browned to your liking.) 4. Divide the greens among four plates and evenly distribute the roasted vegetables on top. Sprinkle with freshly grated cheese and serve with steak or cod, if desired.

Per Serving:

Calories: 227 | fat: 15g | protein: 4g | carbs: 19g | net carbs: 12g | fiber: 7g

Warm Bacon Broccoli Salad

Prep time: 15 minutes | Cook time: 5 minutes | Makes 2 salads

2 cups fresh spinach leaves

¼ cup avocado oil

¼ cup red wine vinegar

1 tablespoon Dijon mustard

½ cup broccoli florets

1 tablespoon olive oil

¼ red onion, thinly sliced

Salt and freshly ground black pepper, to taste

2 or 3 cooked bacon slices, cut widthwise into strips

1. Place the spinach in a large bowl. Set aside. 2. In a small bowl, whisk the avocado oil, vinegar, and mustard. Set aside. 3. In a large skillet over medium-low heat, gently sauté the broccoli in the olive oil for about 4 minutes. Add the warm broccoli to the spinach, letting the broccoli slightly wilt the spinach leaves. 4. Add the red onion to the skillet. Give the dressing another whisk, add it to the bacon and spinach, and toss everything to coat. Season with salt and pepper. Top with the bacon strips and divide between two salad bowls.

Per Serving(1salad):

Calories: 400 | fat: 40g | protein: 6g | carbs: 4g | net carbs: 2g | fiber: 2g

Cajun Pork Belly Chopped Salad

Prep time: 15 minutes | Cook time: 1 hour 45 minutes | Serves 4

1 pound (455 g) side pork belly

1 tablespoon refined avocado oil

1½ tablespoons Cajun seasoning

SALAD:

2 cups (240 g) sliced radishes

3 green onions, sliced

1 bunch fresh cilantro (about 1¾ ounces/50 g), chopped

¼ cup (15 g) chopped fresh

mint

1 large zucchini (about 10½ ounces/300 g), diced

¼ cup (60 ml) refined avocado oil or extra-virgin olive oil

Juice of 2 limes

¼ teaspoon finely ground gray sea salt

2 drops liquid stevia

FOR SERVING (OPTIONAL):

Lime wedges

1. Remove the pork belly from its packaging and place it fat side up on a cutting board. Using a sharp knife, score the top with diagonal lines about ½ inch (1.25 cm) apart. Drizzle the entire pork belly with the avocado oil, and top with the Cajun seasoning. Rub thoroughly. Wrap in plastic wrap and set in the fridge for at least 2 hours and up to 24 hours. 2. When ready to cook the pork belly, preheat the oven to 500°F (260°C) and place the pork belly, fat side up, in a cast-iron or other broiler-safe pan. Cook for 15 minutes, until browned. Reduce the oven temperature to 325°F (163°C) and continue cooking for 1½ hours, or until the top and sides are dark brown and the internal temperature reaches 165°F (74°C). Remove the pork belly from the oven and set it on a cutting board; allow to rest for 5 minutes. 3. Meanwhile, prepare the salad: Place all the ingredients in a large bowl. Toss to combine, then spread out the salad on a large serving platter. 4. Using a sharp knife, slice the pork belly, then arrange the slices on top of the salad. Serve with lime wedges on the side, if desired.

Per Serving:

Calories: 1045 | fat: 105g | protein: 17g | carbs: 7g | net carbs: 4g | fiber: 3g

Zucchini Pasta Salad

Prep time: 5 minutes | Cook time: 0 minutes | Serves 4

4 medium zucchinis, spiral sliced

12 ounces (340 g) pitted black olives, cut in half lengthwise

1 pint (290 g) cherry tomatoes, cut in half lengthwise

½ cup (75 g) pine nuts

¼ cup plus 2 tablespoons (55 g) sesame seeds

⅔ cup (160 ml) creamy Italian dressing or other creamy salad dressing of choice

1. Place all the ingredients in a large mixing bowl. Toss to coat, then divide evenly between 4 serving plates or bowls.

Per Serving:

Calories: 562 | fat: 53g | protein: 9g | carbs: 22g | net carbs: 14g | fiber: 9g

Special Sauce Cobb Salad

Prep time: 15 minutes | Cook time: 10 minutes | Serves 4

4 bacon slices	Dash monk fruit or sweetener
¼ cup mayonnaise	of choice
½ teaspoon coconut vinegar or	8 cherry tomatoes, halved
apple cider vinegar	4 hard-boiled eggs, sliced
¼ teaspoon paprika	1 cup shredded sharp Cheddar
¼ teaspoon garlic powder	cheese
¼ teaspoon onion powder	8 cups chopped romaine lettuce
¼ teaspoon sea salt	or spinach

1. In a large skillet over medium-high heat, cook the bacon until crisp, 5 to 7 minutes. Remove the bacon to a paper towel. 2. While the bacon is cooking, prepare the dressing. In a medium bowl, whisk together the mayonnaise, vinegar, paprika, garlic powder, onion powder, salt, and sweetener. 3. To serve immediately, divide the lettuce among four serving bowls. To each bowl, add 4 tomato halves, 1 sliced egg, ¼ cup Cheddar, 1 crumbled bacon slice, and 1 tablespoon of dressing. Mix well. 4. To assemble and store for future meals, divide and layer the components in four quart-sized, wide-mouth mason jars, adding the ingredients in the following order: 1 tablespoon of dressing, 4 tomato halves, 1 sliced egg, ¼ cup Cheddar, 2 cups of romaine, and top with 1 crumbled bacon slice. Secure the lid tightly and store in the refrigerator. To serve, shake well and empty the jar into a bowl, or you can eat the salad right out of the jar!

Per Serving (1bowl):

Calories: 396 | fat: 34g | protein: 17g | carbs: 5g | net carbs: 3g | fiber: 2g

Marinated Bok Choy Salad

Prep time: 20 minutes | Cook time: 0 minutes | Serves 6

DRESSING:	mustard
⅓ cup (80 ml) extra-virgin olive	¼ teaspoon finely ground gray
oil or refined avocado oil	sea salt
3 tablespoons MCT oil	¼ teaspoon ground black
3 tablespoons apple cider	pepper
vinegar	2 drops liquid stevia
2 tablespoons coconut aminos	SALAD:
4 small cloves garlic, minced	8 cups (900 g) chopped bok
1 (2-inch/5-cm) piece fresh	choy (about 1 large head)
ginger root, minced	⅓ cup (40 g) sliced raw
2 teaspoons prepared yellow	almonds, divided

1. Combine the ingredients for the dressing in a large bowl. 2. Add the bok choy and ¼ cup (30 g) of the sliced almonds. Toss to coat. Cover the bowl and place in the fridge for at least 12 hours, but not longer than 3 days. 3. When ready to serve, divide the salad among 6 bowls and sprinkle each salad with the remaining sliced almonds.

Per Serving:

Calories: 234 | fat: 21g | protein: 4g | carbs: 7g | net carbs: 5g | fiber: 2g

Chicken and Bacon Salad with Sun-Dried Tomato Dressing

Prep time: 10 minutes | Cook time: 5 minutes | Serves 1

2 slices bacon	Pinch each salt and freshly
3 sun-dried tomatoes (packed in	ground black pepper
olive oil)	1 cup Bibb or butter lettuce
1 tablespoon olive oil	leaves
1 teaspoon minced shallots	4 ounces (113 g) cooked
¼ teaspoon garlic powder	chicken breast and/or thigh
½ teaspoon dried oregano	meat, diced (if you use store-
1 teaspoon nutritional yeast	bought, make sure it doesn't
or grated cheese (optional but	contain any added sugar)
recommended)	¼ cup cherry tomatoes, halved
½ teaspoon freshly squeezed	½ avocado, pitted, peeled, and
lemon juice (optional)	diced

1. Heat a shallow skillet over medium heat. When warm, cook the bacon to your desired crispness, about 5 minutes. Turn off the heat and let the bacon sit in the skillet. 2. To make the dressing, in a blender, combine the sun-dried tomatoes, olive oil, shallots, garlic powder, oregano, nutritional yeast or cheese (if using), lemon juice (if using), and salt and pepper. Whirl away until smooth. 3. To construct the salad, put the lettuce on a plate. Top with the chicken, cherry tomatoes, and avocado. Lay the bacon on top (alternatively, you can chop up the bacon and sprinkle it on after you've dressed the salad). If you'd like, pour the bacon pan drippings over the salad (trust me, it's amazing). Spoon on about 1 to 2 tablespoons of dressing and dig in!

Per Serving:

Calories: 858 | fat: 62g | protein: 52g | carbs: 23g | net carbs: 9g | fiber: 14g

Big Mac Salad

Prep time: 10 minutes | Cook time: 15 minutes | Serves 4

Salad	½ cup diced tomato
1 pound lean ground turkey	⅓ cup shredded Cheddar cheese
6 cups chopped iceberg lettuce	1 tablespoon sesame seeds
1 large pickle, sliced into thin	Special Sauce
rounds	¼ cup full-fat mayonnaise
½ cup diced onion	¼ cup no-sugar-added ketchup

1 In a medium skillet over medium heat, cook ground turkey until well done (about 10–15 minutes), stirring regularly. Do not drain fat. Let cool. 2 In a large salad bowl, toss lettuce, pickle, onion, tomato, and shredded cheese. 3 Stir in cooled meat. 4 In a small bowl, mix the sauce ingredients. Add to salad and toss. 5 Sprinkle salad with sesame seeds and serve.

Per Serving:

Calories: 347 | fat: 23g | protein: 25g | carbs: 8g | net carbs: 5g | fiber: 2g

Olive Garden Salad

Prep time: 10 minutes | Cook time: 0 minutes | Serves 4

6 cups chopped iceberg lettuce	3 tablespoons olive oil
2 Roma tomatoes, sliced into rounds	1 tablespoon red wine vinegar
¼ cup sliced red onion	¼ teaspoon garlic powder
1 cup whole pepperoncini	⅛ teaspoon salt
1 cup whole black olives	⅛ teaspoon black pepper
	⅓ cup grated Parmesan cheese

1 Mix all vegetables and olives in a large salad bowl. 2 In a small bowl, mix oil, vinegar, and spices together. 3 Pour dressing over salad, toss, and top with Parmesan cheese. Serve immediately.

Per Serving:

Calories: 217 | fat: 18g | protein: 4g | carbs: 8g | net carbs: 6g | fiber: 2g

Shaved Asparagus Salad with Egg

Prep time: 20 minutes | Cook time: 0 minutes | Serves 4

For the Dressing:	For the Salad:
¼ cup good-quality olive oil	½ pound asparagus stalks (about 20 medium), woody ends snapped off
1½ tablespoons balsamic vinegar	
½ teaspoon minced garlic	4 hardboiled eggs, peeled and chopped
Sea salt, for seasoning	
Freshly ground black pepper, for seasoning	¼ cup chopped pecans

Make the Dressing: Mix the dressing. In a small bowl, stir together the olive oil, vinegar, and garlic. Season with salt and pepper and set it aside. Make the Salad: 1. Prepare the asparagus. Use a vegetable peeler to make long, thin asparagus ribbons, and put them in a large bowl. 2. Mix the salad. Add the eggs, pecans, and dressing to the asparagus and toss to combine the ingredients. 3. Serve. Divide the salad between four plates and serve.

Per Serving:

Calories: 254 | fat: 23g | protein: 8g | carbs: 5g | net carbs: 3g | fiber: 2g

Greek Salad with Avocado

Prep time: 10 minutes | Cook time: 0 minutes | Serves 4

Salad:	1 medium avocado, cut into ½-inch cubes
3 Roma (plum) tomatoes, seeded and chopped	
	½ cup crumbled feta cheese
1 medium cucumber, peeled and cut into ½-inch pieces	¼ medium red onion, thinly sliced
1 green bell pepper, cored, seeded, and cut into ½-inch strips	Dressing:
	¼ cup extra-virgin olive oil
1 cup pitted Kalamata olives	2 tablespoons red wine vinegar
	1 tablespoon chopped fresh

parsley	½ teaspoon pink Himalayan sea salt
1 garlic clove, minced	
1 teaspoon dried oregano	¼ teaspoon freshly ground black pepper
1 teaspoon freshly squeezed lemon juice	

1. To make the salad: In a large bowl, combine the tomatoes, cucumber, bell pepper, olives, avocado, feta, and red onion. 2. To make the dressing: In a small bowl, combine the olive oil, vinegar, parsley, garlic, oregano, lemon juice, salt, and pepper. 3. Toss the salad ingredients until well coated with the dressing.

Per Serving:

Calories: 334 | fat: 31g | protein: 6g | carbs: 12g | net carbs: 6g | fiber: 6g

Blt Wedge Salad

Prep time: 10 minutes | Cook time: 10 minutes | Serves 2

4 bacon slices	Chunky Blue Cheese Dressing)
½ head iceberg lettuce, halved	¼ cup blue cheese crumbles
2 tablespoons blue cheese salad dressing (I use Trader Joe's	½ cup halved grape tomatoes

1. In a large skillet over medium-high heat, cook the bacon on both sides until crispy, about 8 minutes. Transfer the bacon to a paper towel–lined plate to drain and cool for 5 minutes. Transfer to a cutting board, and chop the bacon. 2. Place the lettuce wedges on two plates. Top each with half of the blue cheese dressing, the blue cheese crumbles, the halved grape tomatoes, and the chopped bacon, and serve.

Per Serving:

Calories: 278 | fat: 20g | protein: 15g | carbs: 9g | net carbs: 7g | fiber: 3g

Avocado Salad with Arugula and Red Onion

Prep time: 10 minutes | Cook time: 0 minutes | Serves 2

2 cups arugula, washed and dried	1 tablespoon Dijon mustard
	Salt and freshly ground black pepper, to taste
¼ red onion, thinly sliced	
½ cup olive oil	1 avocado, peeled, halved, pitted, and diced or sliced
¼ cup balsamic vinegar	

1. In a large bowl, combine the arugula and red onion. 2. In a small bowl, whisk together the olive oil, vinegar, mustard, and some salt and pepper. Pour the dressing over the salad and toss well to combine. 3. Divide the salad between two bowls and top each with half an avocado. Season with a bit more salt and pepper and serve.

Per Serving:

Calories: 686 | fat: 70g | protein: 3g | carbs: 11g | net carbs: 3g | fiber: 8g

Classic Egg Salad

Prep time: 10 minutes | Cook time: 0 minutes | serves 4

6 hard-boiled eggs, peeled and chopped	mustard
¼ cup mayonnaise	¼ teaspoon paprika
1 tablespoon finely chopped onions	¼ teaspoon ground black pepper
1 tablespoon dill relish	⅛ teaspoon salt
1 teaspoon prepared yellow	Fresh spinach leaves, for serving (optional)

1. In a medium-sized mixing bowl, stir together all the ingredients until well incorporated. Serve over spinach leaves, if desired. Leftovers can be stored in an airtight container in the refrigerator for up to 3 days.

Per Serving:
Calories: 213 | fat: 18g | protein: 10g | carbs: 1g | net carbs: 1g | fiber: 0g

Taverna-Style Greek Salad

Prep time: 20 minutes | Cook time: 0 minutes | Serves 4

4 to 5 medium tomatoes, roughly chopped	1 teaspoon dried oregano or fresh herbs of your choice, such as parsley, cilantro, chives, or basil, divided
1 large cucumber, peeled and roughly chopped	
1 medium green bell pepper, sliced	½ cup extra-virgin olive oil, divided
1 small red onion, sliced	1 pack feta cheese
16 pitted Kalamata olives	Optional: salt, pepper, and fresh oregano, for garnish
¼ cup capers, or more olives	

1. Place the vegetables in a large serving bowl. Add the olives, capers, feta, half of the dried oregano and half of the olive oil. Mix to combine. Place the whole piece of feta cheese on top, sprinkle with the remaining dried oregano, and drizzle with the remaining olive oil. Season to taste and serve immediately, or store in the fridge for up to 1 day.

Per Serving:
Calories: 320 | fat: 31g | protein: 3g | carbs: 11g | fiber: 4g | sodium: 445mg

Taco Salad

Prep time: 10 minutes | Cook time: 10 minutes | Serves 2

1 tablespoon ghee	1 avocado, cubed
1 pound ground beef	½ cup halved grape tomatoes
Pink Himalayan salt	½ cup shredded cheese (I use Mexican blend)
Freshly ground black pepper	
2 cups chopped romaine	

1. In a large skillet over medium-high heat, heat the ghee. 2. When the ghee is hot, add the ground beef, breaking it up into smaller pieces with a spoon. Stir, cooking until the beef is browned, about 10 minutes. Season with pink Himalayan salt and pepper. 3. Divide the romaine into two bowls. Season with pink Himalayan salt and pepper. 4. Add the avocado and tomatoes, top with the beef and shredded cheese, and serve.

Per Serving:
Calories: 659 | fat: 52g | protein: 48g | carbs: 10g | net carbs: 4g | fiber: 6g

Avocado Caprese Salad

Prep time: 5 minutes | Cook time: 0 minutes | Serves 2

2 cups arugula	4 fresh mozzarella balls, sliced
1 tablespoon olive oil, divided	1 Roma tomato, sliced
Pink Himalayan salt	4 fresh basil leaves, cut into ribbons
Freshly ground black pepper	
1 avocado, sliced	

1. In a large bowl, toss the arugula with ½ tablespoon of olive oil and season with pink Himalayan salt and pepper. 2. Divide the arugula between two plates. 3. Top the arugula with the avocado, mozzarella, and tomatoes, and drizzle with the remaining ½ tablespoon of olive oil. Season with pink Himalayan salt and pepper. 4. Sprinkle the basil on top and serve.

Per Serving:
Calories: 320 | fat: 27g | protein: 13g | carbs: 10g | net carbs: 5g | fiber: 6g

Avocado Egg Salad Lettuce Cups

Prep time: 15 minutes | Cook time: 15 minutes | Serves 2

For The Hardboiled Eggs:	½ teaspoon freshly squeezed lemon juice
4 large eggs	
For The Egg Salad:	4 butter lettuce cups, washed and patted dry with paper towels or a clean dish towel
1 avocado, halved	
Pink Himalayan salt	
Freshly ground black pepper	2 radishes, thinly sliced

To Make The Hardboiled Eggs: 1. In a medium saucepan, cover the eggs with water. Place over high heat, and bring the water to a boil. Once it is boiling, turn off the heat, cover, and leave on the burner for 10 to 12 minutes. 2. Remove the eggs with a slotted spoon and run them under cold water for 1 minute or submerge them in an ice bath. 3. Then gently tap the shells and peel. Run cold water over your hands as you remove the shells. To Make The Egg Salad: 1. In a medium bowl, chop the hardboiled eggs. 2. Add the avocado to the bowl, and mash the flesh with a fork. Season with pink Himalayan salt and pepper, add the lemon juice, and stir to combine. 3. Place the 4 lettuce cups on two plates. Top the lettuce cups with the egg salad and the slices of radish and serve.

Per Serving:
Calories: 258 | fat: 20g | protein: 15g | carbs: 8g | net carbs: 3g | fiber: 5g

Caesar Salad with Anchovies and Pancetta

Prep time: 10 minutes | Cook time: 10 minutes | Serves 2

1 egg yolk, at room temperature	needed
2 garlic cloves, chopped	1 can (2 ounces / 57 g)
2 teaspoons Dijon mustard	anchovies packed in olive oil
Juice from 1 large lemon, at	1 cup extra-virgin olive oil
room temperature	1 cup grated Parmesan cheese
1 teaspoon kosher salt	1 teaspoon butter
½ teaspoon freshly ground	4 ounces (113 g) diced pancetta
black pepper, plus more as	4 cups chopped romaine lettuce

1. In a high-powered blender, combine the egg yolk, garlic, Dijon mustard, lemon juice, salt, pepper, half the anchovies, and ¼ cup oil. Blend for 10 seconds. With the blender running, slowly pour in the remaining oil in a thin stream so the dressing emulsifies. Add in ½ cup of the Parmesan cheese and pulse a few times to combine. 2. Melt the butter in a small skillet and sauté the pancetta until crisp. 3. Toss the lettuce with ½ cup of the dressing. Roughly chop the remaining anchovies and place on top. Sprinkle with the crispy pancetta. Top with Parmesan crisps or the remaining grated Parmesan, and additional freshly ground pepper. If desired, drizzle with more dressing.

Per Serving:
Calories: 602 | fat: 53g | protein: 28g | carbs: 5g | net carbs: 3g | fiber: 2g

Tuscan Kale Salad with Anchovies

Prep time: 15 minutes | Cook time: 0 minutes | Serves 4

1 large bunch lacinato or	chopped
dinosaur kale	2 to 3 tablespoons freshly
¼ cup toasted pine nuts	squeezed lemon juice (from 1
1 cup shaved or coarsely	large lemon)
shredded fresh Parmesan cheese	2 teaspoons red pepper flakes
¼ cup extra-virgin olive oil	(optional)
8 anchovy fillets, roughly	

1. Remove the rough center stems from the kale leaves and roughly tear each leaf into about 4-by-1-inch strips. Place the torn kale in a large bowl and add the pine nuts and cheese. 2. In a small bowl, whisk together the olive oil, anchovies, lemon juice, and red pepper flakes (if using). Drizzle over the salad and toss to coat well. Let sit at room temperature 30 minutes before serving, tossing again just prior to serving.

Per Serving:
Calories: 333 | fat: 27g | protein: 16g | carbs: 12g | fiber: 4g | sodium: 676mg

Simple Crab Salad

Prep time: 5 minutes | Cook time: 0 minutes | Serves 2

⅓ cup mayonnaise, homemade	crab meat, drained
or store-bought	½ cup diced celery
1 teaspoon lemon juice	¼ cup diced red onions
½ teaspoon Dijon mustard	For Serving:
1 teaspoon minced fresh	1 cup coarsely chopped romaine
tarragon leaves	lettuce
½ teaspoon fine sea salt	Freshly ground black pepper
2 (6-ounce / 170-g) cans lump	(optional)

1. Place the mayo, lemon juice, mustard, tarragon, and salt in a bowl. Stir well to combine. Add the crab meat, celery, and onions. Gently fold the ingredients together until well combined. 2. If not using right away, cover the crab salad and store in the fridge for up to 4 days. Do not dress the lettuce with the crab salad until serving. 3. Just before serving, place the crab salad on a bed of romaine lettuce and sprinkle with freshly ground pepper, if desired.

Per Serving:
Calories: 382 | fat: 27g | protein: 31g | carbs: 4g | net carbs: 3g | fiber: 1g

Chapter 7 Snacks and Appetizers

Crispy Parmesan Crackers

Prep time: 10 minutes | Cook time: 5 minutes | Makes 8 crackers

1 teaspoon butter	cheese, shredded or freshly
8 ounces full-fat Parmesan	grated

1. Preheat the oven to 400°F. 2. Line a baking sheet with parchment paper and lightly grease the paper with the butter. 3. Spoon the Parmesan cheese onto the baking sheet in mounds, spread evenly apart. 4. Spread out the mounds with the back of a spoon until they are flat. 5. Bake the crackers until the edges are browned and the centers are still pale, about 5 minutes. 6. Remove the sheet from the oven, and remove the crackers with a spatula to paper towels. Lightly blot the tops with additional paper towels and let them completely cool. 7. Store in a sealed container in the refrigerator for up to 4 days.

Per Serving (1cracker):

Calories: 133 | fat: 11g | protein: 11g | carbs: 1g | net carbs: 1g | fiber: 0g

Bok Choy Salad Boats with Shrimp

Prep time: 8 minutes | Cook time: 2 minutes | Serves 8

26 shrimp, cleaned and deveined	⅓ cup olives, pitted and sliced
2 tablespoons fresh lemon juice	4 tablespoons olive oil
1 cup water	2 tablespoons apple cider vinegar
Sea salt and ground black pepper, to taste	8 Bok choy leaves
4 ounces (113 g) feta cheese, crumbled	2 tablespoons fresh basil leaves, snipped
2 tomatoes, diced	2 tablespoons chopped fresh mint leaves

1. Toss the shrimp and lemon juice in the Instant Pot until well coated. Pour in the water. 2. Lock the lid. Select the Manual mode and set the cooking time for 2 minutes at Low Pressure. 3. When the timer beeps, perform a quick pressure release. Carefully remove the lid. 4. Season the shrimp with salt and pepper to taste, then let them cool completely. 5. Toss the shrimp with the feta cheese, tomatoes, olives, olive oil, and vinegar until well incorporated. 6. Divide the salad evenly onto each Bok choy leaf and place them on a serving plate. Scatter the basil and mint leaves on top and serve immediately.

Per Serving:

Calories: 129 | fat: 11g | protein: 5g | carbs: 3g | net carbs: 2g | fiber: 1g

Cheese Stuffed Mushrooms

Prep time: 15 minutes | Cook time: 8 minutes | Serves 4

1 cup cremini mushroom caps	1 ounce (28 g) Monterey Jack
1 tablespoon chopped scallions	cheese, shredded
1 tablespoon chopped chives	1 teaspoon butter, softened
1 teaspoon cream cheese	½ teaspoon smoked paprika
1 teaspoon sour cream	1 cup water, for cooking

1. Trim the mushroom caps if needed and wash them well. 2. After this, in the mixing bowl, mix up scallions, chives, cream cheese, sour cream, butter, and smoked paprika. 3. Then fill the mushroom caps with the cream cheese mixture and top with shredded Monterey Jack cheese. 4. Pour water and insert the trivet in the instant pot. 5. Arrange the stuffed mushrooms caps on the trivet and close the lid. 6. Cook the meal on Manual (High Pressure) for 8 minutes. 7. Then make a quick pressure release.

Per Serving:

Calories: 45 | fat: 4g | protein: 3g | carbs: 1g | net carbs: 1g | fiber: 0g

Snappy Bacon Asparagus

Prep time: 20 minutes | Cook time: 25 minutes | Serves 6

24 asparagus spears	2 tablespoons olive oil
6 strips no-sugar-added bacon, uncooked	⅛ teaspoon salt

1 My favorite part of preparing asparagus is the SNAP. Grab the "nonpointed" end of stalk and bend until it breaks. This usually happens about an inch from the end with the cut. Now, line up asparagus and cut entire bunch at "snapping" point, making all of your stalks uniform in length. Fancy, right? 2 On a microwave-safe plate, microwave asparagus 2 minutes to soften. Let cool 5 minutes. 3 Lay strip of bacon on a cutting board at 45-degree angle. Lay four asparagus spears centered on bacon in an "up and down" position. 4 Pick up bacon and asparagus where they meet and wrap two ends of bacon around asparagus in opposite directions. 5 Wrap bacon tightly and secure, pinning bacon to asparagus at ends with toothpicks. Don't worry if bacon doesn't cover entire spears. 6 Brush asparagus with olive oil and sprinkle with salt. 7 Heat a medium nonstick skillet over medium heat. Cook asparagus/bacon 3–5 minutes per side while turning to cook thoroughly. Continue flipping until bacon is brown and crispy.

Per Serving:

Calories: 106 | fat: 8g | protein: 5g | carbs: 3g | net carbs: 2g | fiber: 1g

Taco Beef Bites

Prep time: 10 minutes | Cook time: 15 minutes | Serves 6

10 ounces (283 g) ground beef	cheese
3 eggs, beaten	1 teaspoon taco seasoning
⅓ cup shredded Mozzarella	1 teaspoon sesame oil

1. In the mixing bowl mix up ground beef, eggs, Mozzarella, and taco seasoning. 2. Then make the small meat bites from the mixture. 3. Heat up sesame oil in the instant pot. 4. Put the meat bites in the hot oil and cook them for 5 minutes from each side on Sauté mode.

Per Serving:

Calories: 132 | fat: 6g | protein: 17g | carbs: 1g | net carbs: 1g | fiber: 0g

Hushpuppies

Prep time: 10 minutes | Cook time: 15 minutes | Makes 10 hushpuppies

High-quality oil, for frying	½ teaspoon salt
1 cup finely ground blanched almond flour	¼ cup finely chopped onions
1 tablespoon coconut flour	¼ cup heavy whipping cream
1 teaspoon baking powder	1 large egg, beaten

1. Attach a candy thermometer to a Dutch oven or other large heavy pot, then pour in 3 inches of oil and set over medium-high heat. Heat the oil to 375°F. 2. In a medium-sized bowl, stir together the almond flour, coconut flour, baking powder, and salt. Stir in the rest of the ingredients and mix until blended. Do not overmix. 3. Use a tablespoon-sized cookie scoop to gently drop the batter into the hot oil. Don't overcrowd the hushpuppies; cook them in two batches. Fry for 3 minutes, then use a mesh skimmer or slotted spoon to turn and fry them for 3 more minutes or until golden brown on all sides. 4. Use the skimmer or slotted spoon to remove the hushpuppies from the oil and place on a paper towel–lined plate to drain. They are best served immediately.

Per Serving:

Calories: 172 | fat: 14g | protein: 6g | carbs: 5g | net carbs: 3g | fiber: 3g

Olive Pâté

Prep time: 10 minutes | Cook time: 0 minutes | serves 6

1 cup pitted green olives	1 teaspoon freshly ground black
1 cup pitted black olives	pepper
¼ cup cold-pressed olive oil	2 thyme sprigs

1. In a food processor, combine all the ingredients and pulse until the mixture is thick and chunky. 2. Transfer the pâté to a small serving bowl and serve with crackers.

Per Serving:

Calories: 171 | fat: 17g | protein: 0g | carbs: 4g | net carbs: 4g | fiber: 1g

Chinese Spare Ribs

Prep time: 3 minutes | Cook time: 24 minutes | Serves 6

1½ pounds (680 g) spare ribs	1 tablespoon coconut aminos
Salt and ground black pepper, to taste	1 teaspoon ginger-garlic paste
2 tablespoons sesame oil	½ teaspoon crushed red pepper flakes
½ cup chopped green onions	½ teaspoon dried parsley
½ cup chicken stock	2 tablespoons sesame seeds, for serving
2 tomatoes, crushed	
2 tablespoons sherry	

1. Season the spare ribs with salt and black pepper to taste. 2. Set your Instant Pot to Sauté and heat the sesame oil. 3. Add the seasoned spare ribs and sear each side for about 3 minutes. 4. Add the remaining ingredients except the sesame seeds to the Instant Pot and stir well. 5. Secure the lid. Select the Meat/Stew mode and set the cooking time for 18 minutes at High Pressure. 6. When the timer beeps, perform a natural pressure release for 10 minutes, then release any remaining pressure. Carefully remove the lid. 7. Serve topped with the sesame seeds.

Per Serving:

Calories: 336 | fat: 16g | protein: 43g | carbs: 3g | net carbs: 2g | fiber: 1g

Breaded Mushroom Nuggets

Prep time: 15 minutes | Cook time: 50 minutes | Serves 4

24 cremini mushrooms (about 1 pound/455 g)	½ teaspoon finely ground sea salt
2 large eggs	2 tablespoons avocado oil
½ cup (55 g) blanched almond flour	½ cup (120 ml) honey mustard dressing, for serving (optional)
1 teaspoon garlic powder	Special Equipment (Optional):
1 teaspoon paprika	Toothpicks

1. Preheat the oven to 350°F (177°C). Line a rimmed baking sheet with parchment paper or a silicone baking mat. 2. Break the stems off the mushrooms or cut them short so that the stems are level with the caps. 3. Crack the eggs into a small bowl and whisk. 4. Place the almond flour, garlic powder, paprika, and salt in a medium-sized bowl and whisk to combine. 5. Dip one mushroom at a time into the eggs, then use the same hand to drop it into the flour mixture, being careful not to get the flour mixture on that hand. Rotate the mushroom in the flour mixture with a fork to coat on all sides, then transfer it to the lined baking sheet. Repeat with the remaining mushrooms. 6. Drizzle the coated mushrooms with the oil. Bake for 50 minutes, or until the tops begin to turn golden. 7. Remove from the oven and serve with the dressing, if using. If serving to friends and family, provide toothpicks.

Per Serving:

Calories: 332 | fat: 29g | protein: 8g | carbs: 9g | net carbs: 7g | fiber: 2g

Fresh Rosemary Keto Bread

Prep time: 1 hour 45 minutes | Cook time: 55 minutes | serves 6

1½ cups warm water, divided, plus up to ¼ cup more if needed

1 (¼-ounce) packet active dry yeast

1 teaspoon cane sugar

1 cup coconut flour

3 tablespoons ground psyllium husk

1 rosemary sprig

¾ cup tahini

Sea salt

1. In a small bowl, whisk together ½ cup of warm water with the yeast and sugar. Set aside for 10 minutes to allow the yeast to activate and foam. 2. In a separate small mixing bowl, whisk together the coconut flour, psyllium, and rosemary. 3. In a large mixing bowl, stir together the yeast mixture, tahini, and the remaining 1 cup of warm water. 4. Stir the dry ingredients into the wet ingredients, making sure there are no clumps or dry crumbles. If the dough is crumbly or not well combined, add up to ¼ cup of warm water, 1 tablespoon at a time, until the dough comes together. 5. Line a bread pan with parchment paper and press the dough into the pan. If you don't have parchment paper, use a greased pan. Set the dough to rise in a cool, dark place for 90 minutes. It should rise and expand to double its original size. 6. Preheat the oven to 350°F. 7. Bake the bread for 50 to 55 minutes, or until the crust is firm to the touch. 8. While the bread is still warm, remove it from the pan. Let it cool completely before slicing and serving.

Per Serving:

Calories: 278 | fat: 18g | protein: 8g | carbs: 24g | net carbs: 10g | fiber: 14g

Crab Stuffed Mushrooms

Prep time: 10 minutes | Cook time: 20 minutes | Serves 4

1 cup cooked chopped crab

1 cup cream cheese, softened

½ cup grated Parmesan cheese

¼ cup ground almonds

1 scallion, chopped

1 tablespoon chopped fresh

parsley

1 teaspoon minced garlic

12 large button mushrooms, cleaned and stemmed

Olive oil cooking spray

1. Preheat the oven. Set the oven temperature to 375°F. Line a baking sheet with parchment paper. 2. Mix the filling. In a large bowl, stir together the crab, cream cheese, Parmesan, almonds, scallion, parsley, and garlic until everything is well mixed. 3. Precook the mushrooms. Place the mushrooms stem-side up on the baking sheet and lightly spray them with olive oil. Bake them for 2 minutes then drain them stem-side down on paper towels. 4. Stuff the mushrooms. Turn the mushrooms over and place them back on the baking sheet. Spoon about 1½ tablespoons of the filling into each mushroom. 5. Bake the mushrooms. Bake for 15 minutes until the mushrooms are lightly golden and bubbly. 6. Serve. Arrange the mushrooms on a serving platter.

Per Serving:

Calories: 300 | fat: 25g | protein: 16g | carbs: 4g | net carbs: 4g | fiber: 0g

Bar Side Mozzarella Sticks

Prep time: 20 minutes | Cook time: 20 minutes | Makes 16 sticks

3 ounces pork rinds, finely ground

¼ cup grated Parmesan cheese, plus extra for garnish

½ teaspoon dried oregano leaves

½ teaspoon red pepper flakes

½ teaspoon pink Himalayan salt

½ teaspoon ground black pepper

2 large eggs

1 tablespoon heavy whipping cream

8 sticks mozzarella string cheese

2 cups coconut oil, for deep-frying

Low-carb marinara sauce, for serving (optional)

1. Place the pork rinds, Parmesan, oregano, red pepper flakes, salt, and pepper in a shallow dish and combine with a fork. 2. Place the eggs and cream in a separate shallow dish and lightly beat with a fork. 3. Cut each stick of string cheese in half crosswise. Dip each piece in the egg mixture and then in the pork rind mixture. Make sure that each piece has a thick coating. You may have to press the breading into the cheese to ensure an even coat. Place on a plate and freeze for 2 hours. 4. In a 2-quart saucepan, heat the oil over medium-high heat until it reaches between 330°F and 345°F on a deep-fry thermometer. 5. Remove the breaded cheese sticks from the freezer. Fry in batches for 3 to 5 minutes per batch, until golden brown. Use a slotted spoon to remove the sticks from the oil and place on a paper towel–lined plate to drain. Allow to cool for 5 minutes, then garnish with grated Parmesan. Serve with marinara sauce, if desired. 6. Store leftovers in a sealed container in the refrigerator for up to 4 days. Reheat in a preheated 350°F oven for 10 minutes.

Per Serving:

Calories: 356 | fat: 25g | protein: 32g | carbs: 2g | net carbs: 2g | fiber: 0g

Roasted Garlic Bulbs

Prep time: 2 minutes | Cook time: 25 minutes | Serves 4

4 bulbs garlic

1 tablespoon avocado oil

1 teaspoon salt

Pinch of black pepper

1 cup water

1. Slice the pointy tops off the bulbs of garlic to expose the cloves. 2. Drizzle the avocado oil on top of the garlic and sprinkle with the salt and pepper. 3. Place the bulbs in the steamer basket, cut-side up. Alternatively, you may place them on a piece of aluminum foil with the sides pulled up and resting on top of the trivet. Place the steamer basket in the pot. 4. Close the lid and seal the vent. Cook on High Pressure for 25 minutes. Quick release the steam. 5. Let the garlic cool completely before removing the bulbs from the pot. 6. Hold the stem end (bottom) of the bulb and squeeze out all the garlic. Mash the cloves with a fork to make a paste.

Per Serving:

Calories: 44 | fat: 5g | protein: 0g | carbs: 1g | net carbs: 1g | fiber: 0g

Sausage Balls

Prep time: 5 minutes | Cook time: 25 minutes | Makes 2 dozen

1 pound (454 g) bulk Italian sausage (not sweet)	2 teaspoons baking powder
1 cup almond flour	1 teaspoon onion powder
1½ cups finely shredded Cheddar cheese	1 teaspoon fennel seed (optional)
1 large egg	½ teaspoon cayenne pepper (optional)

1. Preheat the oven to 350ºF (180ºC) and line a rimmed baking sheet with aluminum foil. 2. In a large bowl, combine all the ingredients. Use a fork to mix until well blended. 3. Form the sausage mixture into 1½-inch balls and place 1 inch apart on the prepared baking sheet. 4. Bake for 20 to 25 minutes, or until browned and cooked through.

Per Serving:
Calories: 241 | fat: 21g | protein: 11g | carbs: 3g | net carbs: 2g | fiber: 1g

Everything Bagel Cream Cheese Dip

Prep time: 10 minutes | Cook time: 0 minutes | Serves 4

1 (8-ounce / 227-g) package cream cheese, at room temperature	1 tablespoon dried onion, or onion powder
½ cup sour cream	1 tablespoon sesame seeds
1 tablespoon garlic powder	1 tablespoon kosher salt

1. In a small bowl, combine the cream cheese, sour cream, garlic powder, dried onion, sesame seeds, and salt. Stir well to incorporate everything together. Serve immediately or cover and refrigerate for up to 6 days.

Per Serving:
Calories: 291 | fat: 27g | protein: 6g | carbs: 6g | net carbs: 5g | fiber: 1g

Colby Cheese and Pepper Dip

Prep time: 5 minutes | Cook time: 5 minutes | Serves 8

1 tablespoon butter	2 garlic cloves, minced
2 red bell peppers, sliced	1 teaspoon red Aleppo pepper flakes
2 cups shredded Colby cheese	1 teaspoon sumac
1 cup cream cheese, room temperature	Salt and ground black pepper, to taste
1 cup chicken broth	

1. Set your Instant Pot to Sauté and melt the butter. 2. Add the bell peppers and sauté for about 2 minutes until just tender. 3. Add the remaining ingredients to the Instant Pot and gently stir to incorporate. 4. Lock the lid. Select the Manual mode and set the cooking time for 3 minutes at High Pressure. 5. When the timer beeps, perform a quick pressure release. Carefully remove the lid. 6. Allow to cool for 5 minutes and serve warm.

Per Serving:
Calories: 241 | fat: 21g | protein: 11g | carbs: 3g | net carbs: 2g | fiber: 1g

Savory Mackerel & Goat'S Cheese "Paradox" Balls

Prep time: 10 minutes | Cook time: 0 minutes | Makes 10 fat bombs

2 smoked or cooked mackerel fillets, boneless, skin removed	mustard
	1 small red onion, finely diced
4.4 ounces (125 g) soft goat's cheese	2 tablespoons chopped fresh chives or herbs of choice
1 tablespoon fresh lemon juice	¾ cup pecans, crushed
1 teaspoon Dijon or yellow	10 leaves baby gem lettuce

1. In a food processor, combine the mackerel, goat's cheese, lemon juice, and mustard. Pulse until smooth. Transfer to a bowl, add the onion and herbs, and mix with a spoon. Refrigerate for 20 to 30 minutes, or until set. 2. Using a large spoon or an ice cream scoop, divide the mixture into 10 balls, about 40 g/1.4 ounces each. Roll each ball in the crushed pecans. Place each ball on a small lettuce leaf and serve. Keep the fat bombs refrigerated in a sealed container for up to 5 days.

Per Serving (1fatbomb):
Calories: 165 | fat: 12g | protein: 12g | carbs: 2g | net carbs: 1g | fiber: 1g

Burrata Caprese Stack

Prep time: 5 minutes | Cook time: 0 minutes | Serves 4

1 large organic tomato, preferably heirloom	8 fresh basil leaves, thinly sliced
½ teaspoon salt	2 tablespoons extra-virgin olive oil
¼ teaspoon freshly ground black pepper	1 tablespoon red wine or balsamic vinegar
1 (4-ounce / 113-g) ball burrata cheese	

1. Slice the tomato into 4 thick slices, removing any tough center core and sprinkle with salt and pepper. Place the tomatoes, seasoned-side up, on a plate. 2. On a separate rimmed plate, slice the burrata into 4 thick slices and place one slice on top of each tomato slice. Top each with one-quarter of the basil and pour any reserved burrata cream from the rimmed plate over top. 3. Drizzle with olive oil and vinegar and serve with a fork and knife.

Per Serving:
Calories: 109 | fat: 7g | protein: 9g | carbs: 3g | net carbs: 2g | fiber: 1g

Lemon-Butter Mushrooms

Prep time: 10 minutes | Cook time: 4 minutes | Serves 2

1 cup cremini mushrooms, sliced	1 teaspoon almond butter
½ cup water	1 teaspoon grated lemon zest
1 tablespoon lemon juice	½ teaspoon salt
	½ teaspoon dried thyme

1. Combine all the ingredients in the Instant Pot. 2. Secure the lid. Select the Manual mode and set the cooking time for 4 minutes at High Pressure. 3. Once cooking is complete, do a natural pressure release for 5 minutes, then release any remaining pressure. Carefully open the lid. 4. Serve warm.

Per Serving:

Calories: 63 | fat: 5g | protein: 3g | carbs: 3g | net carbs: 2g | fiber: 1g

Wedge Dippers

Prep time: 5 minutes | Cook time: 0 minutes | Serves 4

1 medium head iceberg lettuce (about 6 in/15 cm in diameter)	½ cup (120 ml) ranch dressing

1. Cut the head of lettuce in half, then lay the halves cut side down. Cut each half into 8 wedges, like a pie, for a total of 16 wedges. 2. Serve with the ranch dressing.

Per Serving:

Calories: 132 | fat: 12g | protein: 1g | carbs: 5g | net carbs: 4g | fiber: 1g

Jelly Cups

Prep time: 10 minutes | Cook time: 10 minutes |
Makes 16 jelly cups

Butter Base:	Jelly Filling:
⅔ cup (170 g) coconut butter or smooth unsweetened nut or seed butter	½ cup (70 g) fresh raspberries
	¼ cup (60 ml) water
	3 drops liquid stevia, or 1
⅔ cup (145 g) coconut oil, ghee, or cacao butter, melted	teaspoon confectioners'-style erythritol
2 teaspoons vanilla extract	1½ teaspoons unflavored gelatin
7 drops liquid stevia, or 2 teaspoons confectioners'-style erythritol	Special Equipment:
	16 mini muffin cup liners, or 1 silicone mini muffin pan

1. Set 16 mini muffin cup liners on a tray or have on hand a silicone mini muffin pan. 2. Make the base: Place the coconut butter, melted oil, vanilla, and sweetener in a medium-sized bowl and stir to combine. 3. Take half of the base mixture and divide it equally among the 16 mini muffin cup liners or 16 wells of the mini muffin pan, filling each about one-quarter full. Place the muffin cup liners (or muffin pan) in the fridge. Set the remaining half of the base mixture aside. 4. Make the jelly filling: Place the raspberries, water,

and sweetener in a small saucepan and bring to a simmer over medium heat. Simmer for 5 minutes, then sprinkle with the gelatin and mash with a fork. Transfer to the fridge to set for 15 minutes. 5. Pull the muffin cup liners and jelly filling out of the fridge. Using a ½-teaspoon measuring spoon, scoop out a portion of the jelly and roll it into a ball between your palms, then flatten it into a disc about 1 inch (2.5 cm) in diameter (or in a diameter to fit the size of the liners you're using). Press into a chilled butter base cup. Repeat with the remaining jelly filling and cups. Then spoon the remaining butter base mixture over the tops. 6. Place in the fridge for another 15 minutes before serving.

Per Serving:

Calories: 151 | fat: 15g | protein: 1g | carbs: 3g | net carbs: 1g | fiber: 2g

Classy Crudités and Dip

Prep time: 15 minutes | Cook time: 0 minutes | Serves 8

Vegetables	Sour Cream Dip
1 cup whole cherry tomatoes	2 cups full-fat sour cream
1 cup green beans, trimmed	3 tablespoons dry chives
2 cups broccoli florets	1 tablespoon lemon juice
2 cups cauliflower florets	½ cup dried parsley
1 bunch asparagus, trimmed	½ teaspoon garlic powder
1 large green bell pepper, seeded and chopped	⅛ teaspoon salt
	⅛ teaspoon black pepper

1. Cut vegetables into bite-sized uniform pieces. Arrange in like groups around outside edge of a large serving platter, leaving room in middle for dip. 2. Make dip by combining dip ingredients in a medium-sized decorative bowl and mixing well. 3. Place dip bowl in the center of platter and serve.

Per Serving:

Calories: 146| fat: 10g | protein: 4g | carbs: 9g | net carbs: 6g | fiber: 3g

Spicy Baked Feta in Foil

Prep time: 10 minutes | Cook time: 6 minutes | Serves 6

12 ounces (340 g) feta cheese	1 teaspoon ground paprika
½ tomato, sliced	1 tablespoon olive oil
1 ounce (28 g) bell pepper, sliced	1 cup water, for cooking

1. Sprinkle the cheese with olive oil and ground paprika and place it on the foil. 2. Then top feta cheese with sliced tomato and bell pepper. Wrap it in the foil well. 3. After this, pour water and insert the steamer rack in the instant pot. 4. Put the wrapped cheese on the rack. Close and seal the lid. 5. Cook the cheese on Manual mode (High Pressure) for 6 minutes. Then make a quick pressure release. 6. Discard the foil and transfer the cheese on the serving plates.

Per Serving:

Calories: 178 | fat: 14g | protein: 8g | carbs: 4g | net carbs: 3g | fiber: 1g

Bacon-Cheddar Dip Stuffed Mushrooms

Prep time: 10 minutes | Cook time: 35 minutes |
Serves 12

24 ounces (680 g) baby portobello mushrooms	1 tablespoon chopped fresh parsley
2 tablespoons avocado oil	¾ cup (3 ounces / 85 g) shredded Cheddar cheese
3 ounces (85 g) cream cheese	
¼ cup sour cream	⅓ cup cooked bacon bits
2 cloves garlic, minced	3 tablespoons sliced green onions
1 tablespoon chopped fresh dill	

1. Preheat the oven to 400ºF (205ºC). Line a sheet pan with foil or parchment paper and grease lightly. 2. Remove the stems from the mushrooms and place cavity side up on the baking sheet. Drizzle with the avocado oil. 3. Roast the mushrooms for 15 to 20 minutes, until soft. 4. Meanwhile, in a microwave-safe bowl or a saucepan, melt the cream cheese in the microwave or over low heat on the stove until it's soft and easy to stir. Remove from the heat. 5. Stir the sour cream, garlic, dill, and parsley into the cream cheese. Stir in the Cheddar, bacon, and green onions. 6. When the mushrooms are soft, remove from the oven but leave the oven on. Drain any liquid from the pan and from inside the mushrooms. Pat the cavities dry with paper towels. Use a small cookie scoop or spoon to fill them with the dip mixture. 7. Bake the stuffed mushrooms for 10 to 15 minutes, until hot.

Per Serving:
Calories: 107 | fat: 8g | protein: 4g | carbs: 3g | net carbs: 3g | fiber: 0g

N'Oatmeal Bars

Prep time: 25 minutes | Cook time: 0 minutes |
Makes 16 bars

1 cup (180 g) coconut oil	½ teaspoon vanilla extract
½ cup (95 g) erythritol, divided	10 ounces (285 g) unsweetened baking chocolate, roughly chopped
2 cups (300 g) hulled hemp seeds	
½ cup (50 g) unsweetened shredded coconut	½ cup (120 ml) full-fat coconut milk
⅓ cup (33 g) coconut flour	

1. Line a 9-inch (23-cm) square baking pan with parchment paper, draping it over all sides of the pan for easy lifting. 2. Place the coconut oil and half of the erythritol in a medium-sized saucepan and melt over medium heat, about 2 minutes. Continue to Step 3 if using confectioners'-style erythritol; if using granulated erythritol, continue to cook until the granules can no longer be felt on the back of the spoon. 3. Add the hulled hemp seeds, shredded coconut, coconut flour, and vanilla, stirring until coated. Set aside half of the mixture for the topping. Press the remaining half of the mixture into the prepared pan. 4. Transfer the pan with the base layer to the refrigerator for at least 10 minutes, until set. 5. Meanwhile, prepare the chocolate layer: Place the remaining erythritol, the baking chocolate, and coconut milk in a small saucepan over low heat. Stir frequently until melted and smooth. 6. Take the base out

of the fridge and spoon the chocolate mixture over the base layer, spreading it evenly with a knife or the back of a spoon. If the base hasn't totally set, a couple of hulled hemp seeds will lift up and mix in with the chocolate, so don't rush it. 7. Crumble the reserved hemp seed mixture over the chocolate layer, pressing in gently Cover and refrigerate for 2 to 3 hours or overnight. 8. Cut into 16 bars and enjoy!

Per Serving:
Calories: 311 | fat: 30g | protein: 8g | carbs: 10g | net carbs: 4g | fiber: 5g

Crispy Brussels Sprouts with Bacon

Prep time: 5 minutes | Cook time: 10 minutes | Serves 4

½ pound (227 g) bacon	1 teaspoon salt
1 pound (454 g) Brussels sprouts	½ teaspoon pepper
	½ cup water
4 tablespoons butter	

1. Press the Sauté button and press the Adjust button to lower heat to Less. Add bacon to Instant Pot and fry for 3 to 5 minutes or until fat begins to render. Press the Cancel button. 2. Press the Sauté button, with heat set to Normal, and continue frying bacon until crispy. While bacon is frying, wash Brussels sprouts and remove damaged outer leaves. Cut in half or quarters. 3. When bacon is done, remove and set aside. Add Brussels sprouts to hot bacon grease and add butter. Sprinkle with salt and pepper. Sauté for 8 to 10 minutes until caramelized and crispy, adding a few tablespoons of water at a time as needed to deglaze pan. Serve warm.

Per Serving:
Calories: 387 | fat: 32g | protein: 11g | carbs: 11g | net carbs: 7g | fiber: 4g

Baked Brie with Pecans

Prep time: 5 minutes | Cook time: 10 minutes | Serves 6

1 (¾-pound / 340-g) wheel Brie cheese	2 tablespoons minced fresh rosemary leaves
3 ounces (85 g) pecans, chopped	1½ tablespoons olive oil
2 garlic cloves, minced	Salt and freshly ground black pepper, to taste

1. Preheat the oven to 400ºF (205ºC). 2. Line a baking sheet with parchment paper and place the Brie on it. 3. In a small bowl, stir together the pecans, garlic, rosemary, and olive oil. Season with salt and pepper. Spoon the mixture in an even layer over the Brie. Bake for about 10 minutes until the cheese is warm and the nuts are lightly browned. 4. Remove and let it cool for 1 to 2 minutes before serving.

Per Serving:
Calories: 318 | fat: 29g | protein: 13g | carbs: 3g | net carbs: 2g | fiber: 1g

Cookie Fat Bombs

Prep time: 10 minutes | Cook time: 0 minutes | serves 6

1 cup almond butter

½ cup coconut flour

1 teaspoon ground cinnamon

¼ cup cacao nibs or vegan keto chocolate chips

1. Line a baking sheet with parchment paper. If you don't have parchment paper, use aluminum foil or a greased pan. 2. In a mixing bowl, whisk together the almond butter, coconut flour, and cinnamon. 3. Fold in the cacao nibs. 4. Cover the bowl and put it in the freezer for 15 to 20 minutes. 5. Remove the bowl from the freezer and, using a spoon or cookie scoop, scoop out a dollop of mixture and roll it between your palms to form a ball. Repeat to use all the mixture. 6. Place the fat bombs on a baking sheet and put the sheet in the freezer to chill for 20 minutes until firm.

Per Serving:

Calories: 319 | fat: 26g | protein: 8g | carbs: 18g | net carbs: 8g | fiber: 10g

Broccoli Cheese Dip

Prep time: 5 minutes | Cook time: 10 minutes | Serves 6

4 tablespoons butter

½ medium onion, diced

1½ cups chopped broccoli

8 ounces (227 g) cream cheese

½ cup mayonnaise

½ cup chicken broth

1 cup shredded Cheddar cheese

1. Press the Sauté button and then press the Adjust button to set heat to Less. Add butter to Instant Pot. Add onion and sauté until softened, about 5 minutes. Press the Cancel button. 2. Add broccoli, cream cheese, mayo, and broth to pot. Press the Manual button and adjust time for 4 minutes. 3. When timer beeps, quick-release the pressure and stir in Cheddar. Serve warm.

Per Serving:

Calories: 411 | fat: 37g | protein: 8g | carbs: 4g | net carbs: 3g | fiber: 1g

Brownie Cake

Prep time: 10 minutes | Cook time: 25 minutes | Serves 8

¾ cup (120 g) confectioners'-style erythritol, divided

½ cup plus 3 tablespoons (143 g) coconut oil, ghee, or cacao butter, melted, divided

2 large eggs

2 teaspoons vanilla extract

¾ cup (85 g) blanched almond flour

¼ cup plus 2 tablespoons (30 g) cocoa powder, divided

1 teaspoon baking powder

1. Preheat the oven to 350°F (177°C). Line an 8-inch (20-cm) round cake pan or square baking pan with parchment paper. 2. Combine ½ cup (95 g) of the erythritol, ½ cup (120 ml) of the melted oil, the eggs, and vanilla in a large mixing bowl. 3. In a separate bowl, place the almond flour, ¼ cup (20 g) of the cocoa powder, and the baking powder and whisk with a fork. 4. Add the dry mixture to the wet mixture and mix until smooth. 5. Transfer the batter to the lined pan and smooth with the back of a spoon. Bake for 23 to 25 minutes, until a toothpick inserted in the middle comes out clean. Allow to cool for 30 minutes. 6. Meanwhile, prepare the frosting: Place the remaining ¼ cup (25 g) of erythritol, 3 tablespoons of melted oil, and 2 tablespoons of cocoa powder in a small bowl. Whisk to combine. 7. If you're serving the cake right away, as soon as it's cool, cut into 8 equal pieces, place on plates, and drizzle with the frosting. If you're serving it later, cover the entire cake with the frosting while it's still in the pan and set in the fridge for at least 20 minutes before serving.

Per Serving:

Calories: 207 | fat: 22g | protein: 3g | carbs: 3g | net carbs: 2g | fiber: 2g

Finger Tacos

Prep time: 15 minutes | Cook time: 0 minutes | serves 4

2 avocados, peeled and pitted

1 lime

1 tablespoon tamari

1 teaspoon sesame oil

1 teaspoon ginger powder

1 teaspoon togarashi (optional)

½ cup kale chiffonade

½ cup cabbage chiffonade

10 fresh mint leaves chiffonade

⅓ cup cauliflower rice

1 (0.18-ounce) package nori squares or seaweed snack sheets

1. Put the avocados into a large mixing bowl, and squeeze the lime over them. 2. Roughly mash the avocados with a fork, leaving the mixture fairly chunky. 3. Gently stir in the tamari, sesame oil, ginger powder, and togarashi (if using). 4. Gently fold in the kale, cabbage, mint, and cauliflower rice. 5. Arrange some nori squares on a plate. 6. Use a nori or seaweed sheet to pick up a portion of the avocado mixture and pop it into your mouth.

Per Serving:

Calories: 180 | fat: 15g | protein: 4g | carbs: 13g | net carbs: 5g | fiber: 8g

Cheese Stuffed Bell Peppers

Prep time: 10 minutes | Cook time: 5 minutes | Serves 5

1 cup water

10 baby bell peppers, seeded and sliced lengthwise

4 ounces (113 g) Monterey Jack cheese, shredded

4 ounces (113 g) cream cheese

2 tablespoons chopped scallions

1 tablespoon olive oil

1 teaspoon minced garlic

½ teaspoon cayenne pepper

¼ teaspoon ground black pepper, or more to taste

1. Pour the water into the Instant Pot and insert a steamer basket. 2. Stir together the remaining ingredients except the bell peppers in a mixing bowl until combined. Stuff the peppers evenly with the mixture. Arrange the stuffed peppers in the basket. 3. Lock the lid. Select the Manual mode and set the cooking time for 5 minutes at High Pressure. 4. When the timer beeps, perform a quick pressure release. Carefully remove the lid. 5. Cool for 5 minutes and serve.

Per Serving:

Calories: 226 | fat: 18g | protein: 9g | carbs: 9g | net carbs: 7g | fiber: 1g

90-Second Bread

Prep time: 5 minutes | Cook time: 90 seconds | Serves 1

1 heaping tablespoon coconut flour	1 large egg
½ teaspoon baking powder	1½ tablespoons butter, melted
	Pinch salt

1. In a small, 3- to 4-inch diameter, microwave-safe bowl, combine the coconut flour, baking powder, egg, butter, and salt, and mix until well combined. 2. Place the bowl in the microwave and cook on high for 90 seconds. 3. Dump the bread from the bowl and allow to cool for a couple of minutes. 4. With a serrated knife, cut the bread in half horizontally to make two halves, if desired.

Per Serving:

Calories: 204 | fat: 17g | protein: 8g | carbs: 5g | net carbs: 2g | fiber: 3g

Keto Asian Dumplings

Prep time: 20 minutes | Cook time: 20 minutes | Serves 4

Dipping Sauce:	8 ounces (227 g) shrimp, peeled, deveined, and finely chopped
¼ cup gluten-free soy sauce	
2 tablespoons sesame oil	
1 tablespoon rice vinegar	2 tablespoons gluten-free soy sauce
1 teaspoon chili garlic sauce	
Filling:	½ teaspoon fish sauce
1 tablespoon sesame oil	Salt and freshly ground black pepper, to taste
2 garlic cloves	
1 teaspoon grated fresh ginger	3 scallions, green parts only, chopped
1 celery stalk, minced	
½ onion, minced	1 head napa cabbage, rinsed, leaves separated (about 12 leaves)
1 carrot, minced	
8 ounces (227 g) ground pork	

Make the Dipping Sauce 1. In a small bowl, whisk together the soy sauce, sesame oil, vinegar, and chili garlic sauce. Set aside. Make the Filling 2. In a large skillet over medium heat, heat the sesame oil. 3. Add the garlic, ginger, celery, onion, and carrot. Sauté for 5 to 7 minutes until softened. 4. Add the pork. Cook for 5 to 6 minutes, breaking it up with a spoon, until it starts to brown. 5. Add the shrimp and stir everything together well. 6. Stir in the soy sauce and fish sauce. Season with a little salt and pepper. Give it a stir and add the scallions. Keep it warm over low heat until ready to fill the dumplings. 7. Steam the cabbage leaves: Place the leaves in a large saucepan with just 1 to 2 inches of boiling water. Cook for about 5 minutes or until the leaves become tender. Remove from the water and set aside to drain. 8. Lay each leaf out flat. Put about 2 tablespoons of filling in the center of one leaf. Wrap the leaf over itself, tucking the sides in so the whole thing is tightly wrapped. Secure with a toothpick. Continue with the remaining leaves and filling. Serve with the dipping sauce. Refrigerate leftovers in an airtight container for up to 3 days.

Per Serving (3dumplings):

Calories: 305 | fat: 17g | protein: 27g | carbs: 11g | net carbs: 8g | fiber: 3g

Crunchy Granola Bars

Prep time: 15 minutes | Cook time: 15 minutes | Makes 16 bars

½ cup unsweetened almond butter	¼ teaspoon salt
	2 tablespoons almond flour
2 tablespoons coconut oil	1 cup unsweetened coconut flakes
2 to 4 tablespoons granulated sugar-free sweetener	
	1 cup slivered almonds
1 egg white	1 cup chopped roasted unsalted pecans
1 teaspoon ground cinnamon	
1 teaspoon vanilla extract	1 cup shelled pumpkin seeds

1. Preheat the oven to 350°F (180°C). Line an 8-inch square glass baking dish with parchment paper, letting the paper hang over the sides. 2. In a large glass bowl, combine the almond butter, coconut oil, and sweetener and microwave for 30 seconds, or until the coconut oil is melted. 3. Whisk in the egg white, cinnamon, vanilla extract, and salt until smooth and creamy. 4. Stir in the almond flour, coconut flakes, almonds, pecans, and pumpkin seeds until thoroughly combined. 5. Transfer the mixture into the prepared dish and press down firmly with a spatula to cover the bottom evenly. 6. Bake for 15 minutes, or until crispy and slightly browned around the edges. 7. Allow to cool completely before cutting into 16 bars. Bars can be stored tightly wrapped in the freezer for up to 3 months.

Per Serving:

Calories: 215 | fat: 20g | protein: 6g | carbs: 6g | net carbs: 3g | fiber: 3g

Deviled Eggs with Tuna

Prep time: 10 minutes | Cook time: 8 minutes | Serves 3

1 cup water	1 celery stalk, diced finely
6 eggs	¼ teaspoon Dijon mustard
1 (5-ounce / 142-g) can tuna, drained	¼ teaspoon chopped fresh dill
	¼ teaspoon salt
4 tablespoons mayonnaise	⅛ teaspoon garlic powder
1 teaspoon lemon juice	

1. Add water to Instant Pot. Place steam rack or steamer basket inside pot. Carefully put eggs into steamer basket. Click lid closed. Press the Manual button and adjust time for 8 minutes. 2. Add remaining ingredients to medium bowl and mix. 3. When timer beeps, quick-release the steam and remove eggs. Place in bowl of cool water for 10 minutes, then remove shells. 4. Cut eggs in half and remove hard-boiled yolks, setting whites aside. Place yolks in food processor and pulse until smooth, or mash with fork. Add yolks to bowl with tuna and mayo, mixing until smooth. 5. Spoon mixture into egg-white halves. Serve chilled.

Per Serving:

Calories: 303 | fat: 22g | protein: 20g | carbs: 2g | net carbs: 2g | fiber: 0g

Superpower Fat Bombs

Prep time: 10 minutes | Cook time: 0 minutes | Makes 8 bombs

⅔ cup (145 g) coconut oil, cacao butter, or ghee, melted

¼ cup (40 g) collagen peptides or protein powder

¼ cup (25 g) unflavored MCT oil powder

2 tablespoons cocoa powder

2 tablespoons roughly ground flax seeds

1 tablespoon cacao nibs

1 teaspoon instant coffee granules

4 drops liquid stevia, or 1 tablespoon plus 1 teaspoon confectioners'-style erythritol

Pinch of finely ground sea salt

Special Equipment (Optional): Silicone mold with eight 2-tablespoon or larger cavities

1. Have on hand your favorite silicone mold. I like to use a large silicone ice cube tray and spoon 2 tablespoons of the mixture into each well, which Prep time: 5 minutes | Cook time: 0 minutes | Makes 4 MAKES 8 cubes total. If you do not have a silicone mold, making this into a bark works well, too. Simply use an 8-inch (20-cm) square silicone or metal baking pan; if using a metal pan, line it with parchment paper, draping some over the sides for easy removal. 2. Place all the ingredients in a medium-sized bowl and stir until well mixed and smooth. 3. Divide the mixture evenly among 8 cavities in the silicone mold or pour into the baking pan. Transfer to the fridge and allow to set for 15 minutes if using cacao butter or 30 minutes if using ghee or coconut oil. If using a baking pan, break the bark into 8 pieces for serving.

Per Serving:
Calories: 136 | fat: 12g | protein: 6g | carbs: 3g | net carbs: 1g | fiber: 2g

Cheesecake Balls

Prep time: 15 minutes | Cook time: 0 minutes | Makes 12 balls

Almond Flour Center:

½ cup (55 g) blanched almond flour

2 tablespoons coconut oil or ghee

1 tablespoon confectioners'-style erythritol

Cream Cheese Layer:

1 (8-ounce/225-g) package cream cheese (dairy-free or

regular)

3 tablespoons coconut oil or ghee

¼ cup plus 2 tablespoons (60 g) confectioners'-style erythritol

2 teaspoons ground cinnamon

Cinnamon Sugar Topping:

¼ cup (48 g) granulated erythritol

2 teaspoons ground cinnamon

1. Line a rimmed baking sheet or tray that will fit into your freezer with parchment paper. 2. Make the almond flour center: Place the almond flour, oil, and erythritol in a small bowl. Knead with your hands until incorporated. Separate the mixture into 12 pieces and roll into balls. Place the balls on the lined baking sheet and place in the freezer. 3. Make the cream cheese layer: Place the cream cheese, oil, and erythritol in a small bowl and combine with a fork or handheld mixer. Divide the mixture evenly between 2 bowls.

To one bowl, add the cinnamon and mix until incorporated. Place both bowls in the freezer until the cream cheese has hardened but is still workable and not completely frozen through, about 1 hour. 4. Place the ingredients for the cinnamon sugar topping in a small bowl and whisk with a fork to combine. Set aside. 5. Once the cream cheese mixtures have chilled sufficiently, scoop a teaspoon each of the cinnamon cream cheese mixture and the plain cream cheese mixture and place them side by side on the lined baking sheet. Take the almond flour balls out of the freezer and place one ball between a pair of cream cheese pieces. Pick up the pile and roll between your palms until the almond flour ball is in the middle and the cream cheese surrounds it. Roll the ball in the cinnamon sugar mixture until coated. Place the coated ball back on the lined baking sheet and place in the freezer. 6. Repeat with the remaining almond flour balls, cream cheese mixtures, and cinnamon sugar topping, placing the coated balls on the baking sheet in the freezer as you complete them. 7. Place the coated balls in the freezer to chill for 20 minutes before enjoying.

Per Serving:
Calories: 126 | fat: 13g | protein: 1g | carbs: 2g | net carbs: 1g | fiber: 1g

Creole Pancetta and Cheese Balls

Prep time: 5 minutes | Cook time: 5 minutes | Serves 6

1 cup water

6 eggs

4 slices pancetta, chopped

⅓ cup grated Cheddar cheese

¼ cup cream cheese

¼ cup mayonnaise

1 teaspoon Creole seasonings

Sea salt and ground black pepper, to taste

1. Pour the water into the Instant Pot and insert a steamer basket. Place the eggs in the basket. 2. Lock the lid. Select the Manual mode and set the cooking time for 5 minutes at Low Pressure. 3. When the timer beeps, perform a quick pressure release. Carefully remove the lid. 4. Allow the eggs to cool for 10 to 15 minutes. Peel the eggs and chop them, then transfer to a bowl. Add the remaining ingredients and stir to combine well. 5. Shape the mixture into balls with your hands. Serve chilled.

Per Serving:
Calories: 239 | fat: 19g | protein: 14g | carbs: 3g | net carbs: 3g | fiber: 0g

Cabbage and Broccoli Slaw

Prep time: 5 minutes | Cook time: 10 minutes | Serves 6

2 cups broccoli slaw

½ head cabbage, thinly sliced

¼ cup chopped kale

4 tablespoons butter

1 teaspoon salt

¼ teaspoon pepper

1. Press the Sauté button and add all ingredients to Instant Pot. Stir-fry for 7 to 10 minutes until cabbage softens. Serve warm.

Per Serving:
Calories: 97 | fat: 7g | protein: 2g | carbs: 6g | net carbs: 3g | fiber: 3g

Cauliflower Cheese Balls

Prep time: 5 minutes | Cook time: 21 minutes | Serves 8

1 cup water

1 head cauliflower, broken into florets

1 cup shredded Asiago cheese

½ cup grated Parmesan cheese

2 eggs, beaten

2 tablespoons butter

2 tablespoons minced fresh chives

1 garlic clove, minced

½ teaspoon cayenne pepper

Coarse sea salt and white pepper, to taste

1. Pour the water into the Instant Pot and insert a steamer basket. Place the cauliflower in the basket. 2. Lock the lid. Select the Manual mode and set the cooking time for 3 minutes at High Pressure. 3. When the timer beeps, perform a quick pressure release. Carefully remove the lid. 4. Transfer the cauliflower to a food processor, along with the remaining ingredients. Pulse until everything is well combined. 5. Form the mixture into bite-sized balls and place them on a baking sheet. 6. Bake in the preheated oven at 400ºF (205ºC) for 18 minutes until golden brown. Flip the balls halfway through the cooking time. Cool for 5 minutes before serving.

Per Serving:

Calories: 161 | fat: 13g | protein: 9g | carbs: 4g | net carbs: 3g | fiber: 1g

Red Wine Mushrooms

Prep time: 5 minutes | Cook time: 15 minutes | Serves 2

8 ounces (227 g) sliced mushrooms

¼ cup dry red wine

2 tablespoons beef broth

½ teaspoon garlic powder

¼ teaspoon Worcestershire sauce

Pinch of salt

Pinch of black pepper

¼ teaspoon xanthan gum

1. Add the mushrooms, wine, broth, garlic powder, Worcestershire sauce, salt, and pepper to the pot. 2. Close the lid and seal the vent. Cook on High Pressure for 13 minutes. Quick release the steam. Press Cancel. 3. Turn the pot to Sauté mode. Add the xanthan gum and whisk until the juices have thickened, 1 to 2 minutes.

Per Serving:

Calories: 94 | fat: 1g | protein: 4g | carbs: 8g | net carbs: 6g | fiber: 2g

Keto Taco Shells

Prep time: 5 minutes | Cook time: 20 minutes | Serves 4

6 ounces (170 g) shredded cheese

1. Preheat the oven to 350ºF (180ºC). 2. Line a baking sheet with a silicone baking mat or parchment paper. 3. Separate the cheese into 4 (1½-ounce / 43-g) portions and make small circular piles a few inches apart (they will spread a bit in the oven). Pat the cheese down so all the piles are equally thick. Bake for 10 to 12 minutes or until the edges begin to brown. Cool for just a couple of minutes. 4. Lay a wooden spoon or spatula across two overturned glasses. Repeat to make a second setup, and carefully transfer a baked cheese circle to drape over the length of each spoon or spatula. Let them cool into the shape of a taco shell. 5. Fill with your choice of protein and top with chopped lettuce, avocado, salsa, sour cream, or whatever else you like on your tacos. These taco shells will keep refrigerated in an airtight container for a few days, but they are best freshly made and still a little warm.

Per Serving:

1 taco shell: Calories: 168 | fat: 14g | protein: 11g | carbs: 1g | net carbs: 1g | fiber: 0g

Pesto-Stuffed Mushrooms

**Prep time: 20 minutes | Cook time: 20 minutes |
Makes 1 dozen mushrooms**

1 dozen baby bella mushroom caps, cleaned

8 ounces (227 g) fresh Mozzarella

½ cup pesto

Sea salt and ground black pepper, to taste

1. Preheat the oven to 350ºF (180ºC). 2. Place the mushrooms on a rimmed baking sheet cup side down and bake for 10 minutes, or until some of the moisture is released. 3. While the mushrooms are baking, slice the Mozzarella into small pieces, approximately the size of the mushrooms. 4. Turn the mushrooms cup side up and fill each one with a spoonful of pesto and 1 or 2 pieces of Mozzarella. Return the mushrooms to the oven and bake for about 10 minutes, until golden brown on top. 5. Sprinkle with salt and pepper before serving.

Per Serving:

Calories: 132 | fat: 11g | protein: 4g | carbs: 5g | net carbs: 4g | fiber: 1g

Quick Salsa

**Prep time: 5 minutes | Cook time: 0 minutes | Makes
about 3 cups**

¼ cup fresh cilantro, stems and leaves, finely chopped

1 small red onion, finely chopped

8 roma tomatoes or other small to medium tomatoes, finely chopped

1 small jalapeño pepper, minced, seeded if desired for less heat (optional)

Juice of 1 to 2 limes

Sea salt and ground black pepper, to taste

1. Toss together all the ingredients in a large mixing bowl. Alternatively, place all the ingredients in a food processor and pulse until the desired consistency is reached. 2. Season with salt and pepper to taste. 3. Store in an airtight container in the refrigerator for up to 5 days.

Per Serving:

Calories: 12 | fat: 3g | protein: 1g | carbs: 3g | net carbs: 2g | fiber 1g

Stuffed Jalapeños with Bacon

Prep time: 10 minutes | Cook time: 6 minutes | Serves 2

1 ounce (28 g) bacon, chopped, fried	1 teaspoon chopped green onions
2 ounces (57 g) Cheddar cheese, shredded	2 jalapeños, trimmed and seeded
1 tablespoon coconut cream	

1. Mix together the chopped bacon, cheese, coconut cream, and green onions in a mixing bowl and stir until well incorporated. 2. Stuff the jalapeños evenly with the bacon mixture. 3. Press the Sauté button to heat your Instant Pot. 4. Place the stuffed jalapeños in the Instant Pot and cook each side for 3 minutes until softened. 5. Transfer to a paper towel-lined plate and serve.

Per Serving:
Calories: 216 | fat: 18g | protein: 13g | carbs: 2g | net carbs: 1g | fiber: 1g

Smoked Salmon Cream Cheese Rollups with Arugula and Truffle Oil Drizzle

Prep time: 10 minutes | Cook time: 0 minutes | Serves 4

½ cup cream cheese	salmon
¼ cup plain Greek-style yogurt	¾ cup arugula
2 teaspoons chopped fresh dill	Truffle oil, for garnish
12 slices (½ pound) smoked	

1. Mix the filling. In a small bowl, blend together the cream cheese, yogurt, and dill until the mixture is smooth. 2. Make the rollups. Spread the cream cheese mixture onto the smoked salmon slices, dividing it evenly. Place several arugula leaves at one end of each slice and roll them up. Secure them with a toothpick if they're starting to unroll. 3. Serve. Drizzle the rolls with truffle oil and place three rolls on each of four plates.

Per Serving:
Calories: 234 | fat: 20g | protein: 13g | carbs: 2g | net carbs: 2g | fiber: 0g

Gourmet "Cheese" Balls

Prep time: 1 hour 20 minutes | Cook time: 0 minutes | serves 6

1 cup raw hazelnuts, soaked overnight	1 teaspoon miso paste
¼ cup water	1 teaspoon mustard
2 tablespoons nutritional yeast	½ cup almond flour
1 teaspoon apple cider vinegar	1 cup slivered almonds
	1 teaspoon dried oregano

1. In a high-powered blender, combine the hazelnuts, water, nutritional yeast, vinegar, miso paste, and mustard, and blend until well combined, thick, and creamy. 2. Transfer the mixture to a medium bowl. 3. Slowly stir in the almond flour until the mixture forms a dough-like consistency. Set aside. 4. In a separate, small bowl, toss the almonds and oregano together and set aside. 5. Using a soup spoon or tablespoon, scoop some mixture into your hand and shape it into a bite-size ball. Place the ball on a baking sheet. Repeat until you have used all the mixture (about 2 dozen balls). 6. One by one, roll the hazelnut balls in the almond and oregano mixture until thoroughly coated, placing each coated ball back on the baking sheet. 7. Place the sheet in the refrigerator for 1 hour to allow the balls to set.

Per Serving:
Calories: 308 | fat: 27g | protein: 10g | carbs: 11g | net carbs: 5g | fiber: 6g

Bacon Avocado Mousse Cups

Prep time: 10 minutes | Cook time: 20 minutes | Serves 6

12 bacon slices	Juice of ½ lime
2 or 3 ripe avocados, halved and pitted	Salt and freshly ground black pepper, to taste
½ cup plain Greek yogurt	

1. Preheat the oven to 425ºF (220ºC). 2. Wrap each piece of bacon around the sides and bottom of the wells of a mini muffin tin to create little bacon cups. Bake for 15 to 20 minutes or until the bacon is cooked through and crisp. 3. While the bacon cooks, in a medium bowl, combine the avocado flesh, yogurt, and lime juice. Mix well until combined and smooth. Season with salt and pepper and transfer to a piping bag (or a plastic bag with the tip cut off). 4. Remove the bacon from the oven and cool slightly. Pipe each bacon cup full of avocado mousse. Serve immediately.

Per Serving (2 filled cups):
Calories: 530 | fat: 38g | protein: 31g | carbs: 16g | net carbs: 9g | fiber: 7g

Pizza Bites

Prep time: 5 minutes | Cook time: 10 minutes | Makes 12 pizza bites

12 large pepperoni slices	(approximately 8 ounces / 227 g)
2 tablespoons tomato paste	
12 mini Mozzarella balls	12 fresh basil leaves (optional)

1. Preheat the oven to 400ºF (205ºC). 2. Line each of 12 cups of a mini muffin pan with one pepperoni slice. To make them sit better, use kitchen shears to make three or four small cuts toward the center of the slice, but do not cut too far in—leave the center intact. 3. Bake 5 minutes, remove from the oven, and allow to cool in the pan for 5 to 10 minutes, until somewhat crisp. Keep the oven turned on. 4. Spoon ½ teaspoon of tomato paste into each pepperoni cup and gently spread to coat the bottom. Place a Mozzarella ball and a basil leaf, if using, in each cup. Return muffin pan to the oven and cook another 3 to 5 minutes, until the cheese is melting. 5. Remove pan from the oven and allow the bites to cool for 5 to 10 minutes before serving.

Per Serving:
Calories: 193 | fat: 15g | protein: 11g | carbs: 2g | net carbs: 2g | fiber: 0g

Chapter 8 Stews and Soups

Blue Cheese Mushroom Soup

Prep time: 15 minutes | Cook time: 20 minutes | Serves 4

2 cups chopped white mushrooms	1 teaspoon olive oil
3 tablespoons cream cheese	½ teaspoon ground cumin
4 ounces (113 g) scallions, diced	1 teaspoon salt
4 cups chicken broth	2 ounces (57 g) blue cheese, crumbled

1. Combine the mushrooms, cream cheese, scallions, chicken broth, olive oil, and ground cumin in the Instant Pot. 2. Seal the lid. Select Manual mode and set cooking time for 20 minutes on High Pressure. 3. When timer beeps, use a quick pressure release and open the lid. 4. Add the salt and blend the soup with an immersion blender. 5. Ladle the soup in the bowls and top with blue cheese. Serve warm.

Per Serving:
Calories: 142 | fat: 9g | protein: 10g | carbs: 5g | net carbs: 4g | fiber: 1g

Spaghetti Squash Ramen Soup

Prep time: 15 minutes | Cook time: 1 hour | Serves 4

Spaghetti Squash:	8 cups chicken broth
1 medium (2-pound / 907-g) spaghetti squash	⅓ cup coconut aminos
2 tablespoons avocado oil	1 tablespoon fish sauce (optional)
Sea salt, to taste	1½ teaspoons sea salt, or to taste
Soup:	
1 tablespoon avocado oil	Garnishes:
4 cloves garlic, minced	¼ cup (0.9 ounce / 26 g) chopped green onions
1 tablespoon minced fresh ginger	4 large eggs, soft-boiled, peeled, and cut in half
2 cups (5 ounces / 142 g) shiitake mushrooms, sliced	

1. Preheat the oven to 425ºF (220ºC). Line a baking sheet with foil and grease lightly. 2. Prepare the spaghetti squash: Use a sharp chef's knife to slice the spaghetti squash in half. To make it easier, use the knife to score where you'll be cutting first, then slice. Cut crosswise to yield longer noodles, or lengthwise for shorter ones. Scoop out the seeds. 3. Drizzle the inside of the halves with the avocado oil. Sprinkle lightly with sea salt. 4. Place the spaghetti squash halves on the lined baking sheet cut side down. Roast for 25 to 35 minutes, until the skin pierces easily with a knife. The knife should be able to go in pretty deep with very slight resistance. 5.

Remove from the oven and let the squash rest on the pan (cut side down, without moving) for 10 minutes. Then use a fork to release the strands inside the shells and set aside. 6. Meanwhile, make the soup: In a large soup pot, heat the oil over medium heat. Add the garlic and ginger and sauté for about 1 minute, until fragrant. 7. Add the shiitake mushrooms and sauté for about 5 minutes, or until the mushrooms are soft. 8. Add the chicken broth, coconut aminos, and fish sauce (if using). Add salt to taste (start with 1 teaspoon salt and add more if needed, but I recommend 1½ teaspoons). Bring to a boil, then reduce the heat and simmer for 10 minutes. 9. Add the spaghetti squash noodles to the pot and simmer for 10 to 15 minutes, until hot and flavors develop to your liking. 10. Pour into bowls. Garnish with the green onions and soft-boiled eggs.
Per Serving:
Calories: 238 | fat: 16g | protein: 10g | carbs: 10g | net carbs: 10g | fiber: 0g

Cauliflower Rice and Chicken Thigh Soup

Prep time: 15 minutes | Cook time: 13 minutes | Serves 5

2 cups cauliflower florets	pepper
1 pound (454 g) boneless, skinless chicken thighs	½ cup sliced zucchini
	⅓ cup sliced turnips
4½ cups chicken broth	1 teaspoon dried parsley
½ yellow onion, chopped	3 celery stalks, chopped
2 garlic cloves, minced	1 teaspoon ground turmeric
1 tablespoon unflavored gelatin powder	½ teaspoon dried marjoram
	1 teaspoon dried thyme
2 teaspoons sea salt	½ teaspoon dried oregano
½ teaspoon ground black	

1. Add the cauliflower florets to a food processor and pulse until a ricelike consistency is achieved. Set aside. 2. Add the chicken thighs, chicken broth, onions, garlic, gelatin powder, sea salt, and black pepper to the pot. Gently stir to combine. 3. Lock the lid. Select Manual mode and set cooking time for 10 minutes on High Pressure. 4. When cooking is complete, quick release the pressure and open the lid. 5. Transfer the chicken thighs to a cutting board. Chop the chicken into bite-sized pieces and then return the chopped chicken to the pot. 6. Add the cauliflower rice, zucchini, turnips, parsley, celery, turmeric, marjoram, thyme, and oregano to the pot. Stir to combine. 7. Lock the lid. Select Manual mode and set cooking time for 3 minutes on High Pressure. 8. When cooking is complete, quick release the pressure. 9. Open the lid. Ladle the soup into serving bowls. Serve hot.

Per Serving:
Calories: 247 | fat: 10g | protein: 30g | carbs: 8g | net carbs: 6g | fiber: 2g

"Dolla Store" Pumpkin Soup

Prep time: 15 minutes | Cook time: 25 minutes | Serves 8

2 (9-ounce) packages soy chorizo

6 cups chicken bone broth

½ (15-ounce) can pure pumpkin

2 cups cooked riced cauliflower

1 cup unsweetened coconut milk

1 teaspoon garlic powder

1 teaspoon ground cinnamon

1 teaspoon ground ginger

1 teaspoon ground nutmeg

1 teaspoon paprika

⅛ teaspoon salt

⅛ teaspoon black pepper

1. Place a medium soup pot over medium heat and add all ingredients. Bring to boil while stirring regularly (5–10 minutes). 2. Reduce heat. Let simmer 15 minutes, stirring regularly until desired consistency achieved. 3. Remove from heat, let cool 5 minutes, and serve.

Per Serving:

Calories: 237| fat: 15g | protein: 17g | carbs: 13g | net carbs: 8g | fiber: 5g

Salsa Verde Chicken Soup

Prep time: 5 minutes | Cook time: 10 minutes | Serves 4

½ cup salsa verde

2 cups cooked and shredded chicken

2 cups chicken broth

1 cup shredded cheddar cheese

4 ounces cream cheese

½ teaspoon chili powder

½ teaspoon ground cumin

½ teaspoon fresh cilantro, chopped

Salt and black pepper, to taste

1. Combine the cream cheese, salsa verde, and broth, in a food processor; pulse until smooth. Transfer the mixture to a pot and place over medium heat. Cook until hot, but do not bring to a boil. Add chicken, chili powder, and cumin and cook for about 3-5 minutes, or until it is heated through. 2. Stir in cheddar cheese and season with salt and pepper to taste. If it is very thick, add a few tablespoons of water and boil for 1-3 more minutes. Serve hot in bowls sprinkled with fresh cilantro.

Per Serving:

Calories: 346 | fat: 23g | protein: 25g | carbs: 4g | net carbs: 3g | fiber: 1g

Shrimp Chowder

Prep time: 10 minutes | Cook time: 40 minutes | Serves 6

¼ cup (60 ml) refined avocado oil or melted ghee (if tolerated)

1⅔ cups (140 g) diced mushrooms

⅓ cup (55 g) diced yellow onions

10½ ounces (300 g) small raw shrimp, shelled and deveined

1 can (13½-ounce/400-ml) full-fat coconut milk

⅓ cup (80 ml) chicken bone broth

2 tablespoons apple cider vinegar

1 teaspoon onion powder

1 teaspoon paprika

1 bay leaf

¾ teaspoon finely ground gray sea salt

½ teaspoon dried oregano leaves

¼ teaspoon ground black

pepper

12 radishes (about 6 ounces/170 g), cubed

1 medium zucchini (about 7 ounces/200 g), cubed

1. Heat the avocado oil in a large saucepan on medium for a couple of minutes, then add the mushrooms and onions. Sauté for 8 to 10 minutes, until the onions are translucent and mushrooms are beginning to brown. 2. Add the remaining ingredients, except the radishes and zucchini. Cover and bring to a boil, then reduce the heat to low and simmer for 20 minutes. 3. After 20 minutes, add the radishes and zucchini. Continue to cook for 10 minutes, until the vegetables are fork-tender. 4. Remove the bay leaf, divide among 6 small soup bowls, and enjoy.

Per Serving:

Calories: 301 | fat: 23g | protein: 14g | carbs: 7g | net carbs: 5g | fiber: 2g

Creamy Mushroom Soup

Prep time: 10 minutes | Cook time: 30 minutes | Serves 4

2 slices bacon, cut into ¼-inch dice

2 tablespoons minced shallots or onions

1 teaspoon minced garlic

1 pound (454 g) button mushrooms, cleaned and quartered or sliced

1 teaspoon dried thyme leaves

2 cups chicken bone broth,

homemade or store-bought

1 teaspoon fine sea salt

½ teaspoon freshly ground black pepper

2 large eggs

2 tablespoons lemon juice

For Garnish:

Fresh thyme leaves

MCT oil or extra-virgin olive oil, for drizzling

1. Place the diced bacon in a stockpot and sauté over medium heat until crispy, about 3 minutes. Remove the bacon from the pan, but leave the drippings. Add the shallots and garlic to the pan with the drippings and sauté over medium heat for about 3 minutes, until softened and aromatic. 2. Add the mushrooms and dried thyme and sauté over medium heat until the mushrooms are golden brown, about 10 minutes. Add the broth, salt, and pepper and bring to boil. 3. Whisk the eggs and lemon juice in a medium bowl. While whisking, very slowly pour in ½ cup of the hot soup (if you add the hot soup too quickly, the eggs will curdle). Slowly whisk another cup of the hot soup into the egg mixture. 4. Pour the hot egg mixture into the pot while stirring. Add the cooked bacon, then reduce the heat and simmer for 10 minutes, stirring constantly. The soup will thicken slightly as it cooks. Remove from the heat. Garnish with fresh thyme and drizzle with MCT oil before serving. 5. This soup is best served fresh but can be stored in an airtight container in the fridge for up to 3 days. To reheat, place in a saucepan over medium-low heat until warmed, stirring constantly to keep the eggs from curdling.

Per Serving:

Calories: 185 | fat: 13g | protein: 11g | carbs: 6g | net carbs: 4g | fiber: 2g

Keto Pho with Shirataki Noodles

Prep time: 20 minutes | Cook time: 10 minutes | Makes 4 bowls

8 ounces (227 g) sirloin, very thinly sliced	ground ginger
	8 cups bone broth
3 tablespoons coconut oil (or butter or ghee)	4 (7-ounce / 198-g) packages shirataki noodles, drained and rinsed
2 garlic cloves, minced	
2 tablespoons liquid or coconut aminos	1 cup bean sprouts
	1 scallion, chopped
2 tablespoons fish sauce	1 tablespoon toasted sesame seeds (optional)
1 teaspoon freshly grated or	

1. Put the sirloin in the freezer while you prepare the broth and other ingredients (about 15 to 20 minutes). This makes it easier to slice. 2. In a large pot over medium heat, melt the coconut oil. Add the garlic and cook for 3 minutes. Then add the aminos, fish sauce, ginger, and bone broth. Bring to a boil. 3. Remove the beef from the freezer and slice it very thin. 4. Divide the noodles, beef, and bean sprouts evenly among four serving bowls. Carefully ladle 2 cups of broth into each bowl. Cover the bowls with plates and let sit for 3 to 5 minutes to cook the meat. 5. Serve garnished with the chopped scallion and sesame seeds (if using).

Per Serving (1 bowl):

Calories: 385 | fat: 29g | protein: 23g | carbs: 8g | net carbs: 4g | fiber: 4g

Coconut Red Curry Soup

Prep time: 10 minutes | Cook time: 20 minutes | Serves 4

¼ cup (55 g) coconut oil, or ¼ cup (60 ml) avocado oil	milk
	⅓ cup (80 g) red curry paste
2 cloves garlic, minced	1 teaspoon finely ground sea salt
1 (2-in/5-cm) piece fresh ginger root, peeled and minced	
	FOR SERVING:
1 pound (455 g) boneless, skinless chicken thighs, cut into small cubes	2 medium zucchinis, spiral sliced
	3 green onions, sliced
2 cups (475 ml) chicken bone broth	¼ cup (15 g) fresh cilantro leaves, chopped
1 cup (240 ml) full-fat coconut	

1. Heat the oil in a large saucepan over medium-low heat. Add the garlic and ginger and cook until fragrant, about 2 minutes. 2. Add the chicken thighs, broth, coconut milk, curry paste, and salt. Stir to combine, cover, and bring to a light simmer over medium-high heat. Once simmering, reduce the heat and continue to simmer for 15 minutes, until the flavors meld. 3. Divide the spiral-sliced zucchinis among 4 bowls and top with the curry soup. Sprinkle with the green onions and cilantro before serving.

Per Serving:

Calories: 567 | fat: 40g | protein: 40g | carbs: 11g | net carbs: 10g | fiber: 1g

Butternut Squash Soup with Turmeric & Ginger

Prep time: 5 minutes | Cook time: 35 minutes | serves 8

1 small butternut squash	½ cup dry Marsala wine (optional)
3 tablespoons coconut oil	
3 shallots, coarsely chopped	8 cups miso broth
1-inch knob fresh ginger, peeled and coarsely chopped	1 cup coconut cream
	Cold-pressed olive oil, for drizzling
1-inch knob fresh turmeric root, peeled and coarsely chopped	Handful toasted pumpkin seeds, for garnish (optional)
1 fresh lemongrass stalk, coarsely chopped	

1. Preheat the oven to 365°F. 2. Puncture the squash skin with a fork several times to create air vents. Put the entire squash into a baking dish and bake for 30 minutes or until it is extremely tender. 3. While the squash is baking, heat the oil in a large stockpot over medium heat. Add the shallots, ginger, turmeric, and lemongrass to the pan and sauté until the spices become fragrant and the shallots are tender. 4. Deglaze the pot by pouring in the Marsala wine (if using), and stirring, scraping the bottom of the pot to loosen any stuck bits. Once the alcohol starts to reduce, add the miso broth and turn the heat to low. 5. Remove the squash from oven and poke it with a fork to check for tenderness. Carefully cut the squash in half lengthwise, allowing any liquid to drain out. 6. Once the squash is cool enough to handle, scoop out the seeds. With a paring knife, remove the skin. Roughly chop the squash and add it to the stockpot. 7. Pour the coconut cream into the pot, bring to a simmer, and remove from the heat. 8. Using an immersion blender, blend the soup thoroughly until smooth and velvety. Drizzle with olive oil, and top with toasted pumpkin seeds, if desired. Serve warm.

Per Serving:

Calories: 149 | fat: 13g | protein: 2g | carbs: 10g | net carbs: 9g | fiber: 1g

Kale Curry Soup

Prep time: 10 minutes | Cook time: 15 minutes | Serves 3

2 cups kale	1 teaspoon curry paste
1 teaspoon almond butter	½ cup heavy cream
1 tablespoon fresh cilantro	1 cup chicken stock
½ cup ground chicken	½ teaspoon salt

1. Put the kale in the Instant Pot. 2. Add the almond butter, cilantro, and ground chicken. Sauté the mixture for 5 minutes. 3. Meanwhile, mix the curry paste and heavy cream in the Instant Pot until creamy. 4. Add chicken stock and salt, and close the lid. 5. Select Manual mode and set cooking time for 10 minutes on High Pressure. 6. When timer beeps, make a quick pressure release. Open the lid. 7. Serve warm.

Per Serving:

Calories: 183 | fat: 13g | protein: 10g | carbs: 7g | net carbs: 6g | fiber: 1g

Beef and Cauliflower Soup

Prep time: 10 minutes | Cook time: 14 minutes | Serves 4

1 cup ground beef

½ cup cauliflower, shredded

1 teaspoon unsweetened tomato purée

¼ cup coconut milk

1 teaspoon minced garlic

1 teaspoon dried oregano

½ teaspoon salt

4 cups water

1. Put all ingredients in the Instant Pot and stir well. 2. Close the lid. Select Manual mode and set cooking time for 14 minutes on High Pressure. 3. When timer beeps, make a quick pressure release and open the lid. 4. Blend with an immersion blender until smooth. 5. Serve warm.

Per Serving:

Calories: 106 | fat: 8g | protein: 7g | carbs: 2g | net carbs: 1g | fiber: 1g

Bacon Broccoli Soup

Prep time: 12 minutes | Cook time: 12 minutes | Serves 6

2 large heads broccoli

2 strips bacon, chopped

2 tablespoons unsalted butter

¼ cup diced onions

Cloves squeezed from 1 head roasted garlic, or 2 cloves garlic, minced

3 cups chicken broth or beef broth

6 ounces (170 g) extra-sharp Cheddar cheese, shredded (about 1½ cups)

2 ounces (57 g) cream cheese, softened

½ teaspoon fine sea salt

¼ teaspoon ground black pepper

Pinch of ground nutmeg

1. Cut the broccoli florets off the stems, leaving as much of the stems intact as possible. Reserve the florets for another recipe. Trim the bottom end of each stem so that it is flat. Using a spiral slicer, cut the stems into "noodles." 2. Place the bacon in the Instant Pot and press Sauté. Cook, stirring occasionally, for 4 minutes, or until crisp. Remove the bacon with a slotted spoon and set aside on a paper towel-lined plate to drain, leaving the drippings in the pot. 3. Add the butter and onions to the Instant Pot and cook for 4 minutes, or until the onions are soft. Add the garlic (and, if using raw garlic, sauté for another minute). Add the broth, Cheddar cheese, cream cheese, salt, pepper, and nutmeg and sauté until the cheeses are melted, about 3 minutes. Press Cancel to stop the Sauté. 4. Use a stick blender to purée the soup until smooth. Alternatively, you can pour the soup into a regular blender or food processor and purée until smooth, then return it to the Instant Pot. If using a regular blender, you may need to blend the soup in two batches; if you overfill the blender jar, the soup will not purée properly. 5. Add the broccoli noodles to the puréed soup in the Instant Pot. Seal the lid, press Manual, and set the timer for 1 minute. Once finished, let the pressure release naturally. 6. Remove the lid and stir well. Ladle the soup into bowls and sprinkle some of the bacon on top of each serving.

Per Serving:

Calories: 258 | fat: 19g | protein: 13g | carbs: 9g | net carbs: 8g | fiber: 1g

Cioppino Seafood Soup

Prep time: 10 minutes | Cook time: 30 minutes | Serves 6

2 tablespoons olive oil

½ onion, chopped

2 celery stalks, sliced

1 red bell pepper, chopped

1 tablespoon minced garlic

2 cups fish stock

1 (15-ounce) can coconut milk

1 cup crushed tomatoes

2 tablespoons tomato paste

1 tablespoon chopped fresh basil

2 teaspoons chopped fresh

oregano

½ teaspoon sea salt

½ teaspoon freshly ground black pepper

¼ teaspoon red pepper flakes

10 ounces salmon, cut into 1-inch pieces

½ pound shrimp, peeled and deveined

12 clams or mussels, cleaned and debearded but in the shell

1. Sauté the vegetables. In a large stockpot over medium-high heat, warm the olive oil. Add the onion, celery, red bell pepper, and garlic and sauté until they've softened, about 4 minutes. 2. Make the soup base. Stir in the fish stock, coconut milk, crushed tomatoes, tomato paste, basil, oregano, salt, pepper, and red pepper flakes. Bring the soup to a boil, then reduce the heat to low and simmer the soup for 10 minutes. 3. Add the seafood. Stir in the salmon and simmer until it goes opaque, about 5 minutes. Add the shrimp and simmer until they're almost cooked through, about 3 minutes. Add the mussels and let them simmer until they open, about 3 minutes. Throw out any mussels that don't open. 4. Serve. Ladle the soup into bowls and serve it hot.

Per Serving:

Calories: 377 | fat: 29g | protein: 24g | carbs: 9g | net carbs: 7g | fiber: 2g

Broccoli-Cheese Soup

Prep time: 5 minutes | Cook time: 20 minutes | Serves 4

2 tablespoons butter

1 cup broccoli florets, finely chopped

1 cup heavy (whipping) cream

1 cup chicken or vegetable broth

Pink Himalayan salt

Freshly ground black pepper

1 cup shredded cheese, some reserved for topping (I use sharp Cheddar)

1. In a medium saucepan over medium heat, melt the butter. 2. Add the broccoli and sauté in the butter for about 5 minutes, until tender. 3. Add the cream and the chicken broth, stirring constantly. Season with pink Himalayan salt and pepper. Cook, stirring occasionally, for 10 to 15 minutes, until the soup has thickened. 4. Turn down the heat to low, and begin adding the shredded cheese. Reserve a small handful of cheese for topping the bowls of soup. (Do not add all the cheese at once, or it may clump up.) Add small amounts, slowly, while stirring constantly. 5. Pour the soup into four bowls, top each with half of the reserved cheese, and serve.

Per Serving:

Calories: 383 | fat: 37g | protein: 10g | carbs: 4g | net carbs: 4g | fiber: 0g

Lamb and Broccoli Soup

Prep time: 10 minutes | Cook time: 25 minutes | Serves 4

7 ounces (198 g) lamb fillet, chopped	¼ daikon, chopped
1 tablespoon avocado oil	2 bell peppers, chopped
½ cup broccoli, roughly chopped	¼ teaspoon ground cumin
	5 cups beef broth

1. Sauté the lamb fillet with avocado oil in the Instant Pot for 5 minutes. 2. Add the broccoli, daikon, bell peppers, ground cumin, and beef broth. 3. Close the lid. Select Manual mode and set cooking time for 20 minutes on High Pressure. 4. When timer beeps, use a natural pressure release for 10 minutes, then release any remaining pressure. Open the lid. 5. Serve warm.

Per Serving:

Calories: 169 | fat: 6g | protein: 21g | carbs: 7g | net carbs: 6g | fiber: 1g

Bacon Curry Soup

Prep time: 10 minutes | Cook time: 20 minutes | Serves 4

3 ounces (85 g) bacon, chopped	1 cup coconut milk
1 tablespoon chopped scallions	3 cups beef broth
1 teaspoon curry powder	1 cup Cheddar cheese, shredded

1. Heat the the Instant Pot on Sauté mode for 3 minutes and add bacon. Cook for 5 minutes. Flip constantly. 2. Add the scallions and curry powder. Sauté for 5 minutes more. 3. Pour in the coconut milk and beef broth. Add the Cheddar cheese and stir to mix well. 4. Select Manual mode and set cooking time for 10 minutes on High Pressure. 5. When timer beeps, use a quick pressure release. Open the lid. 6. Blend the soup with an immersion blender until smooth. Serve warm.

Per Serving:

Calories: 398 | fat: 34g | protein: 20g | carbs: 5g | net carbs: 4g | fiber: 1g

Greek Chicken and "Rice" Soup with Artichokes

Prep time: 10 minutes | Cook time: 15 minutes | Serves 4

4 cups chicken stock	divided
2 cups riced cauliflower, divided	8 ounces (227 g) cooked chicken, coarsely chopped
2 large egg yolks	1 (13¾-ounce / 390-g) can
¼ cup freshly squeezed lemon juice (about 2 lemons)	artichoke hearts, drained and quartered
¾ cup extra-virgin olive oil,	¼ cup chopped fresh dill

1. In a large saucepan, bring the stock to a low boil. Reduce the heat to low and simmer, covered. 2. Transfer 1 cup of the hot stock to a blender or food processor. Add ½ cup raw riced cauliflower, the egg yolks, and lemon juice and purée. While the processor or blender is running, stream in ½ cup olive oil and blend until smooth. 3. Whisking constantly, pour the purée into the simmering stock until well blended together and smooth. Add the chicken and artichokes and simmer until thickened slightly, 8 to 10 minutes. Stir in the dill and remaining 1½ cups riced cauliflower. Serve warm, drizzled with the remaining ¼ cup olive oil.

Per Serving:

Calories: 583 | fat: 47g | protein: 26g | carbs: 19g | fiber: 10g | sodium: 189mg

Loaded Fauxtato Soup

Prep time: 5 minutes | Cook time: 20 minutes | serves 4

3 tablespoons salted butter	2 cups shredded sharp cheddar cheese, plus extra for garnish
½ cup chopped white onions	1 cup heavy whipping cream
2 cloves garlic, minced	Salt and ground black pepper
1 (16-ounce) bag frozen cauliflower florets	8 slices bacon, cooked and cut into small pieces, for garnish
2 cups vegetable broth	

1. Melt the butter in a stockpot over medium heat. Sauté the onions and garlic in the butter until the onions are tender and translucent. 2. Add the cauliflower and broth to the pot. Bring to a gentle boil over high heat, then reduce the heat to maintain a simmer and continue cooking until the cauliflower is tender, stirring occasionally, about 15 minutes. 3. Turn the heat down to the lowest setting and add the cheese and cream to the pot. Stir until the cheese is melted and well combined with the rest of the soup. 4. Season to taste with salt and pepper. Serve garnished with extra cheese and bacon pieces. Leftovers can be stored in an airtight container in the refrigerator for up to 5 days.

Per Serving:

Calories: 560| fat: 45g | protein: 5g | carbs: 9g | net carbs: 6g | fiber: 3g

Coconut, Green Beans & Shrimp Curry Soup

Prep time: 10 minutes | Cook time: 15 minutes | Serves 4

2 tablespoons ghee	2 tablespoons red curry paste
1 pound (454 g) jumbo shrimp, peeled and deveined	6 ounces (170 g) coconut milk
	Salt and chili pepper to taste
2 teaspoons ginger-garlic puree	1 bunch green beans, halved

1. Melt ghee in a medium saucepan over medium heat. Add the shrimp, season with salt and black pepper, and cook until they are opaque, 2 to 3 minutes. Remove shrimp to a plate. Add the ginger-garlic puree and red curry paste to the ghee and sauté for 2 minutes until fragrant. 2. Stir in the coconut milk; add the shrimp, salt, chili pepper, and green beans. Cook for 4 minutes. Reduce the heat to a simmer and cook an additional 3 minutes, occasionally stirring. Adjust taste with salt, fetch soup into serving bowls, and serve with cauli rice.

Per Serving:

Calories: 138| fat: 1g | protein: 28g | carbs: 4g | net carbs: 3g | fiber: 1g

Chicken Enchilada Soup

Prep time: 10 minutes | Cook time: 40 minutes | Serves 6

2 (6-ounce / 170-g) boneless, skinless chicken breasts	chilies
½ tablespoon chili powder	2 cups chicken broth
½ teaspoon salt	⅛ cup pickled jalapeños
½ teaspoon garlic powder	4 ounces (113 g) cream cheese
¼ teaspoon pepper	1 cup uncooked cauliflower rice
½ cup red enchilada sauce	1 avocado, diced
½ medium onion, diced	1 cup shredded mild Cheddar cheese
1 (4-ounce / 113-g) can green	½ cup sour cream

1. Sprinkle seasoning over chicken breasts and set aside. Pour enchilada sauce into Instant Pot and place chicken on top. 2. Add onion, chilies, broth, and jalapeños to the pot, then place cream cheese on top of chicken breasts. Click lid closed. Adjust time for 25 minutes. When timer beeps, quick-release the pressure and shred chicken with forks. 3. Mix soup together and add cauliflower rice, with pot on Keep Warm setting. Replace lid and let pot sit for 15 minutes, still on Keep Warm. This will cook cauliflower rice. Serve with avocado, Cheddar, and sour cream.

Per Serving:

Calories: 318 | fat: 19g | protein: 21g | carbs: 10g | net carbs: 7g | fiber: 3g

Tomato Bisque

Prep time: 10 minutes | Cook time: 40 minutes | serves 8

Nonstick coconut oil cooking spray	plus more for drizzling
1 pound heirloom cherry tomatoes, coarsely chopped	2 thyme sprigs
	Sea salt
1 yellow onion, coarsely chopped	Freshly ground black pepper
2 garlic cloves, coarsely chopped	1 lemon, halved
	1 cup coconut cream
¼ cup cold-pressed olive oil,	⅓ cup chopped fresh basil, for garnish

1. Preheat the oven to 400°F. Grease a baking dish with cooking spray and set aside. 2. Combine the tomatoes, onion, and garlic in the baking dish. Drizzle with the olive oil and toss in the thyme. Season with salt and pepper. Top with the lemon halves and roast for 20 minutes or until the tomatoes start to blister. 3. Remove from the oven and transfer the mixture to a large saucepan over low heat. 4. Stir in the coconut cream and bring the soup to a simmer. Cook for 20 minutes to allow the flavors to meld together. 5. Remove and discard the lemon halves. 6. Turn off the heat and blend the soup with an immersion blender until it is silky smooth (adding warm water if necessary to reach desired texture). 7. Finish with cracked black pepper, olive oil drizzle, the basil, and additional salt, if desired.

Per Serving:

Calories: 142 | fat: 14g | protein: 1g | carbs: 7g | net carbs: 5g | fiber: 2g

Bacon Cheddar Cauliflower Soup

Prep time: 15 minutes | Cook time: 30 minutes | Serves 6

1 large head cauliflower, chopped into florets	2 cups chicken broth, or vegetable broth, plus more as needed
¼ cup olive oil	
Salt and freshly ground black pepper, to taste	2 cups heavy (whipping) cream, plus more as needed
12 ounces (340 g) bacon, chopped	½ cup shredded Cheddar cheese, plus more for topping
½ onion, roughly chopped	Sliced scallion, green parts only, or fresh chives, for garnish
2 garlic cloves, minced	

1. Preheat the oven to 400°F (205°C). 2. On a large rimmed baking sheet, toss the cauliflower with the olive oil and season with salt and pepper. Bake for 25 to 30 minutes or until slightly browned. 3. While the cauliflower roasts, in a large saucepan over medium heat, cook the bacon for 5 to 7 minutes until crispy. Transfer the bacon to a paper towel-lined plate to drain; leave the bacon fat in the pan. 4. Return the pan to medium heat and add the onion and garlic. Stir well to combine and sauté for 5 to 7 minutes until the onion is softened and translucent. Season with salt and pepper. 5. Remove the cauliflower from the oven and add it to the pan with the onion and garlic. Stir in the broth and bring the liquid to a simmer. Reduce the heat to low. Cook for 5 to 7 minutes. Remove from the heat. With an immersion blender, carefully blend the soup. Alternatively, transfer the soup to a regular blender (working in batches if necessary), blend until smooth, and return the soup to the pan. 6. Stir in the cream. You may need to add a bit more broth or cream, depending on how thick you like your soup. Add the Cheddar and stir until melted and combined. Spoon the soup into bowls and top with bacon and more Cheddar. Garnish with scallion.

Per Serving (1 cup):

Calories: 545 | fat: 49g | protein: 15g | carbs: 11g | net carbs: 7g | fiber: 4g

Power Green Soup

Prep time: 10 minutes | Cook time: 15 minutes | Serves 6

1 broccoli head, chopped	5 cups veggie stock
1 cup spinach	1 cup coconut milk
1 onion, chopped	1 tablespoon ghee
2 garlic cloves, minced	1 bay leaf
½ cup watercress	Salt and black pepper, to taste

1. Melt the ghee in a large pot over medium heat. Add onion and garlic, and cook for 3 minutes. Add broccoli and cook for an additional 5 minutes. Pour the stock over and add the bay leaf. Close the lid, bring to a boil, and reduce the heat. Simmer for about 3 minutes. 2. At the end, add spinach and watercress, and cook for 3 more minutes. Stir in the coconut cream, salt and black pepper. Discard the bay leaf, and blend the soup with a hand blender.

Per Serving:

Calories: 392 | fat: 38g | protein: 5g | carbs: 7g | net carbs: 6g | fiber: 1g

Buffalo Chicken Soup

Prep time: 7 minutes | Cook time: 10 minutes | Serves 2

1 ounce (28 g) celery stalk, chopped	2 ounces (57 g) Mozzarella, shredded
4 tablespoons coconut milk	6 ounces (170 g) cooked
¾ teaspoon salt	chicken, shredded
¼ teaspoon white pepper	2 tablespoons keto-friendly
1 cup water	Buffalo sauce

1. Place the chopped celery stalk, coconut milk, salt, white pepper, water, and Mozzarella in the Instant Pot. Stir to mix well. 2. Set the Manual mode and set timer for 7 minutes on High Pressure. 3. When timer beeps, use a quick pressure release and open the lid. 4. Transfer the soup on the bowls. Stir in the chicken and Buffalo sauce. Serve warm.

Per Serving:

Calories: 287 | fat: 15g | protein: 33g | carbs: 4g | net carbs: 3g | fiber: 1g

Mushroom Pizza Soup

Prep time: 10 minutes | Cook time: 22 minutes | Serves 3

1 teaspoon coconut oil	½ teaspoon Italian seasoning
¼ cup cremini mushrooms, sliced	1 teaspoon unsweetened tomato purée
5 ounces (142 g) Italian sausages, chopped	1 cup water
½ jalapeño pepper, sliced	4 ounces (113 g) Mozzarella, shredded

1. Melt the coconut oil in the Instant Pot on Sauté mode. 2. Add the mushrooms and cook for 10 minutes. 3. Add the chopped sausages, sliced jalapeño, Italian seasoning, and unsweetened tomato purée. Pour in the water and stir to mix well. 4. Close the lid and select Manual mode. Set cooking time for 12 minutes on High Pressure. 5. When timer beeps, use a quick pressure release and open the lid. 6. Ladle the soup in the bowls. Top it with Mozzarella. Serve warm.

Per Serving:

Calories: 289 | fat: 23g | protein: 18g | carbs: 3g | net carbs: 2g | fiber: 0g

Vegan Pho

Prep time: 10 minutes | Cook time: 20 minutes | serves 8

8 cups vegetable broth	1 (8-ounce) package shirataki
1-inch knob fresh ginger, peeled and chopped	noodles
2 tablespoons tamari	2 cups shredded cabbage
3 cups shredded fresh spinach	2 cups mung bean sprouts
2 cups chopped broccoli	Fresh Thai basil leaves, for garnish
1 cup sliced mushrooms	Fresh cilantro leaves, for
½ cup chopped carrots	garnish
⅓ cup chopped scallions	Fresh mint leaves, for garnish

1 lime, cut into 8 wedges, for   garnish

1. In a large stockpot over medium-high heat, bring the vegetable broth to a simmer with the ginger and tamari. 2. Once the broth is hot, add the spinach, broccoli, mushrooms, carrots, and scallions, and simmer for a few minutes, just until the vegetables start to become tender. 3. Stir in the shirataki noodles, then remove the pot from the heat and divide the soup among serving bowls. 4. Top each bowl with cabbage, sprouts, basil, cilantro, mint, and a lime wedge.

Per Serving:

Calories: 47 | fat: 0g | protein: 3g | carbs: 10g | net carbs: 7g | fiber: 3g

Beef Chili

Prep time: 5 minutes | Cook time: 50 minutes | Serves 4

½ green bell pepper, cored, seeded, and chopped	crushed tomatoes
½ medium onion, chopped	1 cup beef broth
2 tablespoons extra-virgin olive oil	1 tablespoon ground cumin
	1 tablespoon chili powder
1 tablespoon minced garlic	2 teaspoons paprika
1 pound (454 g) ground beef (80/20)	1 teaspoon pink Himalayan sea salt
1 (14-ounce / 397-g) can	¼ teaspoon cayenne pepper

1. In a medium pot, combine the bell pepper, onion, and olive oil. Cook over medium heat for 8 to 10 minutes, until the onion is translucent. 2. Add the garlic and cook for 1 minute longer, until fragrant. 3. Add the ground beef and cook for 7 to 10 minutes, until browned. 4. Add the tomatoes, broth, cumin, chili powder, paprika, salt, and cayenne. Stir to combine. 5. Simmer the chili for 30 minutes, until the flavors come together, then enjoy.

Per Serving:

Calories: 406 | fat: 31g | protein: 22g | carbs: 12g | net carbs: 8g | fiber: 4g

Chicken and Zoodles Soup

Prep time: 25 minutes | Cook time: 15 minutes | Serves 2

2 cups water	2 ounces (57 g) zucchini,
6 ounces (170 g) chicken fillet, chopped	spiralized
1 teaspoon salt	1 tablespoon coconut aminos

1. Pour water in the Instant Pot. Add chopped chicken fillet and salt. Close the lid. 2. Select Manual mode and set cooking time for 15 minutes on High Pressure. 3. When cooking is complete, perform a natural pressure release for 10 minutes, then release any remaining pressure. Open the lid. 4. Fold in the zoodles and coconut aminos. 5. Leave the soup for 10 minutes to rest. Serve warm.

Per Serving:

Calories: 175 | fat: 6g | protein: 25g | carbs: 5g | net carbs: 2g | fiber: 3g

Broccoli and Red Feta Soup

Prep time: 10 minutes | Cook time: 25 minutes | Serves 4

1 cup broccoli, chopped

½ cup coconut cream

1 teaspoon unsweetened tomato purée

4 cups beef broth

1 teaspoon chili flakes

6 ounces (170 g) feta, crumbled

1. Put broccoli, coconut cream, tomato purée, and beef broth in the Instant Pot. Sprinkle with chili flakes and stir to mix well. 2. Close the lid and select Manual mode. Set cooking time for 8 minutes on High Pressure. 3. When timer beeps, make a quick pressure release and open the lid. 4. Add the feta cheese and stir the soup on Sauté mode for 5 minutes or until the cheese melt. 5. Serve immediately.

Per Serving:

Calories: 229 | fat: 18g | protein: 12g | carbs: 6g | net carbs: 5g | fiber: 1g

Thai Shrimp and Mushroom Soup

Prep time: 15 minutes | Cook time: 10 minutes | Serves 6

2 tablespoons unsalted butter, divided

½ pound (227 g) medium uncooked shrimp, shelled and deveined

½ medium yellow onion, diced

2 cloves garlic, minced

1 cup sliced fresh white mushrooms

1 tablespoon freshly grated ginger root

4 cups chicken broth

2 tablespoons fish sauce

2½ teaspoons red curry paste

2 tablespoons lime juice

1 stalk lemongrass, outer stalk removed, crushed, and finely chopped

2 tablespoons coconut aminos

1 teaspoon sea salt

½ teaspoon ground black pepper

13.5 ounces (383 g) can unsweetened, full-fat coconut milk

3 tablespoons chopped fresh cilantro

1. Select the Instant Pot on Sauté mode. Add 1 tablespoon butter. 2. Once the butter is melted, add the shrimp and sauté for 3 minutes or until opaque. Transfer the shrimp to a medium bowl. Set aside. 3. Add the remaining butter to the pot. Once the butter is melted, add the onions and garlic and sauté for 2 minutes or until the garlic is fragrant and the onions are softened. 4. Add the mushrooms, ginger root, chicken broth, fish sauce, red curry paste, lime juice, lemongrass, coconut aminos, sea salt, and black pepper to the pot. Stir to combine. 5. Lock the lid. Select Manual mode and set cooking time for 5 minutes on High Pressure. 6. When cooking is complete, allow the pressure to release naturally for 5 minutes, then release the remaining pressure. 7. Open the lid. Stir in the cooked shrimp and coconut milk. 8. Select Sauté mode. Bring the soup to a boil and then press Keep Warm / Cancel. Let the soup rest in the pot for 2 minutes. 9. Ladle the soup into bowls and sprinkle the cilantro over top. Serve hot.

Per Serving:

Calories: 237 | fat: 20g | protein: 9g | carbs: 9g | net carbs: 6g | fiber: 2g

Chilled Cilantro and Avocado Soup

Prep time: 10 minutes | Cook time: 7 minutes | Serves 6

2 to 3 tablespoons olive oil

1 large white onion, diced

3 garlic cloves, crushed

1 serrano chile, seeded and diced

Salt and freshly ground black pepper, to taste

4 or 5 ripe avocados, peeled,

halved, and pitted

4 cups chicken broth, or vegetable broth

2 cups water

Juice of 1 lemon

¼ cup chopped fresh cilantro, plus more for garnish

½ cup sour cream

1. In a large pan over medium heat, heat the olive oil. 2. Add the onion and garlic. Sauté for 5 to 7 minutes until the onion is softened and translucent. 3. Add the serrano, season with salt and pepper, and remove from the heat. 4. In a blender, combine the avocados, chicken broth, water, lemon juice, cilantro, and onion-garlic-chile mixture. Purée until smooth (you may have to do this in batches), strain through a fine-mesh sieve, and season with more salt and pepper. Refrigerate, covered, for about 3 hours or until chilled through. 5. To serve, top with sour cream and a sprinkle of chopped cilantro. Refrigerate leftovers in an airtight container for up to 1 week.

Per Serving:

Calories: 513 | fat: 45g | protein: 7g | carbs: 20g | net carbs: 8g | fiber: 12g

Chicken Poblano Pepper Soup

Prep time: 10 minutes | Cook time: 20 minutes | Serves 8

1 cup diced onion

3 poblano peppers, chopped

5 garlic cloves

2 cups diced cauliflower

1½ pounds (680 g) chicken breast, cut into large chunks

¼ cup chopped fresh cilantro

1 teaspoon ground coriander

1 teaspoon ground cumin

1 to 2 teaspoons salt

2 cups water

2 ounces (57 g) cream cheese, cut into small chunks

1 cup sour cream

1. To the inner cooking pot of the Instant Pot, add the onion, poblanos, garlic, cauliflower, chicken, cilantro, coriander, cumin, salt, and water. 2. Lock the lid into place. Select Manual and adjust the pressure to High. Cook for 15 minutes. When the cooking is complete, let the pressure release naturally for 10 minutes, then quick-release any remaining pressure. Unlock the lid. 3. Remove the chicken with tongs and place in a bowl. 4. Tilting the pot, use an immersion blender to roughly purée the vegetable mixture. It should still be slightly chunky. 5. Turn the Instant Pot to Sauté and adjust to high heat. When the broth is hot and bubbling, add the cream cheese and stir until it melts. Use a whisk to blend in the cream cheese if needed. 6. Shred the chicken and stir it back into the pot. Once it is heated through, serve, topped with sour cream, and enjoy.

Per Serving:

Calories: 202 | fat: 10g | protein: 20g | carbs: 8g | net carbs: 5g | fiber: 3g

Coconut and Cauliflower Curry Shrimp Soup

Prep time: 5 minutes | Cook time: 2 hours 15 minutes | Serves 4

8 ounces water

1 (13.5-ounce) can unsweetened full-fat coconut milk

2 cups riced/shredded cauliflower (I buy it pre-riced at Trader Joe's)

2 tablespoons red curry paste

2 tablespoons chopped fresh

cilantro leaves, divided

Pink Himalayan salt

Freshly ground black pepper

1 cup shrimp (I use defrosted Trader Joe's Frozen Medium Cooked Shrimp, which are peeled and deveined, with tail off)

1. With the crock insert in place, preheat the slow cooker to high. 2. Add the water, coconut milk, riced cauliflower, red curry paste, and 1 tablespoon of chopped cilantro, and season with pink Himalayan salt and pepper. Stir to combine. 3. Cover and cook on high for 2 hours. 4. Season the shrimp with pink Himalayan salt and pepper, add them to the slow cooker, and stir. Cook for an additional 15 minutes. 5. Ladle the soup into four bowls, top each with half of the remaining 1 tablespoon of chopped cilantro, and serve.

Per Serving:

Calories: 269 | fat: 21g | protein: 16g | carbs: 8g | net carbs: 5g | fiber: 3g

Broccoli Ginger Soup

Prep time: 5 minutes | Cook time: 25 minutes | Serves 4

3 tablespoons coconut oil or avocado oil

1 small white onion, sliced

2 cloves garlic, minced

5 cups (420 g) broccoli florets

1 (13½-ounce/400-ml) can full-fat coconut milk

1½ cups (355 ml) chicken bone broth

1 (2-in/5-cm) piece fresh ginger root, peeled and minced

1½ teaspoons turmeric powder

¾ teaspoon finely ground sea salt

⅓ cup (55 g) collagen peptides (optional)

¼ cup (40 g) sesame seeds

1. Melt the oil in a large frying pan over medium heat. Add the onion and garlic and cook until translucent, about 10 minutes. 2. Add the broccoli, coconut milk, broth, ginger, turmeric, and salt. Cover and cook for 15 minutes, or until the broccoli is tender. 3. Transfer the broccoli mixture to a blender or food processor. Add the collagen, if using, and blend until smooth. 4. Divide among 4 bowls, top each bowl with 1 tablespoon of sesame seeds, and enjoy!

Per Serving:

Calories: 344 | fat: 26g | protein: 13g | carbs: 12g | net carbs: 7g | fiber: 5g

Beef and Mushroom Stew

Prep time: 15 minutes | Cook time: 30 minutes | Serves 4

2 tablespoons coconut oil

1 pound (454 g) cubed chuck roast

1 cup sliced button mushrooms

½ medium onion, chopped

2 cups beef broth

½ cup chopped celery

1 tablespoon sugar-free tomato paste

1 teaspoon thyme

2 garlic cloves, minced

½ teaspoon xanthan gum

1. Press the Sauté button and add coconut oil to Instant Pot. Brown cubes of chuck roast until golden, working in batches if necessary. (If the pan is overcrowded, they will not brown properly.) Set aside after browning is completed. 2. Add mushrooms and onions to pot. Sauté until mushrooms begin to brown and onions are translucent. Press the Cancel button. 3. Add broth to Instant Pot. Use wooden spoon to scrape bits from bottom if necessary. Add celery, tomato paste, thyme, and garlic. Click lid closed. Press the Manual button and adjust time for 35 minutes. When timer beeps, allow a natural release. 4. When pressure valve drops, stir in xanthan gum and allow to thicken. Serve warm.

Per Serving:

Calories: 354 | fat: 25g | protein: 24g | carbs: 4g | net carbs: 2g | fiber: 2g

Chicken and Kale Soup

Prep time: 5 minutes | Cook time: 5 minutes | Serves 4

2 cups chopped cooked chicken breast

12 ounces (340 g) frozen kale

1 onion, chopped

2 cups water

1 tablespoon powdered chicken broth base

½ teaspoon ground cinnamon

Pinch ground cloves

2 teaspoons minced garlic

1 teaspoon freshly ground black pepper

1 teaspoon salt

2 cups full-fat coconut milk

1. Put the chicken, kale, onion, water, chicken broth base, cinnamon, cloves, garlic, pepper, and salt in the inner cooking pot of the Instant Pot. 2. Lock the lid into place. Select Manual and adjust the pressure to High. Cook for 5 minutes. When the cooking is complete, let the pressure release naturally for 10 minutes, then quick-release any remaining pressure. Unlock the lid. 3. Stir in the coconut milk. Taste and adjust any seasonings as needed before serving.

Per Serving:

Calories: 387 | fat: 27g | protein: 26g | carbs: 10g | net carbs: 8g | fiber: 2g

Garlicky Chicken Soup

Prep time: 5 minutes | Cook time: 20 minutes | Serves 6

10 roasted garlic cloves

½ medium onion, diced

4 tablespoons butter

4 cups chicken broth

½ teaspoon salt

¼ teaspoon pepper

1 teaspoon thyme

1 pound (454 g) boneless, skinless chicken thighs, cubed

½ cup heavy cream

2 ounces (57 g) cream cheese

1. In small bowl, mash roasted garlic into paste. Press the Sauté button and add garlic, onion, and butter to Instant Pot. Sauté for 2 to 3 minutes until onion begins to soften. Press the Cancel button. 2. Add Chicken Broth, salt, pepper, thyme, and chicken to Instant Pot. Click lid closed. Press the Manual button and adjust time for 20 minutes. 3. When timer beeps, quick-release the pressure. Stir in heavy cream and cream cheese until smooth. Serve warm.

Per Serving:

Calories: 291 | fat: 21g | protein: 17g | carbs: 4g | net carbs: 3g | fiber: 1g

Chapter 9 Vegetarian Mains

Stuffed Portobellos

Prep time: 10 minutes | Cook time: 8 minutes | Serves 4

3 ounces (85 g) cream cheese, softened
½ medium zucchini, trimmed and chopped
¼ cup seeded and chopped red bell pepper
1½ cups chopped fresh spinach

leaves
4 large portobello mushrooms, stems removed
2 tablespoons coconut oil, melted
½ teaspoon salt

1. In a medium bowl, mix cream cheese, zucchini, pepper, and spinach. 2. Drizzle mushrooms with coconut oil and sprinkle with salt. Scoop ¼ zucchini mixture into each mushroom. 3. Place mushrooms into ungreased air fryer basket. Adjust the temperature to 400°F (204°C) and air fry for 8 minutes. Portobellos will be tender and tops will be browned when done. Serve warm.

Per Serving:
Calories: 151 | fat: 13g | protein: 4g | carbs: 6g | fiber: 2g | sodium: 427mg

Cauliflower Steak with Gremolata

Prep time: 15 minutes | Cook time: 25 minutes | Serves 4

2 tablespoons olive oil
1 tablespoon Italian seasoning
1 large head cauliflower, outer leaves removed and sliced lengthwise through the core into thick "steaks"
Salt and freshly ground black pepper, to taste
¼ cup Parmesan cheese

Gremolata:
1 bunch Italian parsley (about 1 cup packed)
2 cloves garlic
Zest of 1 small lemon, plus 1 to 2 teaspoons lemon juice
½ cup olive oil
Salt and pepper, to taste

1. Preheat the air fryer to 400°F (204°C). 2. In a small bowl, combine the olive oil and Italian seasoning. Brush both sides of each cauliflower "steak" generously with the oil. Season to taste with salt and black pepper. 3. Working in batches if necessary, arrange the cauliflower in a single layer in the air fryer basket. Pausing halfway through the cooking time to turn the "steaks," air fry for 15 to 20 minutes until the cauliflower is tender and the edges begin to brown. Sprinkle with the Parmesan and air fry for 5 minutes longer. 4. To make the gremolata: In a food processor fitted with a metal blade, combine the parsley, garlic, and lemon zest and juice. With the motor running, add the olive oil in a steady stream until the mixture forms a bright green sauce. Season to taste

with salt and black pepper. Serve the cauliflower steaks with the gremolata spooned over the top.

Per Serving:
Calories: 336 | fat: 30g | protein: 7g | carbs: 15g | fiber: 5g | sodium: 340mg

Caprese Eggplant Stacks

Prep time: 5 minutes | Cook time: 12 minutes | Serves 4

1 medium eggplant, cut into ¼-inch slices
2 large tomatoes, cut into ¼-inch slices
4 ounces (113 g) fresh

Mozzarella, cut into ½-ounce / 14-g slices
2 tablespoons olive oil
¼ cup fresh basil, sliced

1. In a baking dish, place four slices of eggplant on the bottom. Place a slice of tomato on top of each eggplant round, then Mozzarella, then eggplant. Repeat as necessary. 2. Drizzle with olive oil. Cover dish with foil and place dish into the air fryer basket. 3. Adjust the temperature to 350°F (177°C) and bake for 12 minutes. 4. When done, eggplant will be tender. Garnish with fresh basil to serve.

Per Serving:
Calories: 97 | fat: 7g | protein: 2g | carbs: 8g | fiber: 4g | sodium: 11mg

Cheese Stuffed Zucchini

Prep time: 20 minutes | Cook time: 8 minutes | Serves 4

1 large zucchini, cut into four pieces
2 tablespoons olive oil
1 cup Ricotta cheese, room temperature
2 tablespoons scallions, chopped
1 heaping tablespoon fresh

parsley, roughly chopped
1 heaping tablespoon coriander, minced
2 ounces (57 g) Cheddar cheese, preferably freshly grated
1 teaspoon celery seeds
½ teaspoon salt
½ teaspoon garlic pepper

1. Cook your zucchini in the air fryer basket for approximately 10 minutes at 350°F (177°C). Check for doneness and cook for 2-3 minutes longer if needed. 2. Meanwhile, make the stuffing by mixing the other items. 3. When your zucchini is thoroughly cooked, open them up. Divide the stuffing among all zucchini pieces and bake an additional 5 minutes.

Per Serving:
Calories: 242 | fat: 20g | protein: 12g | carbs: 5g | fiber: 1g | sodium: 443mg

Vegetarian Chili with Avocado and Sour Cream

Prep time: 10 minutes | Cook time: 25 minutes | Serves 8

2 tablespoons good-quality olive oil

½ onion, finely chopped

1 red bell pepper, diced

2 jalapeño peppers, chopped

1 tablespoon minced garlic

2 tablespoons chili powder

1 teaspoon ground cumin

4 cups canned diced tomatoes

2 cups pecans, chopped

1 cup sour cream

1 avocado, diced

2 tablespoons chopped fresh cilantro

1. Sauté the vegetables. In a large pot over medium-high heat, warm the olive oil. Add the onion, red bell pepper, jalapeño peppers, and garlic and sauté until they've softened, about 4 minutes. Stir in the chili powder and cumin, stirring to coat the vegetables with the spices. 2. Cook the chili. Stir in the tomatoes and pecans and bring the chili to a boil, then reduce the heat to low and simmer until the vegetables are soft and the flavors mellow, about 20 minutes. 3. Serve. Ladle the chili into bowls and serve it with the sour cream, avocado, and cilantro.

Per Serving:
Calories: 332 | fat: 32g | protein: 5g | carbs: 11g | net carbs: 5g | fiber: 6g

Crustless Spanakopita

Prep time: 15 minutes | Cook time: 45 minutes | Serves 6

12 tablespoons extra-virgin olive oil, divided

1 small yellow onion, diced

1 (32-ounce / 907-g) bag frozen chopped spinach, thawed, fully drained, and patted dry (about 4 cups)

4 garlic cloves, minced

½ teaspoon salt

½ teaspoon freshly ground black pepper

1 cup whole-milk ricotta cheese

4 large eggs

¾ cup crumbled traditional feta cheese

¼ cup pine nuts

1. Preheat the oven to 375°F (190°C). 2. In a large skillet, heat 4 tablespoons olive oil over medium-high heat. Add the onion and sauté until softened, 6 to 8 minutes. 3. Add the spinach, garlic, salt, and pepper and sauté another 5 minutes. Remove from the heat and allow to cool slightly. 4. In a medium bowl, whisk together the ricotta and eggs. Add to the cooled spinach and stir to combine. 5. Pour 4 tablespoons olive oil in the bottom of a 9-by-13-inch glass baking dish and swirl to coat the bottom and sides. Add the spinach-ricotta mixture and spread into an even layer. 6. Bake for 20 minutes or until the mixture begins to set. Remove from the oven and crumble the feta evenly across the top of the spinach. Add the pine nuts and drizzle with the remaining 4 tablespoons olive oil. Return to the oven and bake for an additional 15 to 20 minutes, or until the spinach is fully set and the top is starting to turn golden brown. Allow to cool slightly before cutting to serve.

Per Serving:
Calories: 497 | fat: 44g | protein: 18g | carbs: 11g | fiber: 5g | sodium: 561mg

Eggplant Parmesan

Prep time: 15 minutes | Cook time: 17 minutes | Serves 4

1 medium eggplant, ends trimmed, sliced into ½-inch rounds

¼ teaspoon salt

2 tablespoons coconut oil

½ cup grated Parmesan cheese

1 ounce (28 g) 100% cheese crisps, finely crushed

½ cup low-carb marinara sauce

½ cup shredded Mozzarella cheese

1. Sprinkle eggplant rounds with salt on both sides and wrap in a kitchen towel for 30 minutes. Press to remove excess water, then drizzle rounds with coconut oil on both sides. 2. In a medium bowl, mix Parmesan and cheese crisps. Press each eggplant slice into mixture to coat both sides. 3. Place rounds into ungreased air fryer basket. Adjust the temperature to 350°F (177°C) and air fry for 15 minutes, turning rounds halfway through cooking. They will be crispy around the edges when done. 4. Spoon marinara over rounds and sprinkle with Mozzarella. Continue cooking an additional 2 minutes at 350°F (177°C) until cheese is melted. Serve warm.

Per Serving:
Calories: 208 | fat: 13g | protein: 12g | carbs: 13g | fiber: 5g | sodium: 531mg

Greek Vegetable Briam

Prep time: 10 minutes | Cook time: 30 minutes | Serves 4

⅓ cup good-quality olive oil, divided

1 onion, thinly sliced

1 tablespoon minced garlic

¾ small eggplant, diced

2 zucchini, diced

2 cups chopped cauliflower

1 red bell pepper, diced

2 cups diced tomatoes

2 tablespoons chopped fresh parsley

2 tablespoons chopped fresh oregano

Sea salt, for seasoning

Freshly ground black pepper, for seasoning

1½ cups crumbled feta cheese

¼ cup pumpkin seeds

1. Preheat the oven. Set the oven to broil and lightly grease a 9-by-13-inch casserole dish with olive oil. 2. Sauté the aromatics. In a medium stockpot over medium heat, warm 3 tablespoons of the olive oil. Add the onion and garlic and sauté until they've softened, about 3 minutes. 3. Sauté the vegetables. Stir in the eggplant and cook for 5 minutes, stirring occasionally. Add the zucchini, cauliflower, and red bell pepper and cook for 5 minutes. Stir in the tomatoes, parsley, and oregano and cook, giving it a stir from time to time, until the vegetables are tender, about 10 minutes. Season it with salt and pepper. 4. Broil. Transfer the vegetable mixture to the casserole dish and top with the crumbled feta. Broil for about 4 minutes until the cheese is golden. 5. Serve. Divide the casserole between four plates and top it with the pumpkin seeds. Drizzle with the remaining olive oil.

Per Serving:
Calories: 356 | fat: 28g | protein: 11g | carbs: 18g | net carbs: 11g | fiber: 7g

Broccoli-Cheese Fritters

Prep time: 5 minutes | Cook time: 20 to 25 minutes | Serves 4

1 cup broccoli florets
1 cup shredded Mozzarella cheese
¾ cup almond flour
½ cup flaxseed meal, divided
2 teaspoons baking powder
1 teaspoon garlic powder
Salt and freshly ground black pepper, to taste
2 eggs, lightly beaten
½ cup ranch dressing

1. Preheat the air fryer to 400ºF (204ºC). 2. In a food processor fitted with a metal blade, pulse the broccoli until very finely chopped. 3. Transfer the broccoli to a large bowl and add the Mozzarella, almond flour, ¼ cup of the flaxseed meal, baking powder, and garlic powder. Stir until thoroughly combined. Season to taste with salt and black pepper. Add the eggs and stir again to form a sticky dough. Shape the dough into 1¼-inch fritters. 4. Place the remaining ¼ cup flaxseed meal in a shallow bowl and roll the fritters in the meal to form an even coating. 5. Working in batches if necessary, arrange the fritters in a single layer in the basket of the air fryer and spray generously with olive oil. Pausing halfway through the cooking time to shake the basket, air fry for 20 to 25 minutes until the fritters are golden brown and crispy. Serve with the ranch dressing for dipping.

Per Serving:
Calories: 388 | fat: 30g | protein: 19g | carbs: 14g | fiber: 7g | sodium: 526mg

Cheesy Garden Veggie Crustless Quiche

Prep time: 5 minutes | Cook time: 25 minutes | Serves 4

1 tablespoon grass-fed butter, divided
6 eggs
¾ cup heavy (whipping) cream
3 ounces goat cheese, divided
½ cup sliced mushrooms,
chopped
1 scallion, white and green parts, chopped
1 cup shredded fresh spinach
10 cherry tomatoes, cut in half

1. Preheat the oven. Set the oven temperature to 350°F. Grease a 9-inch pie plate with ½ teaspoon of the butter and set it aside. 2. Mix the quiche base. In a medium bowl, whisk the eggs, cream, and 2 ounces of the cheese until it's all well blended. Set it aside. 3. Sauté the vegetables. In a small skillet over medium-high heat, melt the remaining butter. Add the mushrooms and scallion and sauté them until they've softened, about 2 minutes. Add the spinach and sauté until it's wilted, about 2 minutes. 4. Assemble and bake. Spread the vegetable mixture in the bottom of the pie plate and pour the egg-and-cream mixture over the vegetables. Scatter the cherry tomatoes and the remaining 1 ounce of goat cheese on top. Bake for 20 to 25 minutes until the quiche is cooked through, puffed, and lightly browned. 5. Serve. Cut the quiche into wedges and divide it between four plates. Serve it warm or cold.

Per Serving:
Calories: 355 | fat: 30g | protein: 18g | carbs: 5g | net carbs: 4g | fiber: 1g

Vegetable Burgers

Prep time: 10 minutes | Cook time: 12 minutes | Serves 4

8 ounces (227 g) cremini mushrooms
2 large egg yolks
½ medium zucchini, trimmed and chopped
¼ cup peeled and chopped
yellow onion
1 clove garlic, peeled and finely minced
½ teaspoon salt
¼ teaspoon ground black pepper

1. Place all ingredients into a food processor and pulse twenty times until finely chopped and combined. 2. Separate mixture into four equal sections and press each into a burger shape. Place burgers into ungreased air fryer basket. Adjust the temperature to 375ºF (191ºC) and air fry for 12 minutes, turning burgers halfway through cooking. Burgers will be browned and firm when done. 3. Place burgers on a large plate and let cool 5 minutes before serving.

Per Serving:
Calories: 50 | fat: 3g | protein: 3g | carbs: 4g | fiber: 1g | sodium: 299mg

Cauliflower Tikka Masala

Prep time: 10 minutes | Cook time: 20 minutes | Serves 4

For The Cauliflower:
1 head cauliflower, cut into small florets
1 tablespoon coconut oil, melted
1 teaspoon ground cumin
½ teaspoon ground coriander
For The Sauce:
2 tablespoons coconut oil
½ onion, chopped
1 tablespoon minced garlic
1 tablespoon grated ginger
2 tablespoons garam masala
1 tablespoon tomato paste
½ teaspoon salt
1 cup crushed tomatoes
1 cup heavy (whipping) cream
1 tablespoon chopped fresh cilantro

To Make The Cauliflower: 1. Preheat the oven. Set the oven temperature to 425°F. Line a baking sheet with aluminum foil. 2. Prepare the cauliflower. In a large bowl, toss the cauliflower with the coconut oil, cumin, and coriander. Spread the cauliflower on the baking sheet in a single layer and bake it for 20 minutes, until the cauliflower is tender. To Make The Sauce: 1. Sauté the vegetables. While the cauliflower is baking, in a large skillet over medium-high heat, warm the coconut oil. Add the onion, garlic, and ginger and sauté until they've softened, about 3 minutes. 2. Finish the sauce. Stir in the garam masala, tomato paste, and salt until the vegetables are coated. Stir in the crushed tomatoes and bring to a boil, then reduce the heat to low and simmer the sauce for 10 minutes, stirring it often. Remove the skillet from the heat and stir in the cream and cilantro. 3. Assemble and serve. Add the cauliflower to the sauce, stirring to combine everything. Divide the mixture between four bowls and serve it hot.

Per Serving:
Calories: 372 | fat: 32g | protein: 8g | carbs: 17g | net carbs: 10g | fiber: 7g

Mediterranean Filling Stuffed Portobello Mushrooms

Prep time: 10 minutes | Cook time: 35 minutes | Serves 4

4 large portobello mushroom caps	¼ onion, chopped
3 tablespoons good-quality olive oil, divided	2 teaspoons minced garlic
1 cup chopped fresh spinach	1 teaspoon chopped fresh oregano
1 red bell pepper, chopped	2 cups chopped pecans
1 celery stalk, chopped	¼ cup balsamic vinaigrette
½ cup chopped sun-dried tomato	Sea salt, for seasoning
	Freshly ground black pepper, for seasoning

1. Preheat the oven. Set the oven temperature to 350°F. Line a baking sheet with parchment paper. 2. Prepare the mushrooms. Use a spoon to scoop the black gills out of the mushrooms. Massage 2 tablespoons of the olive oil all over the mushroom caps and place the mushrooms on the prepared baking sheet. Set them aside. 3. Prepare the filling. In a large skillet over medium-high heat, warm the remaining 1 tablespoon of olive oil. Add the spinach, red bell pepper, celery, sun-dried tomato, onion, garlic, and oregano and sauté until the vegetables are tender, about 10 minutes. Stir in the pecans and balsamic vinaigrette and season the mixture with salt and pepper. 4. Assemble and bake. Stuff the mushroom caps with the filling and bake for 20 to 25 minutes until they're tender and golden. 5. Serve. Place one stuffed mushroom on each of four plates and serve them hot.

Per Serving:
Calories: 595 | fat: 56g | protein: 10g | carbs: 18g | net carbs: 9g | fiber: 9g

Three-Cheese Zucchini Boats

Prep time: 15 minutes | Cook time: 20 minutes | Serves 2

2 medium zucchini	cheese
1 tablespoon avocado oil	¼ teaspoon dried oregano
¼ cup low-carb, no-sugar-added pasta sauce	¼ teaspoon garlic powder
¼ cup full-fat ricotta cheese	½ teaspoon dried parsley
¼ cup shredded Mozzarella	2 tablespoons grated vegetarian Parmesan cheese

1. Cut off 1 inch from the top and bottom of each zucchini. Slice zucchini in half lengthwise and use a spoon to scoop out a bit of the inside, making room for filling. Brush with oil and spoon 2 tablespoons pasta sauce into each shell. 2. In a medium bowl, mix ricotta, Mozzarella, oregano, garlic powder, and parsley. Spoon the mixture into each zucchini shell. Place stuffed zucchini shells into the air fryer basket. 3. Adjust the temperature to 350°F (177°C) and air fry for 20 minutes. 4. To remove from the basket, use tongs or a spatula and carefully lift out. Top with Parmesan. Serve immediately.

Per Serving:
Calories: 208 | fat: 14g | protein: 12g | carbs: 11g | fiber: 3g | sodium: 247mg

Pesto Spinach Flatbread

Prep time: 10 minutes | Cook time: 8 minutes | Serves 4

1 cup blanched finely ground almond flour	cheese
2 ounces (57 g) cream cheese	1 cup chopped fresh spinach leaves
2 cups shredded Mozzarella	2 tablespoons basil pesto

1. Place flour, cream cheese, and Mozzarella in a large microwave-safe bowl and microwave on high 45 seconds, then stir. 2. Fold in spinach and microwave an additional 15 seconds. Stir until a soft dough ball forms. 3. Cut two pieces of parchment paper to fit air fryer basket. Separate dough into two sections and press each out on ungreased parchment to create 6-inch rounds. 4. Spread 1 tablespoon pesto over each flatbread and place rounds on parchment into ungreased air fryer basket. Adjust the temperature to 350°F (177°C) and air fry for 8 minutes, turning crusts halfway through cooking. Flatbread will be golden when done. 5. Let cool 5 minutes before slicing and serving.

Per Serving:
Calories: 387 | fat: 28g | protein: 28g | carbs: 10g | fiber: 5g | sodium: 556mg

Zucchini Roll Manicotti

Prep time: 15 minutes | Cook time: 30 minutes | Serves 4

Olive oil cooking spray	cheese
4 zucchini	1 tablespoon chopped fresh oregano
2 tablespoons good-quality olive oil	Sea salt, for seasoning
1 red bell pepper, diced	Freshly ground black pepper, for seasoning
½ onion, minced	2 cups low-carb marinara sauce, divided
2 teaspoons minced garlic	½ cup grated Parmesan cheese
1 cup goat cheese	
1 cup shredded mozzarella	

1. Preheat the oven. Set the oven temperature to 375°F. Lightly grease a 9-by-13-inch baking dish with olive oil cooking spray. 2. Prepare the zucchini. Cut the zucchini lengthwise into ⅛-inch-thick slices and set them aside. 3. Make the filling. In a medium skillet over medium-high heat, warm the olive oil. Add the red bell pepper, onion, and garlic and sauté until they've softened, about 4 minutes. Remove the skillet from the heat and transfer the vegetables to a medium bowl. Stir the goat cheese, mozzarella, and oregano into the vegetables. Season it all with salt and pepper. 4. Assemble the manicotti. Spread 1 cup of the marinara sauce in the bottom of the baking dish. Lay a zucchini slice on a clean cutting board and place a couple tablespoons of filling at one end. Roll the slice up and place it in the baking dish, seam-side down. Repeat with the remaining zucchini slices. Spoon the remaining sauce over the rolls and top with the Parmesan. 5. Bake. Bake the rolls for 30 to 35 minutes until the zucchini is tender and the cheese is golden. 6. Serve. Spoon the rolls onto four plates and serve them hot.

Per Serving:
Calories: 342 | fat: 24g | protein: 20g | carbs: 14g | net carbs: 11g | fiber: 3g

Cheesy Broccoli Casserole

Prep time: 10 minutes | Cook time: 35 minutes | Serves 4

2 tablespoons butter
¼ white onion, diced
1 garlic clove, minced
1 pound (454 g) broccoli florets, roughly chopped
Salt, to taste
Freshly ground black pepper, to taste
4 ounces (113 g) cream cheese, at room temperature
1 cup shredded Cheddar cheese, divided
½ cup heavy (whipping) cream
2 eggs

1. Preheat the oven to 350°F (180°C). 2. In a large skillet over medium heat, melt the butter. 3. Add the onion and garlic. Sauté for 5 to 7 minutes until the onion is softened and translucent. 4. Add the broccoli. Season with salt and pepper. Cook for 4 to 5 minutes until just softened. Transfer to a 7-by-11-inch baking dish. 5. In a medium bowl, stir together the cream cheese, ½ cup of Cheddar, the cream, and eggs. Pour over the broccoli. Season with more salt and pepper, and top with the remaining ½ cup of Cheddar. Bake for 20 minutes. Refrigerate leftovers in an airtight container for up to 1 week.

Per Serving:
Calories: 440 | fat: 39g | protein: 16g | carbs: 11g | net carbs: 8g | fiber: 3g

Zucchini Pasta with Spinach, Olives, and Asiago

Prep time: 10 minutes | Cook time: 10 minutes | Serves 4

3 tablespoons good-quality olive oil
1 tablespoon grass-fed butter
1½ tablespoons minced garlic
1 cup packed fresh spinach
½ cup sliced black olives
½ cup halved cherry tomatoes
2 tablespoons chopped fresh basil
3 zucchini, spiralized
Sea salt, for seasoning
Freshly ground black pepper, for seasoning
½ cup shredded Asiago cheese

1. Sauté the vegetables. In a large skillet over medium-high heat, warm the olive oil and butter. Add the garlic and sauté until it's tender, about 2 minutes. Stir in the spinach, olives, tomatoes, and basil and sauté until the spinach is wilted, about 4 minutes. Stir in the zucchini noodles, toss to combine them with the sauce, and cook until the zucchini is tender, about 2 minutes. 2. Serve. Season with salt and pepper. Divide the mixture between four bowls and serve topped with the Asiago.

Per Serving:
Calories: 199 | fat: 18g | protein: 6g | carbs: 4g | net carbs: 3g | fiber: 1g

Herbed Ricotta–Stuffed Mushrooms

Prep time: 10 minutes | Cook time: 30 minutes | Serves 4

6 tablespoons extra-virgin olive oil, divided
4 portobello mushroom caps, cleaned and gills removed
1 cup whole-milk ricotta cheese
⅓ cup chopped fresh herbs
(such as basil, parsley, rosemary, oregano, or thyme)
2 garlic cloves, finely minced
½ teaspoon salt
¼ teaspoon freshly ground black pepper

1. Preheat the oven to 400°F (205°C). 2. Line a baking sheet with parchment or foil and drizzle with 2 tablespoons olive oil, spreading evenly. Place the mushroom caps on the baking sheet, gill-side up. 3. In a medium bowl, mix together the ricotta, herbs, 2 tablespoons olive oil, garlic, salt, and pepper. Stuff each mushroom cap with one-quarter of the cheese mixture, pressing down if needed. Drizzle with remaining 2 tablespoons olive oil and bake until golden brown and the mushrooms are soft, 30 to 35 minutes, depending on the size of the mushrooms.

Per Serving:
Calories: 308 | fat: 29g | protein: 9g | carbs: 6g | fiber: 1g | sodium: 351mg

Three-Cheese Zucchini Boats

Prep time: 15 minutes | Cook time: 20 minutes | Serves 2

2 medium zucchini
1 tablespoon avocado oil
¼ cup low-carb, no-sugar-added pasta sauce
¼ cup full-fat ricotta cheese
¼ cup shredded Mozzarella cheese
¼ teaspoon dried oregano
¼ teaspoon garlic powder
½ teaspoon dried parsley
2 tablespoons grated vegetarian Parmesan cheese

1. Cut off 1 inch from the top and bottom of each zucchini. Slice zucchini in half lengthwise and use a spoon to scoop out a bit of the inside, making room for filling. Brush with oil and spoon 2 tablespoons pasta sauce into each shell. 2. In a medium bowl, mix ricotta, Mozzarella, oregano, garlic powder, and parsley. Spoon the mixture into each zucchini shell. Place stuffed zucchini shells into the air fryer basket. 3. Adjust the temperature to 350°F (177°C) and air fry for 20 minutes. 4. To remove from the basket, use tongs or a spatula and carefully lift out. Top with Parmesan. Serve immediately.

Per Serving:
Calories: 208 | fat: 14g | protein: 12g | carbs: 11g | fiber: 3g | sodium: 247mg

Broccoli Crust Pizza

Prep time: 15 minutes | Cook time: 12 minutes | Serves 4

3 cups riced broccoli, steamed and drained well

1 large egg

½ cup grated vegetarian Parmesan cheese

3 tablespoons low-carb Alfredo sauce

½ cup shredded Mozzarella cheese

1. In a large bowl, mix broccoli, egg, and Parmesan. 2. Cut a piece of parchment to fit your air fryer basket. Press out the pizza mixture to fit on the parchment, working in two batches if necessary. Place into the air fryer basket. 3. Adjust the temperature to 370ºF (188ºC) and air fry for 5 minutes. 4. The crust should be firm enough to flip. If not, add 2 additional minutes. Flip crust. 5. Top with Alfredo sauce and Mozzarella. Return to the air fryer basket and cook an additional 7 minutes or until cheese is golden and bubbling. Serve warm.

Per Serving:

Calories: 87 | fat: 2g | protein: 11g | carbs: 5g | fiber: 1g | sodium: 253mg

Vegetable Vodka Sauce Bake

Prep time: 10 minutes | Cook time: 30 minutes | Serves 4

3 tablespoons melted grass-fed butter, divided

4 cups mushrooms, halved

4 cups cooked cauliflower florets

1½ cups purchased vodka sauce

¾ cup heavy (whipping) cream

½ cup grated Asiago cheese

Sea salt, for seasoning

Freshly ground black pepper, for seasoning

1 cup shredded provolone cheese

2 tablespoons chopped fresh oregano

1. Preheat the oven. Set the oven temperature to 350°F and use 1 tablespoon of the melted butter to grease a 9-by-13-inch baking dish. 2. Mix the vegetables. In a large bowl, combine the mushrooms, cauliflower, vodka sauce, cream, Asiago, and the remaining 2 tablespoons of butter. Season the vegetables with salt and pepper. 3. Bake. Transfer the vegetable mixture to the baking dish and top it with the provolone cheese. Bake for 30 to 35 minutes until it's bubbly and heated through. 4. Serve. Divide the mixture between four plates and top with the oregano.

Per Serving:

Calories: 537 | fat: 45g | protein: 19g | carbs: 14g | net carbs: 8g | fiber: 19g

Chapter 10 Desserts

Traditional Kentucky Butter Cake

Prep time: 5 minutes | Cook time: 35 minutes | Serves 4

2 cups almond flour	1 tablespoon vanilla extract
¾ cup granulated erythritol	½ cup butter, melted
1½ teaspoons baking powder	Cooking spray
4 eggs	½ cup water

1. In a medium bowl, whisk together the almond flour, erythritol, and baking powder. Whisk well to remove any lumps. 2. Add the eggs and vanilla and whisk until combined. 3. Add the butter and whisk until the batter is mostly smooth and well combined. 4. Grease the pan with cooking spray and pour in the batter. Cover tightly with aluminum foil. 5. Add the water to the pot. Place the Bundt pan on the trivet and carefully lower it into the pot using. 6. Set the lid in place. Select the Manual mode and set the cooking time for 35 minutes on High Pressure. When the timer goes off, do a quick pressure release. Carefully open the lid. 7. Remove the pan from the pot. Let the cake cool in the pan before flipping out onto a plate.

Per Serving:

Calories: 179 | fat: 16g | protein: 2g | carbs: 2g | net carbs: 2g | fiber: 0g

Death by Chocolate Cheesecake

Prep time: 20 minutes | Cook time: 70 minutes |
Makes one 9-inch cheesecake

Crust:	3 large eggs
½ cup coconut flour	¾ cup powdered erythritol
½ cup cocoa powder	3 tablespoons cocoa powder
½ cup powdered erythritol	1 teaspoon vanilla extract
½ cup (1 stick) unsalted butter, melted	4 ounces unsweetened baking chocolate (100% cacao)
Filling:	1 tablespoon unsalted butter
3 (8-ounce) packages cream cheese, room temperature	FOR GARNISH (OPTIONAL):
¼ cup plus 2 tablespoons heavy whipping cream	1 ounce unsweetened baking chocolate (100% cacao)

1. Make the crust: Preheat the oven to 350°F. Grease a 9-inch springform pan with coconut oil spray. 2. Put the coconut flour, cocoa powder, and erythritol in a medium-sized mixing bowl and combine using a fork. Pour the melted butter over the dry mixture and combine thoroughly using a rubber spatula. 3. Transfer the crust mixture to the greased pan and press into an even layer across the bottom. Par-bake the crust for 12 minutes. 4. Remove the crust from the oven and lower the oven temperature to 300°F. Allow the crust to cool for at least 20 minutes before adding the filling. 5. Make the filling: Put the cream cheese and cream in a large mixing bowl and beat with a hand mixer until combined and smooth. Add the eggs, erythritol, cocoa powder, and vanilla extract and combine with the mixer. 6. Roughly chop the 4 ounces of chocolate and put it in a microwave-safe bowl with the tablespoon of butter. Microwave in 20-second increments, stirring after each increment, until melted. (Alternatively, melt the chocolate and butter in a small heavy-bottomed saucepan on the stovetop over low heat.) 7. Add the melted chocolate mixture to the rest of the filling ingredients and mix with the hand mixer until smooth and fully incorporated. Pour the filling over the cooled crust and spread evenly with the rubber spatula. 8. Bake the cheesecake for 55 minutes, until a toothpick inserted in the middle comes out clean. Set on a wire baking rack and allow to cool for 15 minutes, then place in the refrigerator until completely set, at least 3 hours. 9. Use a grater or vegetable peeler to grate or shave 1 ounce of chocolate on top of the chilled cheesecake, if desired. Allow to sit at room temperature for 30 minutes prior to serving. 10. To serve, run a knife around the edges to loosen the cheesecake, then remove the rim of the springform pan. Cut into 12 slices. Store in the refrigerator for up to a week or in the freezer for up to 3 months.

Per Serving:

Calories: 398 | fat: 37g | protein: 7g | carbs: 11g | net carbs: 5g | fiber: 6g

Blueberry Fat Bombs

Prep time: 10 minutes | Cook time: 0 minutes |
Makes 12 fat bombs

½ cup coconut oil, at room temperature	½ cup blueberries, mashed with a fork
½ cup cream cheese, at room temperature	6 drops liquid stevia
	Pinch ground nutmeg

1. Line a mini muffin tin with paper liners and set aside. 2. In a medium bowl, stir together the coconut oil and cream cheese until well blended. 3. Stir in the blueberries, stevia, and nutmeg until combined. 4. Divide the blueberry mixture into the muffin cups and place the tray in the freezer until set, about 3 hours. 5. Place the fat bombs in an airtight container and store in the freezer until you wish to eat them.

Per Serving:

Calories: 115 | fat: 12g | protein: 1g | carbs: 1g | net carbs: 1g | fiber: 0g

Strawberry Cheesecake Mousse

Prep time: 10 minutes | Cook time: 0 minutes | Serves 2

4 ounces cream cheese, at room temperature	sweetener or 1 drop liquid stevia
1 tablespoon heavy (whipping) cream	1 teaspoon vanilla extract
1 teaspoon Swerve natural	4 strawberries, sliced (fresh or frozen)

1. Break up the cream cheese block into smaller pieces and distribute evenly in a food processor (or blender). Add the cream, sweetener, and vanilla. 2. Mix together on high. I usually stop and stir twice and scrape down the sides of the bowl with a small rubber scraper to make sure everything is mixed well. 3. Add the strawberries to the food processor, and mix until combined. 4. Divide the strawberry cheesecake mixture between two small dishes, and chill for 1 hour before serving.

Per Serving:

Calories: 221 | fat: 21g | protein: 4g | carbs: 11g | net carbs: 4g | fiber: 1g

Almond Pistachio Biscotti

Prep time: 5 minutes | Cook time: 1 hour 20 minutes | Serves 12

2 cups almond flour or hazelnut flour	2 large eggs
½ packed cup flax meal	2 tablespoons extra-virgin olive oil
½ teaspoon baking soda	1 tablespoon unsweetened almond extract
½ teaspoon ground nutmeg	
½ teaspoon vanilla powder or 1½ teaspoons unsweetened vanilla extract	1 teaspoon apple cider vinegar or fresh lemon juice
¼ teaspoon salt	Optional: low-carb sweetener, to taste
1 tablespoon fresh lemon zest	⅔ cup unsalted pistachio nuts

1. Preheat the oven to 285°F (140°C) fan assisted or 320°F (160°C) conventional. Line one or two baking trays with parchment paper. 2. In a bowl, mix the almond flour, flax meal, baking soda, nutmeg, vanilla, salt, and lemon zest. Add the eggs, olive oil, almond extract, vinegar, and optional sweetener. Mix well until a dough forms, then mix in the pistachio nuts. 3. Form the dough into a low, wide log shape, about 8 × 5 inches (20 × 13 cm). Place in the oven and bake for about 45 minutes. Remove from oven and let cool for 15 to 20 minutes. Using a sharp knife, cut into 12 slices. 4. Reduce the oven temperature to 250°F (120°C) fan assisted or 285°F (140°C) conventional. Lay the slices very carefully in a flat layer on the lined trays. Bake for 15 to 20 minutes, flip over, and bake for 15 to 20 minutes. 5. Remove from the oven and let the biscotti cool down completely to fully crisp up. Store in a sealed jar for up to 2 weeks.

Per Serving:

Calories: 196 | fat: 17g | protein: 7g | carbs: 7g | net carbs: 3g | fiber: 4g

Pumpkin Pie Pudding

Prep time: 10 minutes | Cook time: 20 minutes | Serves 6

Nonstick cooking spray	pumpkin purée
2 eggs	1 teaspoon pumpkin pie spice
½ cup heavy (whipping) cream or almond milk (for dairy-free)	1 teaspoon vanilla extract
¾ cup Swerve	For Serving:
1 (15-ounce / 425-g) can	½ cup heavy (whipping) cream

1. Grease a 6-by-3-inch pan extremely well with the cooking spray, making sure it gets into all the nooks and crannies. 2. In a medium bowl, whisk the eggs. Add the cream, Swerve, pumpkin purée, pumpkin pie spice, and vanilla, and stir to mix thoroughly. 3. Pour the mixture into the prepared pan and cover it with a silicone lid or aluminum foil. 4. Pour 2 cups of water into the inner cooking pot of the Instant Pot, then place a trivet in the pot. Place the covered pan on the trivet. 5. Lock the lid into place. Select Manual and adjust the pressure to High. Cook for 20 minutes. When the cooking is complete, let the pressure release naturally for 10 minutes, then quick-release any remaining pressure. Unlock the lid. 6. Remove the pan and place it in the refrigerator. Chill for 6 to 8 hours. 8. When ready to serve, finish by making the whipped cream. Using a hand mixer, beat the heavy cream until it forms soft peaks. Do not overbeat and turn it to butter. Serve each pudding with a dollop of whipped cream.

Per Serving:

Calories: 188 | fat: 17g | protein: 4g | carbs: 8g | net carbs:6 g | fiber: 2g

Pine Nut Mousse

Prep time: 5 minutes | Cook time: 35 minutes | Serves 8

1 tablespoon butter	1 cup Swerve, reserve 1 tablespoon
1¼ cups pine nuts	
1¼ cups full-fat heavy cream	1 cup water
2 large eggs	1 cup full-fat heavy whipping cream
1 teaspoon vanilla extract	

1. Butter the bottom and the side of a pie pan and set aside. 2. In a food processor, blend the pine nuts and heavy cream. Add the eggs, vanilla extract and Swerve and pulse a few times to incorporate. 3. Pour the batter into the pan and loosely cover with aluminum foil. Pour the water in the Instant Pot and place the trivet inside. Place the pan on top of the trivet. 4. Close the lid. Select Manual mode and set the timer for 35 minutes on High pressure. 5. In a small mixing bowl, whisk the heavy whipping cream and 1 tablespoon of Swerve until a soft peak forms. 6. When timer beeps, use a natural pressure release for 15 minutes, then release any remaining pressure and open the lid. 7. Serve immediately with whipped cream on top.

Per Serving:

Calories: 184 | fat: 19g | protein: 3g | carbs: 2g | net carbs: 2g | fiber: 0g

Peanut Butter Mousse

Prep time: 10 minutes | Cook time: 0 minutes | Serves 4

1 cup heavy (whipping) cream

¼ cup natural peanut butter

1 teaspoon alcohol-free pure

vanilla extract

4 drops liquid stevia

1. In a medium bowl, beat together the heavy cream, peanut butter, vanilla, and stevia until firm peaks form, about 5 minutes. 2. Spoon the mousse into 4 bowls and place in the refrigerator to chill for 30 minutes. 3. Serve.

Per Serving:

Calories: 280 | fat: 28g | protein: 6g | carbs: 4g | net carbs: 3g | fiber: 1g

Coconut Cupcakes

Prep time: 5 minutes | Cook time: 10 minutes | Serves 6

4 eggs, beaten

4 tablespoons coconut milk

4 tablespoons coconut flour

½ teaspoon vanilla extract

2 tablespoons erythritol

1 teaspoon baking powder

1 cup water

1. In the mixing bowl, mix up eggs, coconut milk, coconut flour, vanilla extract, erythritol, and baking powder. 2. Then pour the batter in the cupcake molds. 3. Pour the water and insert the trivet in the instant pot. 4. Place the cupcakes on the trivet. 5. Lock the lid. Select the Manual mode and set the cooking time for 10 minutes on High Pressure. Once the timer goes off, perform a natural pressure release for 5 minutes, then release any remaining pressure. Carefully open the lid. 6. Serve immediately.

Per Serving:

Calories: 85 | fat: 5.7g | protein: 4.7g | carbs: 9.1g | net carbs: 6.8g | fiber: 2.3g

Angel Food Mug Cake with Strawberries

Prep time: 5 minutes | Cook time: 15 minutes | Serves 2

¼ cup egg whites

Pinch of cream of tartar

¼ teaspoon vanilla extract

1/16 teaspoon almond extract (optional)

¼ cup (1 ounce / 28 g) blanched almond flour

2 tablespoons erythritol

⅛ teaspoon sea salt

Whipped cream or whipped coconut cream, for serving (optional)

¼ cup (1½ ounces / 43 g) strawberries, sliced

1. If using the oven method, preheat the oven to 350ºF (180ºC). 2. In a medium bowl, with an electric hand mixer, beat the egg whites with the cream of tartar for a couple of minutes at high speed, until stiff peaks form. Beat in the vanilla and almond extract. 3. In another medium bowl, stir together the almond flour, erythritol, and sea salt. Gently fold the flour mixture into the egg whites, being careful not to break them down. 4. Divide the batter between two 4-ounce / 113-g ramekins or two small mugs. 5. Oven method: Place the ramekins in the oven and bake for about 15 minutes, until the tops of the cakes are firm and an inserted toothpick comes out mostly clean (a few crumbs are fine). Microwave method: Place the ramekins in the microwave for 70 to 90 seconds, until the tops of the cakes are firm and an inserted toothpick comes out mostly clean (a few crumbs are fine). 6. If desired, garnish with whipped cream (or whipped coconut cream for a dairy-free version). Serve with the sliced strawberries on top.

Per Serving:

Calories: 104 | fat: 7g | protein: 6g | carbs: 8g | net carbs: 3g | fiber: 5g

Rhubarb Microwave Cakes

Prep time: 5 minutes | Cook time: 0 minutes | Serves 2

1 large egg

3 tablespoons refined avocado oil or macadamia nut oil

1 tablespoon plus 1 teaspoon confectioners'-style erythritol

¼ teaspoon vanilla extract or powder

¼ cup (32 g) roughly ground flax seeds

1 teaspoon ground cinnamon

¼ teaspoon ground nutmeg

¼ teaspoon baking powder

1 (2½-in/6.5-cm) piece rhubarb, diced

1 to 2 fresh strawberries, hulled and sliced, for garnish (optional)

1. Place the egg, oil, erythritol, and vanilla in a small bowl. Whisk to combine. 2. In a separate small bowl, place the flax seeds, cinnamon, nutmeg, and baking powder. Stir to combine, then add to the bowl with the wet ingredients. 3. Add the diced rhubarb to the bowl and stir until coated. 4. Divide the mixture between two 8-ounce (240-ml) ramekins, coffee cups, or other small microwave-safe containers. Microwave for 2 to 2½ minutes, until a toothpick inserted in the middle comes out clean. Garnish with strawberry slices, if desired.

Per Serving:

Calories: 303 | fat: 28g | protein: 6g | carbs: 7g | net carbs: 2g | fiber: 6g

Nut Butter Cup Fat Bomb

Prep time: 5 minutes | Cook time: 0 minutes | Serves 8

½ cup crunchy almond butter (no sugar added)

½ cup light fruity extra-virgin olive oil

¼ cup ground flaxseed

2 tablespoons unsweetened

cocoa powder

1 teaspoon vanilla extract

1 teaspoon ground cinnamon (optional)

1 to 2 teaspoons sugar-free sweetener of choice (optional)

1. In a mixing bowl, combine the almond butter, olive oil, flaxseed, cocoa powder, vanilla, cinnamon (if using), and sweetener (if using) and stir well with a spatula to combine. Mixture will be a thick liquid. 2. Pour into 8 mini muffin liners and freeze until solid, at least 12 hours. Store in the freezer to maintain their shape.

Per Serving:

Calories: 239 | fat: 24g | protein: 4g | carbs: 5g | net carbs: 2g | fiber: 3g

Zucchini Bread

Prep time: 10 minutes | Cook time: 40 minutes | Serves 12

2 cups coconut flour

2 teaspoons baking powder

¾ cup erythritol

½ cup coconut oil, melted

1 teaspoon apple cider vinegar

1 teaspoon vanilla extract

3 eggs, beaten

1 zucchini, grated

1 teaspoon ground cinnamon

1. In the mixing bowl, mix coconut flour with baking powder, erythritol, coconut oil, apple cider vinegar, vanilla extract, eggs, zucchini, and ground cinnamon. 2. Transfer the mixture into the air fryer basket and flatten it in the shape of the bread. 3. Cook the bread at 350°F (177°C) for 40 minutes.

Per Serving:

Calories: 135 | fat: 14g | protein: 2g | carbs: 4g | net carbs: 3g | fiber: 1g

Jelly Pie Jars

Prep time: 20 minutes | Cook time: 15 minutes | Serves 8

Coconut oil, for the jars

Pie Base:

1 cup (110 g) blanched almond flour

1 tablespoon plus 1½ teaspoons whisked egg (about ½ large egg)

1 tablespoon lard

2 drops liquid stevia

¼ teaspoon ground cinnamon

Pinch of finely ground gray sea salt

Jam Filling:

1½ heaping cups (260 g) fresh blackberries

⅓ cup (80 ml) water

1½ teaspoons vanilla extract

3 drops liquid stevia

¼ cup (38 g) chia seeds

1½ teaspoons balsamic vinegar

Almond Butter Topping:

¾ cup (210 g) unsweetened smooth almond butter

¼ cup (60 ml) melted coconut oil or ghee (if tolerated)

1 teaspoon ground cinnamon

2 to 4 drops liquid stevia

For Garnish (Optional):

16 to 24 fresh blackberries

1. Preheat the oven to 325°F (163°C). Grease eight 4-ounce (120-ml) mason jars with a dab of coconut oil and set on a rimmed baking sheet. 2. To prepare the base, place the ingredients for the base in a large bowl and mix with a fork until fully combined. 3. Divide the dough evenly among the jars, pressing it in firmly and evening it out with your fingers. Place the jars back on the baking sheet and bake for 15 to 17 minutes, until the tops are golden. Remove from the oven and allow to cool completely, at least 30 minutes. Meanwhile, make the filling. 4. To prepare the jam filling, place the blackberries, water, vanilla, and stevia in a medium-sized saucepan. Cook, covered, over medium heat for 5 minutes. 5. Reduce the heat to low and add the chia seeds and balsamic vinegar. Cook, uncovered, for another 3 to 4 minutes, stirring frequently, until the mixture has thickened. Transfer the mixture to a heat-safe bowl and set aside to cool to room temperature, at least 30 minutes. 6. To prepare the almond butter topping, place the topping ingredients in a small bowl and whisk to combine. 7. To assemble, divide the cooled jam filling among the jars, being sure to keep the layer as flat as possible. Then add the almond butter topping, pouring it in slowly to avoid spillover. Transfer the assembled jars to the fridge to cool for 30 minutes. 8. Before serving, top each jar with 2 or 3 blackberries, if desired. Enjoy!

Per Serving:

Calories: 388 | fat: 32g | protein: 11g | carbs: 13g | net carbs: 4g | fiber: 9g

Ultimate Chocolate Cheesecake

Prep time: 10 minutes | Cook time: 50 minutes | Serves 12

2 cups pecans

2 tablespoons butter

16 ounces (454 g) cream cheese, softened

1 cup powdered erythritol

¼ cup sour cream

2 tablespoons cocoa powder

2 teaspoons vanilla extract

2 cups low-carb chocolate chips

1 tablespoon coconut oil

2 eggs

2 cups water

1. Preheat oven to 400°F (205°C). Place pecans and butter into food processor. Pulse until dough-like consistency. Press into bottom of 7-inch springform pan. Bake for 10 minutes then set aside to cool. 2. While crust bakes, mix cream cheese, erythritol, sour cream, cocoa powder, and vanilla together in large bowl using a rubber spatula. Set aside. 3. In medium bowl, combine chocolate chips and coconut oil. Microwave in 20-second increments until chocolate begins to melt and then stir until smooth. Gently fold chocolate mixture into cheesecake mixture. 4. Add eggs and gently fold in, careful not to overmix. Pour mixture over cooled pecan crust. Cover with foil. 5. Pour water into Instant Pot and place steam rack on bottom. Place cheesecake on steam rack and click lid closed. Press the Manual button and adjust time for 40 minutes. When timer beeps, allow a natural release. Carefully remove and let cool completely. Serve chilled.

Per Serving:

Calories: 461 | fat: 40g | protein: 5g | carbs: 20g | net carbs: 15g | fiber: 5g

Crustless Cheesecake Bites

Prep time: 10 minutes | Cook time: 30 minutes | Serves 4

4 ounces cream cheese, at room temperature

¼ cup sour cream

2 large eggs

⅓ cup Swerve natural sweetener

¼ teaspoon vanilla extract

1. Preheat the oven to 350°F. 2. In a medium mixing bowl, use a hand mixer to beat the cream cheese, sour cream, eggs, sweetener, and vanilla until well mixed. 3. Place silicone liners (or cupcake paper liners) in the cups of a muffin tin. 4. Pour the cheesecake batter into the liners, and bake for 30 minutes. 5. Refrigerate until completely cooled before serving, about 3 hours. Store extra cheesecake bites in a zip-top bag in the freezer for up to 3 months.

Per Serving:

Calories: 169 | fat: 15g | protein: 5g | carbs: 18g | net carbs: 2g | fiber: 0g

Mint–Chocolate Chip Ice Cream

Prep time: 10 minutes | Cook time: 30 minutes | Serves 2

½ tablespoon butter	(whipping) cream, divided
1 tablespoon Swerve natural sweetener	¼ teaspoon peppermint extract
10 tablespoons heavy	2 tablespoons sugar-free chocolate chips (I use Lily's)

1. Put a medium metal bowl and your hand-mixer beaters in the freezer to chill. 2. In a small, heavy saucepan over medium heat, melt the butter. Whisk in the sweetener and 5 tablespoons of cream. 3. Turn the heat up to medium-high and bring the mixture to a boil, stirring constantly. Turn the heat down to low and simmer, stirring occasionally, for about 30 minutes. You want the mixture to be thick, so it sticks to the back of a spoon. 4. Stir in the peppermint extract. 5. Pour the thickened mixture into a medium bowl and refrigerate to cool. 6. Remove the metal bowl and the mixer beaters from the freezer. Pour the remaining 5 tablespoons of cream into the bowl. With the electric beater, whip the cream until it is thick and fluffy and forms peaks. Don't overbeat, or the cream will turn to butter. Take the cream mixture out of the refrigerator. 7. Using a rubber scraper, gently fold the whipped cream into the cooled mixture. 8. Transfer the mixture to a small metal container that can go in the freezer (I use a mini loaf pan since I only make enough for two). 9. Mix in the chocolate chips, and cover the container with foil or plastic wrap. 10. Freeze the ice cream for 4 to 5 hours before serving, stirring it twice during that time.

Per Serving:

Calories: 325 | fat: 33g | protein: 3g | carbs: 17g | net carbs: 4g | fiber: 4g

No-Churn Peanut Butter Ice Cream

Prep time: 15 minutes | Cook time: 12 minutes | Makes roughly 3 cups

2 cups heavy whipping cream	2 tablespoons natural creamy peanut butter, plus extra for topping (optional)
3 tablespoons unsalted butter, plus extra for topping (optional)	
⅔ cup powdered erythritol	1 teaspoon vanilla extract
4 large egg yolks	⅛ teaspoon xanthan gum

1. Put the cream, butter, and erythritol in a medium-sized heavy-bottomed saucepan over medium-high heat. Mix using a whisk until the sweetener has dissolved. Bring to a boil, then lower the heat and simmer rapidly for 5 to 7 minutes, until slightly thickened. Remove from the heat and let cool for about 15 minutes, until just warm to the touch. 2. Put the egg yolks in a large mixing bowl and mix using a hand mixer until lightened to a pale yellow color, 30 to 45 seconds. Add the peanut butter and vanilla extract and combine with the mixer. 3. Slowly add the cooled cream mixture to the egg yolk mixture while mixing with the hand mixer. Add the xanthan gum and continue to mix until a frothy layer has formed on the top. 4. Pour the ice cream mixture into an 8 by 4-inch loaf pan and place in the freezer for 30 minutes. Mix with a spoon, then return the pan to the freezer for another 30 minutes. Mix again, then return the pan to the freezer until the ice cream is hard enough to scoop, at least 3 more hours. 5. Allow the ice cream to sit out at room temperature for 10 minutes prior to serving. If desired, garnish each serving with a spoonful of peanut butter or with a quick peanut butter drizzle (as shown in the photo), made by combining equal parts peanut butter and butter in a microwave-safe bowl, microwaving until the butter has melted, and then combining them with a spoon until smooth. 6. Store in a sealed container in the freezer for up to a week.

Per Serving:

Calories: 392 | fat: 41g | protein: 5g | carbs: 4g | net carbs: 3g | fiber: 1g

Five-Minute Keto Cookie Dough

Prep time: 5 minutes | Cook time: 0 minutes | Makes 20 dough balls

8 ounces (227 g) cream cheese, at room temperature	½ teaspoon vanilla extract
6 tablespoons butter or ghee, at room temperature	½ to 1 teaspoon monk fruit or stevia, or more (optional)
½ cup peanut butter (or almond butter)	¼ teaspoon sea salt
¼ cup granulated sweetener (such as erythritol)	¼ cup stevia-sweetened chocolate chips (or >90% dark chocolate chunks)

1. In a large bowl, mix together the cream cheese and butter using an electric hand mixer. 2. Add the peanut butter, granulated sweetener, vanilla, monk fruit, and salt and mix again until well combined. Taste and adjust the sweetness to your liking. 3. Fold in the chocolate chips and then use a tablespoon or small scoop to form 20 dough balls. Arrange the dough balls on a plate or baking sheet. 4. Let chill in the refrigerator for 1 hour and store in an airtight container for up to 3 weeks.

Per Serving (1 dough ball):

Calories: 123 | fat: 11g | protein: 2g | carbs: 4g | net carbs: 3g | fiber: 1g

Protein Powder Doughnut Holes

Prep time: 25 minutes | Cook time: 6 minutes | Makes 12 holes

½ cup blanched finely ground almond flour	½ teaspoon baking powder
½ cup low-carb vanilla protein powder	1 large egg
½ cup granular erythritol	5 tablespoons unsalted butter, melted
	½ teaspoon vanilla extract

1. Mix all ingredients in a large bowl. Place into the freezer for 20 minutes. 2. Wet your hands with water and roll the dough into twelve balls. 3. Cut a piece of parchment to fit your air fryer basket. Working in batches as necessary, place doughnut holes into the air fryer basket on top of parchment. 4. Adjust the temperature to 380°F (193°C) and air fry for 6 minutes. 5. Flip doughnut holes halfway through the cooking time. 6. Let cool completely before serving.

Per Serving:

1 hole: Calories: 89 | fat: 7g | protein: 5g | carbs: 2g | net carbs: 1g | fiber: 1g

Chocolate Mousse

1½ tablespoons heavy (whipping) cream

4 tablespoons butter, at room temperature

1 tablespoon unsweetened

cocoa powder

4 tablespoons cream cheese, at room temperature

1 tablespoon Swerve natural sweetener

1. In a medium chilled bowl, use a whisk or fork to whip the cream. Refrigerate to keep cold. 2. In a separate medium bowl, use a hand mixer to beat the butter, cocoa powder, cream cheese, and sweetener until thoroughly combined. 3. Take the whipped cream out of the refrigerator. Gently fold the whipped cream into the chocolate mixture with a rubber scraper. 4. Divide the pudding between two dessert bowls. 5. Cover and chill for 1 hour before serving.

Per Serving:

Calories: 486 | fat: 50g | protein: 4g | carbs: 5g | net carbs: 4g | fiber: 1g

Rich Chocolate Mug Cake

½ cup almond flour

2 tablespoons coconut flour

2 tablespoons cocoa powder

1¼ teaspoons baking powder

1 tablespoon monk fruit sweetener, granulated form

¼ cup melted grass-fed butter

2 eggs

½ teaspoon vanilla extract

½ cup keto-friendly chocolate chips like Lily's Dark Chocolate Chips

1. Mix the dry ingredients. In a medium bowl, stir together the almond flour, coconut flour, cocoa powder, baking powder, and sweetener. 2. Finish the batter. Stir in the melted butter, eggs, and vanilla until everything is well combined. Stir in the chocolate chips. 3. Cook and serve. Divide the batter between two large mugs and microwave them on high for 90 seconds, or until the cakes are cooked. Serve them immediately.

Per Serving:

Calories: 383 | fat: 35g | protein: 11g | carbs: 12g | net carbs: 5g | fiber: 7g

Crustless Creamy Berry Cheesecake

16 ounces (454 g) cream cheese, softened

1 cup powdered erythritol

¼ cup sour cream

2 teaspoons vanilla extract

2 eggs

2 cups water

¼ cup blackberries and strawberries, for topping

1. In large bowl, beat cream cheese and erythritol until smooth.

Add sour cream, vanilla, and eggs and gently fold until combined. 2. Pour batter into 7-inch springform pan. Gently shake or tap pan on counter to remove air bubbles and level batter. Cover top of pan with tinfoil. Pour water into Instant Pot and place steam rack in pot. 3. Carefully lower pan into pot. Press the Cake button and press the Adjust button to set heat to More. Set time for 40 minutes. When timer beeps, allow a full natural release. Using sling, carefully lift pan from Instant Pot and allow to cool completely before refrigerating. 4. Place strawberries and blackberries on top of cheesecake and serve.

Per Serving:

Calories: 153 | fat: 13g | protein: 3g | carbs: 14g | net carbs: 14g | fiber: 0g

Orange–Olive Oil Cupcakes

1 large egg

2 tablespoons powdered sugar-free sweetener (such as stevia or monk fruit extract)

½ cup extra-virgin olive oil

1 teaspoon almond extract

Zest of 1 orange

1 cup almond flour

¾ teaspoon baking powder

⅛ teaspoon salt

1 tablespoon freshly squeezed orange juice

1. Preheat the oven to 350°F (180°C). Place muffin liners into 6 cups of a muffin tin. 2. In a large bowl, whisk together the egg and powdered sweetener. Add the olive oil, almond extract, and orange zest and whisk to combine well. 3. In a small bowl, whisk together the almond flour, baking powder, and salt. Add to wet ingredients along with the orange juice and stir until just combined. 4. Divide the batter evenly into 6 muffin cups and bake until a toothpick inserted in the center of the cupcake comes out clean, 15 to 18 minutes. 5. Remove from the oven and cool for 5 minutes in the tin before transferring to a wire rack to cool completely.

Per Serving (1 cupcake):

Calories: 280 | fat: 27g | protein: 4g | carbs: 8g | net carbs: 6g | fiber: 2g

Chocolate Almond Smoothie

2 cups ice cubes

1 cup heavy (whipping) cream

1 cup water

¼ cup canned coconut cream

3 tablespoons almond butter

2 tablespoons cocoa powder

½ teaspoon liquid stevia

1. In a high-speed blender, combine the ice cubes, cream, water, coconut cream, almond butter, cocoa powder, and stevia. Blend on high speed until the mixture is smooth, then serve immediately.

Per Serving:

Calories: 669 | fat: 68g | protein: 10g | carbs: 13g | net carbs: 8g | fiber: 5g

Coconut–White Chocolate Fudge

Prep time: 10 minutes | Cook time: 0 minutes |
Makes 16 squares

Coconut oil for greasing	powder
1 cup full-fat unsweetened coconut milk	1 teaspoon vanilla extract
4 ounces (113 g) unsweetened cacao/cocoa butter, chopped	¼ teaspoon sea salt
	⅛ teaspoon ground cinnamon (optional)
½ cup coconut butter/manna	½ teaspoon sweetener of choice
⅓ cup vanilla-flavored collagen	(optional)

1. Grease an 8-inch square pan with oil and then line it with a piece of parchment paper, pressing down so that it sticks and evenly covers the pan. 2. In a medium saucepan over low heat, melt together the coconut milk, cacao butter, and coconut butter, stirring occasionally, until smooth. Remove from the heat and whisk in the collagen powder, vanilla, salt, and cinnamon (if using). Taste the mixture and then add the sweetener (if using), adjusting the sweetness to your liking. 3. Pour the mixture into the prepared pan and spread evenly. Refrigerate overnight. 4. Cut into 16 squares and store in an airtight container in the refrigerator for up to 2 weeks.

Per Serving (1 square):
Calories: 148 | fat: 15g | protein: 2g | carbs: 2g | net carbs: 1g | fiber: 1g

Caramelized Pumpkin Cheesecake

Prep time: 15 minutes | Cook time: 45 minutes | Serves 8

Crust:	16 ounces (454 g) cream
1½ cups almond flour	cheese, softened
4 tablespoons butter, melted	½ cup granulated erythritol
1 tablespoon Swerve	2 eggs
1 tablespoon granulated erythritol	¼ cup pumpkin purée
	3 tablespoons Swerve
½ teaspoon ground cinnamon	1 teaspoon vanilla extract
Cooking spray	¼ teaspoon pumpkin pie spice
Filling:	1½ cups water

1. To make the crust: In a medium bowl, combine the almond flour, butter, Swerve, erythritol, and cinnamon. Use a fork to press it all together. 2. Spray the pan with cooking spray and line the bottom with parchment paper. 3. Press the crust evenly into the pan. Work the crust up the sides of the pan, about halfway from the top, and make sure there are no bare spots on the bottom. 4. Place the crust in the freezer for 20 minutes while you make the filling. 5. To make the filling: In a large bowl using a hand mixer on medium speed, combine the cream cheese and erythritol. Beat until the cream cheese is light and fluffy, 2 to 3 minutes. 6. Add the eggs, pumpkin purée, Swerve, vanilla, and pumpkin pie spice. Beat until well combined. 7. Remove the crust from the freezer and pour in the filling. Cover the pan with aluminum foil and place it on the trivet. 8. Add the water to the pot and carefully lower the trivet into the pot. 9. Set the lid in place. Select the Manual mode and set the cooking time for 45 minutes on High Pressure. When the timer goes off, do a quick pressure release. Carefully open the lid. 10. Remove the trivet and cheesecake from the pot. Remove the foil from the pan. The center of the cheesecake should still be slightly jiggly. 11. Let the cheesecake cool for 30 minutes on the counter before placing it in the refrigerator to set. Leave the cheesecake in the refrigerator for at least 6 hours before removing the sides and serving.

Per Serving:
Calories: 407 | fat: 36g | protein: 10g | carbs: 7g | net carbs: 4g | fiber: 3g

Lemonade Fat Bomb

Prep time: 10 minutes | Cook time: 0 minutes | Serves 2

½ lemon	2 teaspoons Swerve natural
4 ounces cream cheese, at room temperature	sweetener or 2 drops liquid stevia
2 ounces butter, at room temperature	Pinch pink Himalayan salt

1. Zest the lemon half with a very fine grater into a small bowl. Squeeze the juice from the lemon half into the bowl with the zest. 2. In a medium bowl, combine the cream cheese and butter. Add the sweetener, lemon zest and juice, and pink Himalayan salt. Using a hand mixer, beat until fully combined. 3. Spoon the mixture into the fat bomb molds. (I use small silicone cupcake molds. If you don't have molds, you can use cupcake paper liners that fit into the cups of a muffin tin.) 4. Freeze for at least 2 hours, unmold, and eat! Keep extras in your freezer in a zip-top bag so you and your loved ones can have them anytime you are craving a sweet treat. They will keep in the freezer for up to 3 months.

Per Serving:
Calories: 404 | fat: 43g | protein: 4g | carbs: 8g | net carbs: 4g | fiber: 1g

Debauchery Chocolate Brownies

Prep time: 10 minutes | Cook time: 30 minutes | Serves 16

¾ cup unsalted butter, softened	1 cup Lily's sugar-free chocolate chips
3 large eggs	
¾ cup Carbquik, divided	¾ cup unsweetened cocoa
1 cup powdered 0g net carb sweetener	powder
	½ teaspoon salt
½ cup finely chopped pecans	

1 Preheat oven to 325°F. Grease and "flour" an 8" × 8" pan (using 1 tablespoon Carbquik). 2 In a large bowl, beat butter with eggs. 3 In a medium bowl, combine the dry ingredients and add to the large bowl. Mix in the remaining ingredients to form batter. 4 Spread mixture into pan and bake 30 minutes. Use a toothpick to tell if it's done by poking it into center—it should come out clean. 5 Cut into sixteen portions and serve while still warm.

Per Serving:
Calories: 184 | fat: 17g | protein: 4g | carbs: 23g | net carbs: 15g | fiber: 8g

Quick Blackberry Cobbler for Two

Prep time: 5 minutes | Cook time: 2 minutes | serves 2

1½ cups fresh blackberries	¼ cup (½ stick) cold salted
¼ teaspoon liquid stevia	butter, cubed
¼ teaspoon vanilla extract	½ teaspoon baking powder
¼ cup finely ground blanched almond flour	Whipped cream, for serving (optional)

1. Grease a 2-cup microwave-safe baking dish. 2. In a small bowl, gently combine the blackberries, stevia, and vanilla extract, then pour the mixture into the prepared baking dish. 3. In a small bowl, use a fork to stir together the almond flour and baking powder, then add the butter and continue stirring with the fork until a crumbly mixture forms. Sprinkle the mixture evenly over the blackberries. 4. Microwave for 1½ to 2 minutes, checking every 30 seconds, until the blackberries are bubbly and the topping is lightly browned; microwave cook times vary according to wattage. Allow the cobbler to cool for 10 minutes. Serve with whipped cream, if desired.

Per Serving:

Calories: 328 | fat: 30g | protein: 4g | carbs: 13g | net carbs: 6g | fiber: 7g

Almond Chai Truffles

Prep time: 200 minutes | Cook time: 0 minutes |
Serves 10

½ cup (140 g) unsweetened smooth almond butter	liquid stevia ½ teaspoon vanilla extract or powder
¼ cup plus 2 tablespoons (90 g) cacao butter, melted	Pinch of finely ground gray sea salt
1 tablespoon plus 1 teaspoon chai spice (recipe below)	3 tablespoons almonds, roasted Special Equipment:
1 tablespoon confectioners'-style erythritol or 2 to 4 drops	10 mini paper liners (optional)

1. Combine the almond butter, cacao butter, chai spice, erythritol, vanilla, and salt in a medium-sized bowl and stir to combine. Place in the fridge to set for 30 to 45 minutes, until firm yet still pliable. 2. Meanwhile, put the roasted almonds in a small baggie, seal, and cover with a kitchen towel. Bash with a mallet or the bottom of a mug until the pieces are no larger than ⅛ inch (3 mm). Pour the pieces into a small bowl. 3. Line a rimmed baking sheet with parchment paper or a silicone baking mat. 4. Remove the truffle mixture from the fridge and break it up with a fork until no clumps larger than a pencil eraser remain. Scoop up a tablespoon of the mixture and roll it quickly between your palms, then place it in the bowl with the roasted almond pieces and toss to coat. Once coated, transfer to the prepared baking sheet. Clean your hands so as not to transfer the almond pieces to the truffle mixture. Repeat with the remaining dough, making 10 truffles total. 5. Serve the truffles in mini paper liners, if desired. They are best when consumed at room temperature.

Per Serving:

Calories: 196 | fat: 18g | protein: 4g | carbs: 4g | net carbs: 2g | fiber: 2g

Flourless Chocolate Cake

Prep time: 10 minutes | Cook time: 42 minutes |
Makes one 9-inch cake

5 ounces unsweetened baking chocolate (100% cacao)	5 large eggs
	1 cup powdered erythritol
½ cup (1 stick) plus 2 tablespoons unsalted butter	½ cup cocoa powder
	½ teaspoon baking powder

1. Preheat the oven to 350°F and grease a 9-inch springform pan with coconut oil spray. 2. Put the chocolate and butter in a small microwave-safe bowl and microwave for 30 seconds. Stir and microwave for another 30 seconds, then stir again. If the chocolate is not fully melted, continue to microwave in 20- to 30-second intervals, stirring after each interval. Set aside. 3. Crack the eggs into a large bowl and mix with a hand mixer until frothy. Slowly pour in the melted chocolate as you keep mixing. Set aside. 4. Put the erythritol, cocoa powder, and baking powder in a small bowl and combine using a fork. In 2 batches, add the dry mixture to the wet mixture and combine using the mixer until you have a thick batter. 5. Pour the batter into the greased springform pan and bake for 40 minutes, or until a toothpick inserted in the center of the cake comes out clean. Allow to rest in the pan for 15 minutes prior to cutting and serving. To serve, run a knife around the edges to loosen the cake, then remove the rim of the springform pan and cut into 8 slices. 6. Store leftover cake in a sealed container or gallon-sized zip-top plastic bag for up to a week.

Per Serving:

Calories: 296 | fat: 26g | protein: 7g | carbs: 8g | net carbs: 2g | fiber: 6g

Pecan Clusters

Prep time: 10 minutes | Cook time: 8 minutes | Serves 8

3 ounces (85 g) whole shelled pecans	2 teaspoons confectioners' erythritol
1 tablespoon salted butter, melted	½ teaspoon ground cinnamon
	½ cup low-carb chocolate chips

1. In a medium bowl, toss pecans with butter, then sprinkle with erythritol and cinnamon. 2. Place pecans into ungreased air fryer basket. Adjust the temperature to 350°F (177°C) and air fry for 8 minutes, shaking the basket two times during cooking. They will feel soft initially but get crunchy as they cool. 3. Line a large baking sheet with parchment paper. 4. Place chocolate in a medium microwave-safe bowl. Microwave on high, heating in 20-second increments and stirring until melted. Place 1 teaspoon chocolate in a rounded mound on ungreased parchment-lined baking sheet, then press 1 pecan into top, repeating with remaining chocolate and pecans. 5. Place baking sheet into refrigerator to cool at least 30 minutes. Once cooled, store clusters in a large sealed container in refrigerator up to 5 days.

Per Serving:

Calories: 104 | fat: 10g | protein: 1g | carbs: 3g | net carbs: 2g | fiber: 1g

Coconut Lemon Squares

3 eggs	½ teaspoon vanilla extract
2 tablespoons grass-fed butter, softened	½ cup Swerve, or more to taste
½ cup full-fat coconut milk	¼ cup lemon juice
½ teaspoon baking powder	1 cup blanched almond flour

1. In a large bowl, mix together the eggs, butter, coconut milk, baking powder, vanilla, Swerve, lemon juice, and flour. Stir thoroughly, until a perfectly even mixture is obtained. 2. Next, pour 1 cup filtered water into the Instant Pot, and insert the trivet. Transfer the mixture from the bowl into a well-greased, Instant Pot-friendly pan (or dish). 3. Using a sling if desired, place the dish onto the trivet, and cover loosely with aluminum foil. Close the lid, set the pressure release to Sealing, and select Manual. Set the Instant Pot to 40 minutes on High Pressure, and let cook. 4. Once cooked, let the pressure naturally disperse from the Instant Pot for about 10 minutes, then carefully switch the pressure release to Venting. 5. Open the Instant Pot, and remove the dish. Let cool, cut into 6 squares, serve, and enjoy!

Per Serving:

Calories: 166 | fat: 15g | protein: 6g | carbs: 3g | net carbs: 2g | fiber: 1g

Chocolate Pudding

2 ripe avocados, halved and pitted	1 to 2 teaspoons liquid stevia or monk fruit extract (optional)
¼ cup unsweetened cocoa powder	½ teaspoon ground cinnamon (optional)
¼ cup heavy whipping cream, plus more if needed	¼ teaspoon salt
2 teaspoons vanilla extract	Whipped cream, for serving (optional)

1. Using a spoon, scoop out the ripe avocado into a blender or large bowl, if using an immersion blender. Mash well with a fork. 2. Add the cocoa powder, heavy whipping cream, vanilla, sweetener (if using), cinnamon (if using), and salt. Blend well until smooth and creamy, adding additional cream, 1 tablespoon at a time, if the mixture is too thick. 3. Cover and refrigerate for at least 1 hour before serving. Serve chilled with additional whipped cream, if desired.

Per Serving:

Calories: 205 | fat: 18g | protein: 3g | carbs: 12g | fiber: 9g | sodium: 156mg

Birthday Cheesecake

Crust	softened
2 cups blanched almond flour	¾ cup full-fat sour cream
⅓ cup unsalted butter, melted	1¼ cups 0g net carb sweetener
3 tablespoons 0g net carb sweetener	3 large eggs, room temperature
1 teaspoon pure vanilla extract	1 tablespoon lemon juice
Cheesecake Filling	1½ teaspoons pure vanilla extract
32 ounces full-fat cream cheese,	

1. Preheat oven to 350°F. 2. Generously grease the sides of a 9" springform pan. Cut some parchment paper to line the bottom and grease it as well. 3. For the crust, mix the almond flour, melted butter, sweetener, and vanilla in a medium bowl. Finished product will be dry. Spread and pack crust evenly onto bottom of the pan. Bake crust 10–15 minutes or until golden brown. 4. Using an electric mixer, in a large bowl, beat softened cream cheese, sour cream, and sweetener on low speed while ensuring there are not too many bubbles in the mix. Beat eggs in one at a time. Stop and scrape bowl periodically to ensure all ingredients completely mix. Beat in lemon juice and vanilla extract. 5. Pour batter on top of cooked crust and level the top. Bake 50–60 minutes until center is almost set. 6. Remove from oven. Use a sharp knife to cut around edge. Let cool 10 minutes. Refrigerate in pan 4 hours. Release from the pan when ready to serve.

Per Serving:

Calories: 343 | fat: 28g | protein: 9g | carbs: 8g | net carbs: 7g | fiber: 1g

Appendix 1 Measurement Conversion Chart

MEASUREMENT CONVERSION CHART

VOLUME EQUIVALENTS(DRY)

US STANDARD	METRIC (APPROXIMATE)
1/8 teaspoon	0.5 mL
1/4 teaspoon	1 mL
1/2 teaspoon	2 mL
3/4 teaspoon	4 mL
1 teaspoon	5 mL
1 tablespoon	15 mL
1/4 cup	59 mL
1/2 cup	118 mL
3/4 cup	177 mL
1 cup	235 mL
2 cups	475 mL
3 cups	700 mL
4 cups	1 L

WEIGHT EQUIVALENTS

US STANDARD	METRIC (APPROXIMATE)
1 ounce	28 g
2 ounces	57 g
5 ounces	142 g
10 ounces	284 g
15 ounces	425 g
16 ounces (1 pound)	455 g
1.5 pounds	680 g
2 pounds	907 g

VOLUME EQUIVALENTS(LIQUID)

US STANDARD	US STANDARD (OUNCES)	METRIC (APPROXIMATE)
2 tablespoons	1 fl.oz.	30 mL
1/4 cup	2 fl.oz.	60 mL
1/2 cup	4 fl.oz.	120 mL
1 cup	8 fl.oz.	240 mL
1 1/2 cup	12 fl.oz.	355 mL
2 cups or 1 pint	16 fl.oz.	475 mL
4 cups or 1 quart	32 fl.oz.	1 L
1 gallon	128 fl.oz.	4 L

TEMPERATURES EQUIVALENTS

FAHRENHEIT(F)	CELSIUS(C) (APPROXIMATE)
225 °F	107 °C
250 °F	120 °C
275 °F	135 °C
300 °F	150 °C
325 °F	160 °C
350 °F	180 °C
375 °F	190 °C
400 °F	205 °C
425 °F	220 °C
450 °F	235 °C
475 °F	245 °C
500 °F	260 °C

Appendix 2 The Dirty Dozen and Clean Fifteen

The Dirty Dozen and Clean Fifteen

The Environmental Working Group (EWG) is a nonprofit, nonpartisan organization dedicated to protecting human health and the environment Its mission is to empower people to live healthier lives in a healthier environment. This organization publishes an annual list of the twelve kinds of produce, in sequence, that have the highest amount of pesticide residue-the Dirty Dozen-as well as a list of the fifteen kinds ofproduce that have the least amount of pesticide residue-the Clean Fifteen.

THE DIRTY DOZEN	THE CLEAN FIFTEEN
• The 2016 Dirty Dozen includes the following produce. These are considered among the year's most important produce to buy organic:	• The least critical to buy organically are the Clean Fifteen list. The following are on the 2016 list:

THE DIRTY DOZEN		THE CLEAN FIFTEEN	
Strawberries	Spinach	Avocados	Papayas
Apples	Tomatoes	Corn	Kiw
Nectarines	Bell peppers	Pineapples	Eggplant
Peaches	Cherry tomatoes	Cabbage	Honeydew
Celery	Cucumbers	Sweet peas	Grapefruit
Grapes	Kale/collard greens	Onions	Cantaloupe
Cherries	Hot peppers	Asparagus	Cauliflower
		Mangos	

• *The Dirty Dozen list contains two additional itemskale/collard greens and hot peppers-because they tend to contain trace levels of highly hazardous pesticides.*

• *Some of the sweet corn sold in the United States are made from genetically engineered (GE) seedstock. Buy organic varieties of these crops to avoid GE produce.*

Appendix 3 Recipes Index

53984245R00077